For Joanne and Jonathan

Because, as Jose Rizal put it, the youth is the hope of our future

Published by
Straits Times Press Pte Ltd
English/Malay/Tamil Media Group
Mezzanine Floor, Information Resource Centre
Level 3, Podium Block, Singapore Press Holdings
1000 Toa Payoh North, News Centre, Singapore 318994
Tel: (65) 6319 6319 Fax: (65) 6319 8258
stpressbooks@sph.com.sg, www.stpressbooks.com.sg

Straits Times Press
General Manager, Susan Long
Publishing Manager, Lee Hui Chieh
Creative Director, Lock Hong Liang
Marketing and Operations Manager, Ilangoh Thanabalan
Sales Manager, Irene Lee
Book Editor, Kelly Pang

Cover art and design by Lock Hong Liang

All dollars ($) in this book are Singapore dollars (SGD)
unless specifically defined otherwise.

Printed in Singapore

**National Library Board, Singapore
Cataloguing-in-Publication Data**
Name(s): Chua, Mui Hoong.
Title: Singapore, disrupted / Chua Mui Hoong.
Description: Singapore : Straits Times Press Pte Ltd, [2018]
Identifier(s): OCN 1030874442 | ISBN 978-981-4747-92-9
(paperback)
Subject(s): LCSH: Singapore–Politics and government—
21st century. | Singapore—
Social conditions–21st century. | Singapore--Economic
conditions–21st century.
Classification: DDC 305.80095957–dc23

SINGAPORE,
DISRUPTED

Essays on a nation at the crossroads of change

CHUA MUI HOONG

Straits Times Press

CONTENTS

—

ACKNOWLEDGEMENTS
—

Journalism is a privilege and a responsibility. The privilege lies in being a witness to events as they unfold and the access we have to people; and the responsibility requires that we be fair witnesses to history and honest critics of the society we observe up close. It has been my privilege to be a journalist with The Straits Times since 1991.

I have written thousands of articles over a 27-year stint as a journalist. For this compilation, I picked articles centred on four themes, grouped into four chapters.

The first chapter looks at inequality and the class divide, which I consider the biggest current threat to Singapore. This chapter includes many articles I wrote over the years on life in the HDB (Housing and Development Board) heartlands – the core of Singapore life.

The second chapter looks at the broad theme of disruption that is transforming Singapore. In these articles, I articulate the challenges facing sectors from retail to the media; and try to draw out some possible responses.

The third chapter includes articles on politics I wrote over the years, on elections, the nature of political leadership, and social safety nets. If there is a single theme in these essays, it is a reminder about the importance of political leaders remaining in touch with the heart of Singapore life.

The fourth and last chapter is a collection of my articles on Lee Kuan Yew and Lee Hsien Loong, both of whom I interviewed at various points in my career.

This book would not be possible without the encouragement, support and hard work on the part of many editors and colleagues over the years who challenged and probed my ideas. They include, in chronological order: Han Fook Kwang, Cheong Yip Seng, Leslie Fong,

Patrick Daniel, Zuraidah Ibrahim, Warren Fernandez and Sumiko Tan.

I am also immensely grateful to Professor Tommy Koh for reading the manuscript and writing the foreword despite the short notice, and to Chan Heng Chee, Peter Ho, Koh Tai Ann and Fook Kwang for their endorsements of the book.

Good friends and family have provided wise counsel. They include my late parents Lou Hui Ngo and Chua Soon Kuan, who anchored my views on the realities of life; my siblings Lee Hoong and Daniel and his wife Lyn; and my nephew Jonathan and niece Joanne Chua, who provided so much fodder for my early columns. Among my many intellectual sparring partners, two have been invaluable: Adeline Sum has heard the genesis of the ideas in many of these articles, and wrestled with me mentally, sharpening my arguments; and Leonard Leow has challenged my worldview on countless occasions, often offering me perspectives I could not have reached on my own.

Finally, thanks are due to my publishers especially Susan Long for cajoling me into doing this compilation; Kelly Pang the book editor, and the team at Straits Times Press. I am grateful too to Audrey Quek, my fellow Opinion editor, who steadfastly manned the fort while I took time off my regular duties to work on this book.

Many people I interviewed, quoted and interacted with over the years gave generously of their time and views and shaped my intellectual formation – my gratitude extends to all of them.

Finally, a special Thank You to my readers over the years, many of whom have written to me – first in cards or letters via snail mail, and then through e-mail or on Facebook – to agree, disagree, console, argue, scold, praise, and otherwise just engage me.

FOREWORD

I thank my good friend, Chua Mui Hoong, for giving me the pleasure of contributing the foreword for this important book.

My friendship with Mui Hoong began in 2003. On March 12, 2003, the World Health Organisation (WHO) issued a global health alert on cases of atypical pneumonia, later named as severe acute respiratory syndrome or Sars. A Singapore tourist caught the virus in Hong Kong and brought it back to Singapore. It spread like wildfire. By the time WHO took Singapore off the list of Sars-affected territories on May 30, 2003, 33 Singaporeans had lost their lives and 238 people were infected. When faced with a crisis, some countries rise to the challenge while others fall apart. Singapore survived the test of fire.

The Singapore Government asked the Institute of Policy Studies (IPS), of which I was then Chairman, to publish a truthful and reflective book on the crisis. I chaired an interministerial committee of senior officials for the book project. I was asked to pick a writer from a shortlist of journalists from The Straits Times. I chose Mui Hoong because I admired her columns. She wrote an excellent book, *A Defining Moment: How Singapore Beat Sars*, which was published in 2004.

Our paths crossed again when the editor of The Straits Times, Warren Fernandez, invited me to contribute a monthly op-ed to the newspaper. My two editors were Mui Hoong and Lydia Lim. Lydia has been succeeded by Audrey Quek.

I am an avid reader of newspapers. I have read most of the columns included in this book. I enjoyed reading them again. I especially like the four new essays she has written, to introduce the four chapters of the book, namely, The Class Divide, The Brave New World of Disruption, Politics in Singapore and Chronicles from the Court of Lee. It is worth buying the book just to read these thoughtful essays.

I regard Chua Mui Hoong as one of the best journalists of Singapore. She writes with a brilliant mind, a warm heart, and integrity. She is not afraid to praise or to criticise any one, any institution, including the Government. No reasonable person can question her objectivity and fairness. She loves Singapore and Singaporeans, especially our working class and heartlanders. In spite of her success, she has never forgotten her roots. Her gentle voice is a voice of conscience from our heartland.

TOMMY KOH

Ambassador-at-Large, Ministry of Foreign Affairs
Professor of Law, National University of Singapore

INTRODUCTION
—

Singapore is at a crossroads.

The theme of this book is Singapore, Disrupted. The title is a reference to Singapore's development, which faces disruption from all quarters.

Disruption is the shorthand word used to describe the wave of economic and social transformation unleashed by the cauldron of technological and engineering advancements that makes big data, robotics and artificial intelligence, among other wonders, possible. As a small, open economy, Singapore will be buffeted by these forces, even as we do our best to be nimble and flexible, and capitalise on the opportunities these present – just as we always have.

In addition to economic disruption, the geopolitical landscape also poses challenges, as a rising China asserts its influence in the region, and the United States becomes a more unpredictable world power. The rising threats posed by terrorism, cyber attacks and state-sponsored fake news campaigns to derail elections add to a global climate of anxiety. Within Singapore, a young population is coming of age, probing and pushing sociopolitical boundaries even as they face a future where the jobs they trained for might disappear before they even have a chance to climb the job ladder.

The scale of disruption in all spheres of life requires not just good economic management, but a reordering of our entire society. As many others have noted, the future economy will thrive on innovation and entrepreneurship. No economic planner can tell parents what jobs are in store for their children, or what courses they should study, when no one even knows what kind of new jobs are available tomorrow. The smart parent or education minister knows the best way to help young people get ready for such a future is to go beyond the traditional training of the mind in academic subjects, and equip them with life skills like discipline, initiative and co-working abilities, and arm them with digital literacy.

The old way of doing things in Singapore is under pressure to change.

. The success of the economy no longer depends on whether a small coterie of smart planners places their Big Bet correctly on the right industries. From betting on a few big sectors, Singapore is now seeding thousands of start-ups and research initiatives, in hopes that some will bear fruit. When the future is legion, with many permutations, every person, every worker, every student, has to be able to adapt and respond to changing circumstances. This requires a very different kind of society from what Singaporeans have become used to.

The success of Singapore as a country will depend less and less on a small group of leaders who can think big and execute big projects well, and more and more on how we organise ourselves overall, and whether we can harness the innate skills of each person.

To take just one small example: Big ticket attractions like the zoo, casinos and Gardens by the Bay may attract tourists to Singapore once, but no tourist will return if his daily experience and encounters in Singapore lack heart and warmth. Increasingly, it will be the small, intimate, experiential encounters that will keep tourists coming back for more. In other words, the success of Singapore, even as a tourist destination, can't depend on a few attractions; it has to depend on every hotel staff, Airbnb host, private-hire car driver, tour guide, restaurant waiter, and every other person who comes into contact with the tourists.

Whether we like it or not, Singapore society is in a state of disruption wrought by a confluence of forces technological, geopolitical and demographic. How we respond to it will determine our place in the disrupted world.

What has changed

Singapore's disruption began – if such things can ever be said to have a distinct beginning – in 2011, with the momentous General Election of that year which saw the People's Action Party (PAP) lose six seats and receive its lowest ever vote share of 60.1 per cent. By most developed country standards, that would have been a landslide victory; for Singapore, it jolted the ruling party into some soul-searching and a decisive policy shift towards more income redistribution.

What has changed in this period of disruption in the sociopolitical landscape?

Fraying consensus

First, there is a fraying consensus on what Singapore stands for and its future. The old way of doing things that brought the country success is being questioned by many people, including from within the country's own establishment circles.

In economic management, alternative models are being put forward, centred around developing local enterprises rather than relying on foreign multinationals; relying less on cheap foreign labour and raising skills and wages for locals; and lowering land costs to channel more profit share from capital to labour.

In social policy, lively discussions abound on whether Singapore can go for slower growth and a less punishing pace of life; and if it can have a more Nordic system with more universal benefits.

In the political realm, debate is rapidly polarising into those who think Singapore's future remains glowing in the hands of the PAP, and those who argue an alternative would be better.

Elite fragmentation

The second thing that has changed post-2011: elite fragmentation.

It is notable that all four candidates who stood in the 2011 Presidential Election were members of the establishment. The winning candidate Tony Tan is a former deputy prime minister. The first runner-up Tan Cheng Bock was a long-serving MP from the PAP. Tan Jee Say was a member of the elite Administrative Service that runs the country. Tan Kin Lian used to help former PM Goh Chok Tong run his PAP party branch. He was also head of Income, the insurance cooperative of the labour movement (NTUC) that has a symbiotic relationship with the PAP that is affirmed each May Day.

Members of the erstwhile establishment are breaking ranks and coming out to compete with each other for political positions. Tan Jee Say, for example, contested the 2011 General Election under the Singapore Democratic Party banner.

Most interesting of all is the way elite members are now offering alternatives to established positions of policy. Some offer sustained, well-reasoned critiques of the Singapore system, such as the one from Donald Low and Sudhir Thomas Vadaketh *(Hard Choices: Challenging The Singapore Consensus)*. Others use their social media influence to good effect, commenting on issues. A group of them is behind the Future of Singapore Forum, a self-described "non-partisan Internet research and discussion forum" that organises talks on Singapore issues. Its first forum in January 2017 featured former GIC senior economist Yeoh Lam Keong. The six-part video is available online and has attracted several thousand viewers.

Some write occasional papers or commentaries that irk the establishment. Kishore Mahbubani, then dean of the Lee Kuan Yew School of Public Policy, faced a volley of sharp rebuttals when he wrote an article in The Straits Times published in July 2017 saying Singapore should behave like a small state, by which he meant it should be more prudent in its foreign policy. His viewpoint was interpreted as a criticism of Singapore's China policy and indeed of the current Cabinet. He stepped down as dean in December 2017, and is on sabbatical before his retirement is due in 2019.

The public debate on foreign policy alarmed some Singaporeans, but as I argued in a commentary then, the country will certainly see more contestation of views in the coming years. It is vital that we develop the art of debating contentious issues in a way that helps the country open up parameters for new ideas, not close them down.

Singapore needs a fresh, more adaptive way to govern and manage the economy. In politics and society, it needs to give up on its vertical, command-and-control *modus operandi* and learn the art of horizontal relations – to learn to engage respectfully across sectors, listen and understand, seek common ground, and collaborate to find solutions. And when no common ground is possible, we need to learn to disagree civilly.

The most glaring example of elite fragmentation came when members of Prime Minister Lee Hsien Loong's own family broke out in a quarrel over what to do with their late father Lee Kuan Yew's family home. As the three Lee siblings traded words on Facebook and via public statements, the country was distressed over the public airing of dirty family linen. Most pernicious of all were accusations of abuse of power and dynastic ambitions made by the younger Lees against their elder brother, the Prime Minister. These were not substantiated, and were debated and dismissed in Parliament, but still left a sting as they were not met with the usual battery of lawsuits for defamation that such comments would normally attract.

Myth of exceptionalism punctured

A fraying consensus and a public display of elite fragmentation have both led to the puncturing of the myth of exceptionalism that has prevailed in Singapore for decades.

For years, leaders in Singapore justified its system of soft authoritarianism by arguing that Singapore's small, multiracial society in a geopolitical quagmire required strong social controls and skilful political management by a small corps of carefully selected and groomed leaders. Entering public service was likened to joining the priesthood – political and public service was exalted. Singapore had to stand out from its neighbours – by being clean, incorruptible, efficient, superior – to function as a First World oasis in a Third World region.

The years after 2011 have punctured that myth. As I wrote in a column in 2013, that was the year Singapore lost its aura of invincibility, when sex-for-favours corruption scandals broke out, and a riot erupted in Little India among migrant workers.

The constant infrastructure problems – breakdowns on the MRT, floods, and falling trees that caused injury and even death – also eroded confidence.

Then in 2017, scandal engulfed Keppel Corp, a government-linked company, over its operations in Brazil. Many Singaporeans were shocked to learn that Keppel had engaged in bribery to secure contracts; others were astounded at the naivete of those so shocked. What transpired was a kind of collective wringing of the hands in despair and a loss of innocence.

If a Singapore success story like Keppel had engaged in bribery, can

Singapore still claim to be so incorruptible? Perhaps Singapore was not so exceptional after all.

The gap between the "best" and the rest

As elite squabbles become more commonplace, and as more members of the establishment become critics, it is inevitable that citizens start to question two things: if the system still works, and if the leaders in that system are still worth their salt (or multi-million-dollar salaries).

On the first, there is plenty of discussion online and off on what needs fixing about Singapore – its education system, its system of recruiting and rewarding public and political service officials, its economic management, its information and media management approach, its healthcare system; the list goes on. It is a measure of the level of engagement that many Singaporeans have with the country and its system that so many citizens are deeply involved in such discussions in their personal and professional realms.

As a journalist, I too have taken part in some of those discussions. I've covered, observed, and commented on many issues in over 27 years as a political columnist. One issue that has always troubled me is the class divide. I wrote about the issue in 1987 as an intern in The Straits Times; it was the subject of my first feature when I started work as a full-time reporter in 1991; and I continued to write about it incessantly through the years. By 2018, as I write this, the issues of income inequality and class have resurfaced.

Rising inequality is a feature of the modern world, not just Singapore. More thinkers are now arguing that the neoliberal global order that believes in open borders and free trade has created uneven benefits across countries, and within countries. The gap between the top 10 per cent and the remaining 90 per cent has fuelled discontent. In Singapore, the gap between the "best" and the rest risks becoming invidious. Here, the divide is not of income or birth; it is one of academic achievement transmuted into professional success as administrators and corporate chiefs.

As for the second question – do officials deserve their salaries? – the issue is an emotional one, not only about merit or deservedness, but about identity and empathy.

Personally, I think the emotional gulf has widened between government and people, after the Government introduced a pay formula to peg the salaries of Cabinet ministers and Administrative Service officers (the elite rungs of the civil service, from which permanent secretaries and heads of statutory boards are typically picked) to the top pay of private-sector professionals. As I wrote several times over the years, that pay formula has altered the subtle relationship between people and government, shifting the basis of the relationship from a moral to a transactional one.

The pay formula was never strictly adhered to, as it moved up and down with the economy; and was countercyclical as it lagged real data. (For example, the benchmark used pay data from a few years ago. If pay then was high, but the economy is today in recession, adhering to it would mean giving ministers a pay rise when the economy is down – which would be politically untenable.)

The formula has been adjusted several times over the years. In its current incarnation, it is pegged to "the median income of the top 1,000 Singapore citizens income earners, with a 40 per cent discount to reflect the ethos of political service" as the Public Service Division puts it. Entry-level ministers' average package comes up to about $600,000 a year, with another $400,000 or so in variable bonus.

Part of the bonus, called the National Bonus made up of three months' pay, is based on four criteria: real GDP growth rate, unemployment rate, and the real growth rates of the median income and the income of the bottom 20 per cent of Singapore citizens. The changed formula, especially the criteria pegged to socioeconomic conditions like wage growth, is an improvement from the original. But it remains a lightning rod for criticism.

High salaries have catapulted public and political service officials from the ranks of the top 10 per cent into the tiers of the top 1 per cent. A pay formula pegged to the top 1,000 income earners, out of a workforce of about two million, puts one in the top 0.05 per cent. A 40 per cent "discount" off that rate might lower the tier somewhat, perhaps to the top 0.1 per cent – and certainly still comfortably within the top 1 per cent range.

These days, it is the gap beween the top 1 per cent and the rest that is particularly troubling. Economists like Joseph Stiglitz have written about how globalisation benefits the plutocrats. As I write this in March 2018, a report from Oxfam estimates that 82 per cent of wealth generated in 2017 went to the top 1 per cent.

In Singapore, too, the gap between the top 1 per cent and the top 10 per cent is also surfacing, as the upper middle-class looks with envy at the lifestyles of the Ultra Rich – people who went to school with them and used to be their neighbours.

New York Times columnist David Brooks highlighted this in an article in 2011, describing this as Blue Inequality, a reference to the Democrat Party base of urban populations: "...If you live in these big cities, you see people similar to yourself, who may have gone to the same college, who are earning much more while benefiting from low tax rates, wielding disproportionate political power, gaining in prestige and contributing seemingly little to the social good. That is the experience of Blue Inequality."

As I wrote in several commentaries, Singapore faces a similar bifurcation in its society: a growing gap between the elite and the masses. I consider this gap, or class divide, particularly corrosive because it strikes at the heart of what makes us proud to be Singaporean: a society of immigrants, descendants of farmers, coolies, street hawkers, who built a First World city to be proud of, whose offspring have gone on to top global leagues in performance in the academic, cultural and sporting fields.

In Singapore, for decades, talent has risen to the top naturally, regardless of wealth, family, connections. If family background now starts to matter, if people's connections help determine their future success, then we will become a more troubled society. Sadly, there are signs that we are indeed becoming more class-conscious. Our education policies that give priority admission to alumni parents or parents with grassroots or community experience are examples. It requires political will to dismantle such systems of privilege. The good thing is that awareness is rising, with outspoken academics and observers writing and speaking out on these. It remains to be seen if these will translate into concrete policy changes, the way the 2011 General Election results sparked real change in social policy.

If not tackled, the gap between the "best" and the rest will become the brink at which the Singapore Dream falters.

Future dreams

A fraying consensus; elite contestation; questioning of what makes Singapore exceptional; and rising inequality driving a wedge between the "best" and the rest. These add up to a rather toxic brew for Singapore.

What's next? How should the country – especially the Government – respond?

A reordering of society, I would argue, is in order. This means a changing in mores, so that we stop prioritising the elite and laud the "best", and give more people the tools to make a difference.

In the political realm, especially, the need for reform is acute; but sadly, this is the one arena where change is glacial. The "PAP-knows-best" mentality continues to be dominant. This can be dangerous for the country in an age of disruption, as no central group of leaders can possibly claim to be on top of everything.

In this respect, I was glad that the Government chose to convene a Select Committee to listen to expert views on how to regulate the spread of "fake news" or deliberate online falsehoods. But even then, this was a throwback to the 1990s, when such parliamentary committees were often convened.

Genuine change can come only when the Government is prepared to cede and share power with the people. This means being more transparent and subjecting itself to more scrutiny.

A Freedom of Information Act has been touted periodically, but this has always been rejected. Singapore's political landscape is so far from being ready for such an Act that more modest milestone targets should be considered.

The Government can, for example, start by trusting its researchers. Over the years, various people have told me that much interesting research is commissioned by the Government, but the results, data and reports are usually confined to small circles. Sometimes, these researchers write up a portion of their results for The Straits Times Opinion pages, but I often get that there is a lot more they can share that might offer a different, more nuanced, more messy picture of Singapore, if they were allowed to.

The Government can also trust the mainstream media more. As I argue in articles on disruption in the media sector, letting go of attempts to control the media frees us to be more robust in our reporting and commentary. The local media then stands a better chance of winning the battle for the minds and hearts of Singaporean readers, so that we can keep telling the Singapore Story amidst the onslaught of global information.

Most of all, the Government can learn to trust Singapore citizens more. This is, after all, a remarkable electorate that has chosen to return the PAP to power in 12 consecutive general elections since independence, calibrating its approval or disapproval finely to nudge the ruling party to change.

In this tango, the people push, the PAP Government steps back a little. As a younger generation comes of age, the tempo of the dance accelerates; if the Government's steps remain slow, the tango will become out of sync, and then what will happen? Disharmony for sure in the short term; and in the long term, even a change of dance partner.

But it need not be thus.

1

THE CLASS DIVIDE

I grew up in a working-class family but it wasn't until my university days that I became conscious of class.

My parents were first-generation migrants from China who sold food for a living. They eked out a living first as itinerant hawkers, and then as hawkers resettled into government-run hawker centres. My parents spoke the Teochew dialect to me, and I learnt English and Mandarin only when I went to primary school. The first day of school, the teacher went round asking every student some question in English. I didn't understand a word. But all the pupils replied with their name, so I deduced she was asking us our names. When it was my turn, I gave my name, which is pronounced in Teochew the way it is phonetically spelt in English – Chua Mui Hoong. To my relief, it appeared to be the correct answer.

But I couldn't bluff my way through school for long. Soon, the teacher had to stand over me to give me hurried instructions in dialect so I could understand what she wanted us to do.

Fortunately for those of my generation from similar non-English speaking homes, the teachers taught us the rudiments of the English language from scratch. I learnt my ABCs, my Ps and Qs, and my grammar. I learnt to read and write, and to speak English. Once I discovered the gift of the English language, I couldn't stop. I haven't stopped talking, reading, writing and being vocal since!

My primary school was racially and socioeconomically diverse.

It was in Newton, near the kampung where I grew up, surrounded by landed houses. I remember a gentle girl with an Arabic name who lived in one of the bungalows nearby. I played Barbie dolls at the Bukit Timah house of an Indian-Muslim girl, who learnt Mandarin with the Chinese students. Among my classmates were the daughters of the school canteen noodle seller, a cleaner, teachers and bankers.

I did well in school and managed to get into Raffles Girls' Secondary School. Back then, in the 1980s, RGS was not an "elite" school. You needed to do well in the Primary School Leaving Examination to get in, as entry was based on exam scores, but many of my classmates were not from "elite" homes. I had classmates who lived in Housing Board flats like I did, and others who lived in rental flats, landed homes or condos. We knew each other's backgrounds, but the ethos of the school was down-to-earth and not snobbish. We didn't compare our parents' occupations, incomes or car model, family holiday plans, or other symbols of wealth or social status. But unlike my primary school, RGS was less racially diverse. Almost all my classmates in Secondary 1, and then Secondary 3 when we were streamed into subject clusters, were Chinese.

I went on from RGS to Raffles Junior College, joining the Humanities programme targeted at helping students interested in pursuing humanities to vie for scholarships to study at Oxbridge or the Ivy League universities. I got an Overseas Merit Scholarship from the Singapore Government to study English literature in Cambridge University in the United Kingdom. It came with a bond and I had to come back to Singapore and teach for eight years.

Class consciousness

My consciousness about class arose in my Cambridge days. The

Singaporean students were divided into two large groups: the "government scholars" or those studying there on government scholarships; and the "Pa Ma scholars" who were funded by their parents.

To be sure, most of us mixed across the income and class divide. But there were differences in lifestyle, and I was old enough at 18 to understand the differences. I was living on my £300-a-month scholarship allowance, and maintained a tight budget so I could save up for holidays. I couldn't afford restaurant dinners. Some of my wealthier friends would offer to give me a treat. As one friend told me once, she would rather pay for a nice dinner for both of us than have to endure another mediocre college dinner! I realised that just as I wouldn't want my friends to impose their (affluent) lifestyle on me, it wasn't fair to impose my standard of living on them all the time too. So I learnt to receive graciously, with gratitude, and with a promise to myself that one day, when I had the means, I would pass on that generosity to others. I've retold that story many times since, when I treat students, volunteer workers, or people younger than me who are just starting out in their careers. Just pass it forward, I say.

In Cambridge, I was surrounded by vestiges of a class-ridden society. Cambridge undergraduates in the 1980s lived an ivory tower life. There was a "bedder" or cleaning lady who would make our beds, clean our rooms and wash up our cups in the kitchen sink – every day. College meals were provided at a reasonable fee. We lived in heated furnished rooms; in my second year, I had a suite with a bedroom and living room. If a light bulb blew in my study desk lamp, I just rang the "porter" who would come by to change it for me. (Yes, they didn't just change bulbs in hard-to-reach ceiling lights, they would change even the bulb in the lamp on your study table.)

At Formal Hall dinners, we donned our gowns over suit and tie for men, and dresses for women, and sat down for a meal in the dining room – invariably a grand wood-panelled hall several hundreds of years old, with portraits of stern-looking, white-haired, white-whiskered men staring down at us. The working-class girl from the Singapore heartlands was living surrounded by privilege – indeed, was living in privilege – in Cambridge.

In my second year, I came back to Singapore for the summer, and worked as an intern at The Straits Times. I was attached to the lifestyle section, and spent a few pleasant weeks writing up briefs, reviewing books, and writing a feature on the class divide, called "Children of the Establishment". I just interviewed my obliging Cambridge friends and friends of friends for the feature.

I started work at The Straits Times in 1991. I had decided to switch from the teaching service to journalism, and luckily for me, my new employer was prepared to pay the Singapore Government the bonded sum for my eight years of service.

I've remained a grateful and fulfilled journalist since. Over the years, I've written about many issues, some closer to my heart than others. Class is one of them.

Singapore prides itself on being a classless society. This was especially so in the 1970s, 1980s and 1990s. The country was pell-mell headed for industrialisation, progress, and rapid development. Anyone with an education was valued, and those with ability and drive quickly rose through the ranks.

Class receded into the background. This was the period of young people who became heads of department in their 20s, of the street noodle seller's son who became a deputy prime minister (Wong Kan Seng) or the taxi-driver's son who became head of civil service (Lim Siong Guan).

Most important of all, such advancement was unremarkable –

many people lived through the transformation of Singapore from Third World to First in their own personal lives, catapulting from a shared room in an attap house with an outhouse toilet in their childhood to a cushy condo, or a landed house with a garden and art on their wall, in retirement.

But somewhere along the line, we took our eyes away for a few seconds too long, and dropped the ball on social mobility and class.

The class divide became a hot topic for discussion in late 2017 into 2018. This followed a survey by the Institute of Policy Studies that showed quite definitively that class, not race or religion, was the biggest divide in Singapore society. The survey identified two matrices of class difference as being important: the housing type you live in (public HDB or private housing) and the school you went to (so-called "elite" schools like RGS, the one I went to, versus mainstream schools). It found that if you went to one type of school and lived in one type of housing, your social contacts and networks tended to also come from similar backgrounds.

Now that I am into middle age, and my working-class parents have long passed on, I find that my social networks are indeed congregating along class lines. It is so easy, in comfortable, cushy Singapore, to insulate yourself from the hurly-burly of life, and to forget that for many families, life remains a struggle.

My family background has kept me grounded as a journalist.

When I was assigned to write a feature on social class after a new book on the class divide came out in 1991, I interviewed a *zichar* cook who became a *karung guni* man. He was the friend of a family member. A few years later, when I had to find someone who did not have a Singapore passport to interview for a feature, I asked my mother for help. She played card games with the neighbourhood *ah ma* and *ah pek*. One of her close *kaki*, who was born in Singapore and raised a family here, had never left the country. I wrote up her story. I remember my boss asking how I managed to find such people to interview – this was in the period before social media and the Internet, when old-fashioned telephoning and word of mouth prevailed. I didn't tell him I just asked my mother!

Sociologist Teo You Yenn's 2018 book, *This Is What Inequality Looks Like*, recounts in moving detail her experiences moving from the physical and emotional landscape of her research subjects who are often mired in poverty back to her own comfortable middle-class lifestyle.

Like her, I have felt that dissonance as I move from my work life – where I hobnob, lunch or have chats with senior political and public figures – to my personal life, where I used to sit and chat with my Teochew-speaking mother in a coffee shop and hear her neighbourhood tales or commiserate with her grumbles on the rising prices of fish in the market; or spend time with relations and friends who are low-wage workers who receive Workfare, ComCare or get grocery vouchers from their MP.

As I wrote in some of my commentaries, there are two Singapores – a wealthy one where life is good and we live in our condo-and-car bubble, and another where life is a struggle. There are also two Singapores in the psyche – an official universe where people are rational and knowledgeable, and a parallel universe where rumour and "fake news" thrive, and always have, long before the notion of fake news was ever created. The politician who wants to win votes, and minds – never mind hearts – must be familiar with the underground parallel universe. In Singapore's context, that parallel universe resides, if it can be said to reside in any physical space, in the Housing Board heartlands.

I wrote a column called Heartlanders for several years, offering a viewpoint of life in Singapore from the heartlands. The centre of gravity in political life in Singapore remains the heartlands, where the majority of Singaporeans live, work and play. Yet too few of the senior officials I know – and even journalists – live in the heartlands. HDB estates have become places you "upgrade" out of, not residences where you build an identity and your future.

As Singapore develops economically and matures as a society, we risk having those two separate worlds remain distinct and isolated from each other.

Have we become an academic aristocracy?

In sociology, scholars talk of social distance – the distance that emerges among groups on racial, class, gender or sexuality lines. People of a group tend to hang out with one another from the same group. More worryingly, there is affective social distance, which is the idea that those of one group identify with and feel more for others in the same group.

There is also normative social distance, or the notion that you tend to think people like yourself are the "norm", the insiders who should get the rewards in a system. And then there is interactional social distance, which measures how much interaction takes place across social groups.

Applying these theories to Singapore, you can see how one group of Singaporeans who has risen to become part of the "ruling" elite can over time create a system that rewards people like themselves and lose empathy for others.

Affective social distance results when the academically gifted in Singapore who go on to have good jobs and assume leadership positions in the public or private sector feel a sense of kinship with those like themselves. They may feel alienated, or different, from the masses.

With normative social distance, they assume that people like themselves are the natural winners of the system. They feel they should be the "insiders" who get assigned plum roles in the professions. Not surprisingly, the public-sector elite, many of whom come from similar academic backgrounds, then appoint one another to the boards of the many government agencies, government-linked companies and Temasek-linked companies. The same kind of background is sought for political leadership positions, with the ruling PAP recruiting from the same ranks. Perhaps this is why the Cabinet remains the stronghold of those bonded scholars who come back from overseas universities to work in the public sector. Like-minded people tend to feel more comfortable with each other. Policymakers may then structure policies that reward people like themselves and unconsciously discriminate against those who are different. It would be hard for a group like this to accept, let alone welcome, someone from the private sector into its inner rungs.

Over time, Singapore's meritocracy has hardened around its edges. From a fluid meritocracy where people from all backgrounds have a shot at climbing the socioeconomic ladder, we are in danger of becoming an academic aristocracy, with a ruling class of scholar-administrators who permeates the public-sector and political ranks, and whose reach extends into the corporate world when they leave the public sector for private-sector positions. To diversify the political leadership, the PAP has sought to recruit people from more diverse backgrounds, but this has proved challenging.

Singapore is very fortunate that this scholar-administrator class has proven to be generally capable and clean. For now, this academic aristocracy, I believe, has its heart in the right place and wants to do right by Singaporeans.

But Singapore is at a juncture in its development when its leadership model needs to be disrupted. The scholar-administrator model of running the country has been effective, but may not be so in the future. Technological disruption is upending jobs; social behaviours are becoming unmoored from tradition and hierarchy; and millennials' expectations of a good life are no longer grounded solely on material achievements.

Like the rest of the industrialised world, Singapore is changing rapidly. My fear is that the pace of change is faster than our society or institutions can cope with.

A society with more rigid class divides is less resilient than one where people know they can cross social divides with ease. In the latter kind of society, cohesion, cooperation and compassion come more naturally.

I believe Singapore's academic-based system of meritocracy needs to evolve. Already, many critics have pointed to the limits of Singapore's competitive exam-based academic meritocracy, which has bred a generation of hypercompetitive students who try to top exams by winning that extra 0.01 point to secure a place in that cherished school or to win that prestigious scholarship.

The concept of a "compassionate meritocracy" has been put forth by some political leaders in Singapore as a way to blunt the sharp edges of Singapore's competitive system. In a compassionate meritocracy, the emphasis is on helping others, and making sure the playing field is level so all can kick off at more equal starting points.

A compassionate meritocracy also calls on those who succeed on merit to lend a helping hand to those who are disadvantaged. While this is a laudable goal, I think this merely perpetuates class divisions in a different dimension. The academic aristocracy, already imbued with a sense of entitlement and privilege, may then feel morally justified to feel like benefactors in the system, bestowing on lesser creatures the largesse of their generous assistance. Any system that pits one group as benefactor and another as recipient remains an unequal one.

If you have an A student coach a C student in Math, and the C student gets a B, you may be running a compassionate meritocracy in helping the C student attain grades higher than he could have gotten himself. But they are all operating under the same underlying system that values the A student more and gives him more status, more autonomy and maybe even more moral agency. The system remains unequal, even if the C student has been helped to attain a B.

Many schools had Community Involvement Programmes (CIP) where students spent time on a voluntary project, such as tutoring fellow students or visiting a welfare home. Such programmes may expose students of privilege to others' poverty or hardship. But they also perpetuate a system where one group is considered the norm, the insider, the privileged, and others the rank outsider to be "helped". In 2012, the CIP was replaced with a more holistic programme called Values in Action where the focus shifted from providing community service to developing desired values in students.

To build empathy and awareness of privilege, schools can do more than expose students to people from diverse backgrounds. They can create systems of differences, where a diverse range of skills and values becomes privileged.

Schools should turn their academic-oriented curriculum topsy-turvy now and then. Get students to work together on a DIY project. Dig a garden in school and tend to it. Put together a go-kart engine and race the car. Work on a class quilt. Put up a light and dance show.

Students can be assigned such projects, which should be examinable. They should be grouped randomly. So when the student who gets A in Math finds out he is hopeless with a drill bit, or a needle, and needs coaching in these motor skills from the student who usually gets a C in English, he will naturally learn empathy, humility, and a renewed respect for other kinds of talents his classmates have. The student who gets a D in Science may find she excels in designing and planting a herb garden and develop renewed confidence.

I realised the limits of an academic aristocracy quite late in my life. At 29, I learnt to drive. I went through two sets of driving instructors, gave up and enrolled in one of the big driving schools that had a more systematic syllabus. I took the driving test three times, and finally passed, after spending thousands of dollars. I realised how lucky I was that Singapore society values paper qualifications, as I was good at passing exams. If driving skills were the arbiter of pay and status, I would be among the low-income for sure – and a very stressed low-wage worker at that. When I took up watercolour painting lessons and then golf lessons, in my 30s, I had similar feelings. If any of these fine motor skills had been the normative ones to have, I would languish at the bottom of the status pile.

Rather than an academic aristocracy or even a compassionate meritocracy that puts academic merit at the top, I think Singapore should strive to be a meritocracy of many skills. Whatever skill you are good at deserves to be valued and respected. This requires that all kinds of skills should be paid a good wage in the marketplace. This is where I think Singapore can do better for its workers.

In Singapore, low-wage jobs are often those which are open to cheap foreign labour. The conventional mantra is that these are jobs Singaporeans don't want. But maybe Singaporeans don't want these jobs because they pay so little. And they pay so little because wages are arguably depressed by the easy presence of large numbers of foreign workers – in the cleaning sector, in construction, in kitchen preparation work.

If wages rise to $15, $20 an hour, will Singaporeans take up these jobs? I would bet Yes, especially if work conditions improve. Instead of expecting people to work split shifts, restaurants can design the work into two distinct blocks and pay per hour. Those who value part-time or flexi-hours will then be attracted to do these jobs.

Right now, there is one sector where wages have gone up swiftly, from the $5-$10 an hour range, to $15-$20. This is the domestic cleaning service sector, where higher-income households hire a part-time cleaner to clean their homes for a few hours a week. Foreign domestic maids living in Singapore are typically contracted to work for only one family and are not allowed to "moonlight" for others. Many families, however, don't want a live-in domestic maid, only a part-time one. Without cheap foreign substitutes, families who want a part-time maid need to rely on locals – and are forced to pay accordingly. And because of the willingness of these higher-income families to pay for a part-time maid, wages for such work have risen. Observing the rise in domestic work wages over the years has led me to wonder if similar tightenings of foreign worker numbers can cause a wage rise in other typically low-wage jobs.

Higher wages for skills is only one part of the equation of equalising the class divide. People want good pay, and also dignity, respect, and to feel valued. Over the decades, Singapore has become a society where certain skills are valued a lot more than others, where a certain class of people is respected more, and feels more valued. The flip side of this system of privilege is that entire groups of people with less "valued" skills are made to feel less worthy. This is corrosive.

In the past, people who worked with their hands could feel proud of what they did. They worked hard, and honestly, providing for their children, some of whom would go on to get good jobs and become leaders in their own right. Their pride stemmed from their labour, and their hopes in their children.

Today, blue-collar workers may feel a sense of shame that they remain in lower-status jobs when their friends or neighbours have surpassed them. When they look at their children and compare them to the children of their friends or neighbours, they may feel not hope, but despair, at whether their children can ever catch up, and a corresponding sense of guilt, wondering if they have failed their children.

Class divides will always be a feature of any society. Human beings belong to the primate family, arguably hard-wired to establish social pecking orders of dominance and status. But tendency is not destiny. As reasonable, compassionate human beings, we must struggle against the primal tendency to establish hierarchy. Most of all, we have to scan our social and political systems and try to make sure they give equal chances of success to people from different groups, not just those most like "us".

WHAT A KARUNG GUNI MAN TAUGHT ME ABOUT CLASS

17 November 1991

A fortnight ago I spent a day trailing a *karung guni* man, Ian Lim, on his rounds. It was instructive, not so much for what I learnt about the rag-and-bone trade as for what I learnt about Singaporeans and social distinctions.

What was most interesting was that friends and colleagues who read my article on Ian and social class invariably asked me one of two questions: How I had come to know Ian Lim at all; and how a *karung guni* man could be called Ian.

The questions revealed several things, among them the wonder that I, an English-educated graduate, should know a dialect-speaking, secondary-school dropout like Ian; and the incredulity that a working-class person, an "Ah Beng" sort of person, should have, in the words of a colleague, "an upmarket English name" like Ian.

This disbelief, more than anything else, was instructive. It revealed the gap which exists between different groups in our society.

To be amazed that a *karung guni* man should call himself Ian, or conversely, that an up-and-coming executive should be called Tan Ah Kow (and with no Christian name) is to make glib assumptions that reduce complex humanity to the level of mere types.

More than that, for a country like Singapore, it is to begin treading the dangerous road towards social differentiation that plagues other modern societies like Britain, where the way you speak, dress and walk immediately betrays your social origins, helps determine the way you are treated in restaurants or in shops, and influences your chances in life.

Recently, a quiet concern has arisen in some circles that socioeconomic gaps have widened in our society and are more significant than differences of race or language.

In July, for example, at a forum on the census results, Chief Statistician Paul Cheung warned that class differences would be increasingly marked across society as a whole.

Hitherto, when talk of social class in Singapore cropped up, two arguments were traditionally used to prove that Singapore is a "classless" society.

The first argument goes something like this: Home ownership and ownership of consumer durables like a refrigerator, washing machine, television or video recorder indicate that the majority of Singaporeans are well-off and lead comfortable lives.

Singapore is a classless – by which is meant a largely middle-class – society.

No doubt a larger proportion of Singaporeans own their own homes and many things besides than is the case in many other countries.

But, as sociologists have pointed out, ownership of "luxury" items is not a class indicator simply because what constitutes luxury to some may be necessities to others.

The second argument is even simpler. Social mobility is high in Singapore, the proof being those who have done well with neither money nor connections to aid them.

It is true that children of taxi-drivers or hawkers, the two groups that appear synonymous with the working class, do make it to become President's Scholars with reassuring regularity every year.

But in giving ourselves a well-deserved pat on our back for the meritocracy on which our school system is based and for the conspicuous absence of poverty on our streets, we are perhaps guilty of overlooking another point.

This is that different groups of Singaporeans do not understand each other – distanced, regrettably, by how much money one has, what job one holds and how many pieces of paper qualifications one possesses.

Class distinctions exist not only in societies where clear lines are drawn, but where the accident of one's birth determines the quality of one's life.

Class distinctions also exist in a society when there is little interaction between different social groups.

One's network of friends will usually tend to consist of people similar to onself, but when social networks begin to harden into social categories, then class differences begin to emerge.

And class differences consist primarily in the perception of one social group by another.

The comfortably-off rub shoulders with myriad of working-class characters, those of the hawker/taxi-driver/salesgirl brigade, only when these services are required. In the process, the working class appears two-dimensional, perhaps suspect, and different.

And so, to some in the middle class, the working class appears to be dirty, crass, vulgar, potentially violent and criminal, backward, and irresponsible voters who misuse the ballot box.

This is sad.

Now, some might argue that class differences are a can of worms best left untouched. Endemic in this view is the belief that man is born unequal and that even where equality of opportunity exists, achievement – and hence rewards – will be unequal. So why talk about something that is inevitable, they might ask.

But looking around me today, I cannot help but feel that already, the can of worms has been left untouched too long, and that, in the way of maggots, worms have bred more worms and are threatening to spill out of the can.

Not talking about class and simply pretending that it does not exist will not make the problem go away. If left unfettered, class differences could prove a threat to the cohesion of our very young society.

REAL INCOME DIVIDE

Moving into a new neighbourhood has highlighted class differences

6 November 2011

I was at a Dempsey cafe with some friends when a stray comment got me thinking about Singapore, social class and lifestyle experiences.

What do you do on weekends, I was asked.

Nothing much, I replied. My favourite weekend morning activity is to have breakfast at a hawker centre and read the papers.

Oh yes, he nodded. Just to soak in the atmosphere?

I was puzzled by the comment. In the two seconds it took me to process why, the conversation had moved on.

And then I realised why. I have lived in everything from an attap house to a landed property to a condominium, but I always returned to Housing Board flats.

Hawker centres, coffee shops and the rhythm of HDB life represent my native habitat. It is places such as Dempsey I go to, to soak in the atmosphere. And even then, I avoid weekend evenings when the trendy turn out in droves, and go there on quiet weekdays.

I moved to an HDB estate in the west five months ago. Since then, I've realised two things. One, I remain at heart an HDB kid. Two, I had become used to certain comforts of a middle-class life. I had assumed they were just common habits of an increasingly affluent Singapore, but living here has sensitised me to just how subtle but real the gap is between the working class and the middle class.

In the Bukit Timah condominium where I used to live, every other car was a BMW, an Audi or a Mercedes, with a few Lamborghinis and Porsches. This is the UMI – upper middle-income – class.

Many are millionaires. According to a Boston Consulting Group report in June, Singapore has the highest concentration of millionaire households in the world, with 16 per cent of all households boasting at least $1 million in assets under management. That's 170,000 households out of 1.13 million.

In Bishan where I also used to live, the carparks even of HDB estates are full of Japanese sedans and big cars, with a sprinkling of European luxury cars. This is the solid middle class, the HDB burgher.

In my current estate, every other vehicle is a van, pick-up or lorry of some kind. I glance at the registered addresses on the vehicle, and I know most of those driving these vehicles home are not the bosses. My guess is they are the delivery drivers, the maintenance technicians. This is working-class Singapore.

For the average HDB working-class family, life remains a struggle. I see it around me. HDB shops have bare cement floors and fewer wares. Children play unsupervised by adults. When I changed my curtains, I packed my old ones into a bag, affixed a label that said "Fits Master Bedroom" and left it at the foot of my block. It was gone when I returned from breakfast.

My categorisation of Singapore groups are, of course, generalisations based on anecdotal experiences. But anecdote can be the basis of insight.

In middle-class Bishan, I enjoyed the convenience of HDB life with its coffee shops, but I also had easy access to the organic food stores and deluxe cafes I enjoyed. Here in the west, the merchandise and shop mix is different.

I went shopping for Dryel. That's the dry-cleaning kit that comes with a zipped-up bag and sheets of chemical cleaners you can use in your dryer, so you can dry-clean your silk dresses at home. I used to have no problems finding it in my old neighbourhoods. In my new estate, I couldn't find it in a few supermarkets. I asked one sales staff and was greeted with a stare, a loud question and a shake of the head. If you think about it, it's not surprising. Not many HDB families have a clothes dryer, so why would they need Dryel?

I gave up, and returned to my old haunt, the Cold Storage at Guthrie House, a tiny supermarket with an amazing knack of stocking things every household – okay, every UMI household – can need. There was Dryel. And nice bread. And nice pate to go with said bread.

I came to see that there are not just two Singapores: the heartlanders and the rest.

Among the heartlanders, there is the middle class and the working class.

And, I am coming to realise, there is another subset of the UMI class. If the UMI is the top 20 per cent, the top 1 per cent would be the Ultra Rich. My totally subjective definition of this group is that they earn at least $2 million a year, live in Good Class Bungalow areas or penthouse condominium apartments, and fly First or Business Class on holiday.

These folks apologise for their homes being "only 5,000 sq ft" – as one interviewee once told me. Their numbers will grow, if Singapore continues to do well, and attract Asia's rising super class.

So there you have at least four groups: the working class and the middle class among the heartlanders; and in the private property group, you have the UMI and the Ultra Rich.

So long as social boundaries are porous, and the average heartlander can move from the working to the middle to the UMI group, the Singapore Dream remains alive.

The new twist in the old debate on inequality, though, is the gap among the elite: between the top 20 per cent and the top 1 per cent.

New York Times columnist David Brooks wrote last week of this Blue Inequality fuelled by zooming incomes of the top 1 per cent.

"Within each profession, the top performers are now paid much better than the merely good or average performers. If you live in these big cities, you see people similar to yourself... who are earning much more while benefiting from low tax rates, wielding disproportionate political power, gaining in prestige and contributing seemingly little to the social good."

I have a feeling the anger over high ministerial salaries is fuelled in part by Blue Inequality. Some critics of the high ministerial pay policy come from the UMI class, and don't see why folks who went to school or used to work in the same office with them should be propelled into the Ultra Rich group once they enter politics, thanks to multi-million-dollar salaries paid out of the public purse.

It's easy to target the Ultra Rich as Public Enemy No. 1, as the other social groups can band together against them.

But that battle is not really relevant to the lives of the working class. For this group, what matter most are a job that pays enough for a life without strife and good schools for their children. For this group that forks out only for essentials, a set of made-to-measure curtains is a luxury.

GAP BETWEEN RULING ELITE AND MASSES IS BIGGEST POLITICAL RISK FOR THE PAP

26 October 2014

What might cause the People's Action Party (PAP) to lose power? This was the subject of a lecture by Mr Ho Kwon Ping, erstwhile dissident journalist turned establishment businessman and latterly the Institute of Policy Studies' first S R Nathan Fellow for the Study of Singapore.

Mr Ho painted three scenarios of how the PAP might lose dominance: a freak election result; an internal party split; and a massive loss of confidence in the PAP, due perhaps to corruption. He also cited factors that would erode support for the PAP: demography, its organisational structure and the relative strength of the opposition.

These are perfectly lucid analyses but also predictable, as he himself noted. It was his comments on what made Singapore less governable that I found more insightful. He cited four factors that would make Singapore harder to govern, regardless of which party is in power.

These are:

"First, the ability of governments to control information will continue to erode, despite sometimes frantic and illogical attempts to stem it."

"Second, it will be increasingly difficult to hold the political centre together in the midst of polarising extremes."

"Third, diminution in the stature of political leadership will encourage the rise of so-called 'non-constructive' politics."

"Fourth, maintaining an ethos of egalitarianism in an increasingly unequal society will require more than just political oratory."

On the last point, Mr Ho added: "The gulf between rich and poor

Singaporeans, not only in terms of wealth but also in terms of values, is probably more than ever before, and is continuing to widen."

My take on this is that what makes Singapore less governable is also what might cause the PAP to lose power: the growing gap between rich and poor.

As Mr Ho points out, the gulf is widening, not only in income, but in values.

I think the biggest and most dangerous political divide in Singapore that can arise is that between the political and socioeconomic elite and the hoi polloi.

We already see this happening in jurisdictions elsewhere. In Hong Kong, chief executive C.Y. Leung said in an interview last week that if Hong Kong had free elections with candidates nominated by the public, then the largest sector of society would likely dominate the electoral process.

"If it's entirely a numbers game and numeric representation, then obviously you'd be talking to the half of the people in Hong Kong who earn less than US$1,800 (S$2,250) a month," he said in comments published by the Wall Street Journal and International New York Times.

A few weeks ago, Mr Wang Zhenmin, a regular adviser to Beijing, had made a similar point, when he said greater democratic freedom in Hong Kong must be balanced against the city's powerful business elite who would have to share their "slice of the pie" with voters.

"The business community is in reality a very small group of elites in Hong Kong who control the destiny of the economy in Hong Kong. If we ignore their interests, Hong Kong capitalism will stop," he had said in August.

Such views are not the sole preserve of defenders of undemocratic Hong Kong's system. Even leaders of the world's freest country, the United States, are wont to express such a view in private.

Think back to Republican candidate Mitt Romney in the 2012 US

Presidential Election. At a private $50,000-a-head fundraising dinner, he responded to a question on his campaign strategy by dissing the 47 per cent of voters who were dependent on government aid and paid no taxes, who would support Democrat incumbent Barack Obama.

He said: "There are 47 per cent who are with him, who are dependent upon government, who believe that they are victims, who believe the government has a responsibility to care for them, who believe that they are entitled to healthcare, to food, to housing, to you-name-it. That that's an entitlement. And the government should give it to them. And they will vote for this president no matter what... These are people who pay no income tax... My job is not to worry about those people. I'll never convince them they should take personal responsibility and care for their lives."

Mr Romney later claimed the comments, which were secretly videotaped by a bartender at the dinner, were taken out of context.

As New York Times' columnist Paul Krugman noted this week: "The political right has always been uncomfortable with democracy. No matter how well conservatives do in elections, no matter how thoroughly free-market ideology dominates discourse, there is always an undercurrent of fear that the great unwashed will vote in left-wingers who will tax the rich, hand out largesse to the poor, and destroy the economy."

Mr Krugman describes America as being caught in a struggle between the plutocrats and the democrats, the way some depict the struggle in Hong Kong.

In Singapore, we don't see such a striking dichotomy – yet.

But if you were to read some of the comments online, you can see the rise of such polarised views – such as when bloggers and commenters paint the PAP as a bunch of self-serving elite people who pay themselves multi-million-dollar salaries to perpetuate a system in which they and their family members can become very rich.

We start to see the seeds of distrust being sowed – and a clear wedge driven between people and government, when activists demand the "return" of Central Provident Fund money – as though CPF monies are not clearly the sole property of each CPF member, as though they can be pilfered by a dishonest government.

Nor is it just some among the literate digerati who are at risk of sowing distrust.

When leaders and those in the elite shake their heads at a government policy and mutter that the PAP is "becoming populist", they too drive a wedge between the government and the governed, as though doing something that makes a government popular is a bad thing for the country.

It can be, but it need not be.

A good government first needs to create the conditions for business to flourish. Then it needs to spend and redistribute the wealth created to maintain harmony and fairness in a society, to enhance citizens' wellbeing. Doing the latter is not being populist.

Spending money to ensure universal health coverage is not populist – just the responsibility of any decent, humane government that has the wherewithal to do so.

Helping the jobless and underemployed get back into the job marketplace via wage subsidies and training is not populist – just good old common sense to get people back onto their feet.

Nor is spending on early childhood education to help poor children do well in school populist – just good investment in these kids' futures.

If a government has rich state coffers, but its people feel stressed and anxious at every stage of their lives, it cannot be a good government.

A good government strikes a balance between collecting enough for a country's future, and spending enough for the present.

It has to satisfy the elite generating most of the wealth, and the masses whose labour helps sustain it. The 47 per cent, the ones who earn below US$1,800 a month.

MIND THE PARALLEL UNIVERSE OF LOCAL POLITICS

20 April 2007

Those who observe Singapore politics know that there are two versions of reality in Singapore politics. I call it the theory of parallel universes.

One version is the "official" point of view, forcefully (often persuasively) articulated by government leaders, and reported by the mainstream media. Many Singaporeans buy into this version most of the time. According to received wisdom in this tradition, citizens are a law-abiding, hardworking lot. When they voice disagreement with authority, they do so with civility and respect for the other's position and feelings (they "give face", to use a colloquialism).

But there's an entire parallel universe of views, made up of common folk and, increasingly, netizens. In this world, citizens are sceptical and cynical, prone to believing the worst of public figures.

When they disagree with some policy or politician, they don't give quarter in their comments in coffee shops, cocktail parties or online. Rumour, gossip, biting comments and dark humour characterise this parallel universe.

The mainstream media, being a responsible creature, doesn't report rumour and gossip, so you don't read much of such *kopitiam* chat in The Straits Times.

As a political reporter, I sometimes sit for hours in Parliament listening to ministers' views on a policy, and then am subject the next morning to the parallel universe of ordinary folks, which says it was all nonsense.

I have come to understand that both universes have their own laws, valid claims to reality, and offer important perspectives on an issue. Politics in Singapore cannot be understood without knowing both worlds.

When I'm in the "official" universe, I accept its ground rules. In the parallel universe, a different part of my brain and feelings is engaged.

The theory of the parallel universes helps explain some things in politics, especially the way different groups of people end up with completely different perceptions of the same issue.

The most recent example is the debate over the decision to raise civil service and ministers' pay. To some people, the public response was reasonable and muted; others think the response was vociferously angry.

It all depends on which universe you've been living in. In the "official" universe, the Prime Minister's decision to forgo his salary increases was applauded. Indeed, even among the heartlanders of the parallel universe, many thought it was a good move.

But go into the parallel universe of coffee-shop mutterings and the Internet, and a very different picture emerges. There, conspiracy theories abound: that it represented a retreat from the decision to raise salaries; that it was a PR (public relations) move; and the most cynical of all, that it was a tax avoidance move, since donations to some charity receive double tax deductions.

Other examples of parallel universe thinking abound.

One vivid example is from August 2003. This was when then-Prime Minister Goh Chok Tong recounted an old urban legend that in 1990, Mr Lee Hsien Loong had a disagreement with and slapped fellow Cabinet minister S. Dhanabalan. Mr Goh told the story to stress that it was not true. Official universe thinking: story debunked conclusively.

But in the recounting, many people got the wrong impression.

Eating *mee pok* with my mother one morning around that period, I was bemused when she said in Teochew: "Lee Hsien Loong *pah kiling gia*", using a phrase that means "to hit an Indian".

I explained to her that it was not the case, that Mr Goh himself said it was not true, and told her to tell all her neighbourhood *kaki* that was the case.

Sometimes, comments from the parallel universe spill into official discourse.

Back in 1996 amid a booming property market, talk swirled that Mr Lee Kuan Yew and then-deputy PM Lee Hsien Loong had bought luxury apartments from developer HPL at discounts.

This was the parallel universe in action. The "official" response? To bring the talk into the open. A series of statements from regulators, the developer and the Lees ensued. Then-PM Goh ordered an investigation, which showed no wrongdoing. For good measure, the whole issue was extensively debated in Parliament.

What could have been a disaster for the Government ended up buttressing its reputation for impartiality and incorruptibility, as the episode showed the resilience of a system which could subject the former PM and the deputy PM to scrutiny.

Another example when the parallel universe of gossip penetrated the hallowed halls of Parliament was during the recent debate on ministers' pay.

For years, some people have muttered unkind things about Dr Lee Boon Yang being "just a vet" who did not deserve ministerial million-dollar salaries. PM Lee Hsien Loong brought that talk into the open to rebut it, and defuse it with humour. Back in the 1960s, said PM Lee, many bright students studied veterinary science because pig farming was a big part of the economy. As for Dr Lee, he had many skills. If there were more vets like him, said PM Lee to laughter in Parliament, he wanted their names.

The HPL and "vet" examples suggest one good approach to dealing with the two universes: expose the parallel universe to a good dose of light from the "official" universe.

Some rudimentary knowledge of quantum physics may help. I was surprised to discover when I Googled the term this week, that the theory of parallel universes has a respected history in science.

The theory was formulated by physicists in the 1950s and 1960s, as one way to make sense of the new discoveries of quantum physics and general relativity that challenged people's ideas of a linear, straightforward universe.

One kind of parallel universe in physics is an anti-matter universe, made up of anti-particles, which are particles that are the antithesis of those in the world of matter.

It's all quite arcane. But what is interesting for this article is that when you expose small amounts of anti-matter to large doses of matter, then the anti-matter gets annihilated. So maybe one way to deal with the anti-matter parallel universe of heartfelt, but often ill-informed, discourse is to expose it to doses of "official" matter.

Politicians in Singapore ignore the parallel universe at their peril. To be effective, a good MP (and political reporter) needs footholds in both worlds.

This is why the People's Action Party traditionally values so-called "grassroots MPs" with traction in the parallel universe, who can shape opinion in that world.

For, like it or not, the parallel universe is a fact of life in Singapore politics and its discourse cannot be dismissed. And as physicists will tell you, sometimes, universes collide.

INEQUALITY IS A THREAT
– NAME IT, AND FACE IT

Singapore must not become a society where people feel the system is stacked against them, favouring a minority

18 February 2018

Thirty years ago, as an intern for The Straits Times, I worked on a two-part feature on "Children of the Establishment".

It was both an easy and difficult feature to do. I was then studying at Cambridge University on a government scholarship. All I did was talk to my friends and friends of friends. They included offspring of a diplomat, university professor, senior lawyer, doctors, and others in establishment circles. My university mates were, well, just mates. We talked. They were not at all snobbish or arrogant.

But it was also a difficult assignment because I was writing about class, and although I went to college with them, I stood on the other side of the divide, as a child of working-class parents.

I wrote up some interviews and then concluded the series with a short piece on my own reflections.

I noted that most of the families knew each other, and most had close friends from the same socioeconomic circles.

I wrote that it was reassuring that wealth had not bred decadence, but a sense of responsibility and a strong work ethic. But, I also added: "In a society where eight out of 10 live in Housing Board flats, these people show a disturbing unawareness of the other end of society. Most have little interaction with people from different, less privileged backgrounds."

Fast forward 30 years, and the issue of the class divide has resurfaced, with a vengeance.

An Institute of Policy Studies (IPS) survey on social capital put hard numbers to what many Singaporeans have noticed anecdotally and spoken about privately: that despite our aspiration to be a meritocratic society with high social mobility, we may in fact be coming even more class-riven.

The Straits Times report on the survey, published in December, put it starkly in the first sentence: "The sharpest social divisions in Singapore may now be based on class, instead of race or religion."

The survey asked Singaporeans where they lived, what schools they went to, and who their friends and associates were. It found that those who live in public housing have ties to 4.3 people in public housing and 0.8 people in private.

People who studied in "non-elite" schools had ties to 3.9 people who went to similar schools, and ties to only 0.4 people who studied in "elite" schools.

What the survey shows is a concentration of social networks around class differentiators such as housing type and schools attended.

It is clear that Singapore's once egalitarian, easy-going society is stratifying.

Prime Minister Lee Hsien Loong acknowledged this in Parliament this month. Responding to an MP's question, he said: "The issues of mitigating income inequality, ensuring social mobility and enhancing social integration are critical. If we fail – if widening income inequalities result in a rigid and stratified social system, with each class ignoring the others or pursuing its interests at the expense of others – our politics will turn vicious, our society will fracture and our nation will wither."

I agree with PM Lee that left unchecked, inequality will turn Singapore's cohesive politics vicious, fracture our society, and wither our nation. I was glad he didn't mince his words. It's time to talk about inequality with the seriousness the issue deserves.

But I think the issue goes beyond income inequality to one of wider social inequalities that are embedded in our system.

This is because inequality is not about absolute deprivation, unlike poverty. When families are poor, a hand up or a handout can help them move into more comfortable lives.

But inequality is a structural impediment. Inequality is about how a society's policies, structures, assumptions and decisions work together to create advantage for some groups, and obstacles for others.

We can see how politics globally have become fragmented as societies are driven apart by competing interests, and when people feel that the country's systems are unequal and stacked against them.

We must not allow that to happen in Singapore.

In Singapore, we have started to tackle income inequality in a concerted manner. As PM Lee and other government leaders have noted, the Gini coefficient that measures income inequality fell from 0.470 in 2006 to 0.458 in 2016, its lowest in a decade. When government taxes and transfers are factored in, the 2016 figure is even lower at 0.402.

Programmes like the Workfare Income Supplement, and transfers to help low-wage workers boost their retirement savings or help them cope with the goods and services tax, all raise income levels at the bottom. As a society, we also continue to have fairly good intergenerational social mobility.

But will it continue to be so?

I got to thinking about this after reading a fascinating new book by sociologist Teo You Yenn, titled *This is What Inequality Looks Like*.

You Yenn's book is a mix of ethnography and analysis. She writes about structures of inequality that many of us are oblivious to, drawing on stories of the people she has done research on.

Hers is a gently probing, insistent voice, unpacking assumptions behind common practices and beliefs in Singapore to reveal the unequal structures that sometimes trap people in poverty and insecurity. (I recommend this book be read by every politician and civil servant, especially those involved in administering social policy.)

For example, insisting on housing subsidies being funnelled to married parents leaves out precisely the most vulnerable children – those with unmarried parents who are more likely to be struggling to cope.

Rather than devote more resources to the most vulnerable young, inequality is perpetuated through the generations by denying them housing subsidies given liberally to those from intact families.

What saddens me most in reading the book and the news reports around the IPS survey is the realisation that Singapore society has changed for the worse in the 30 years since I wrote that feature about "Children of the Establishment".

This is especially the case for our education system. Once a conveyor belt for meritocracy, propelling many a taxi driver's son or hawker's daughter along a pathway to academic achievement and a well-paying job with good social standing, our education system risks becoming a bastion of privilege, where the powerful and well-connected protect access to the nation's well-regarded primary schools for their own kind.

And with the complicated through-train system, getting into the "right" primary school can secure your secondary school education – and as we know now from the IPS survey – even a lifetime of access to networks that can come in useful in your working life.

Class plays a role too, as parents who have the time to volunteer to gain priority access tend to have more secure, well-paying jobs, or are homemakers married to spouses with those kinds of jobs.

To be sure, there is nothing very nefarious about privilege being passed on – it is the trait of societies that stratification is transmitted to future generations, as parents pass on their socioeconomic advantages to their children. So the taxi driver's son who managed to get into a brand-name school in the past and becomes a lawyer, thus joining the elite ranks, will pass on his advantages and alumni access to his son. That lawyer's son may then gain a coveted place in a brand-name school, depriving today's taxi driver's son of one.

In that way, those without connections today will find it harder to break into circles of privilege than those in the past. This is a very simplistic example, but is illustrative of how societies can become stratified along socioeconomic status over time.

The system of giving priority admission for alumni members and community volunteers has continued for decades, despite its clearly detrimental effect on social cohesion, creating a society where connections determine what school your child goes to. In my view, the negative social effects outweigh positive effects, such as maintaining school tradition.

In 2013, PM Lee highlighted the problem of some popular primary schools becoming "closed institutions" open only to those with alumni or family connections to the school. The Government has since kept at least one class of 40 places open in all schools, for those without connections to the school.

Today, we have Workfare, the Progressive Wage Model and any number of schemes to boost the incomes of those with low-paying jobs. As PM Lee made clear, income inequality is now being dealt with seriously.

Still, I think other aspects of the inequality debate deserve a hearing. Our school admission policy is just one rather obvious example of how inequality is allowed to perpetuate. Are other social policies exacerbating inequality?

Unlike low-wage workers or poverty, inequality is harder to root out because it can't be captured by one figure or income. Inequality is always about relativities: relative access to public goods, relative privilege, relative well-being.

And its effects are more insidious.

Inequality will eat away at our sense of society, if people start to doubt that the Singapore system is fair to all – especially those without wealth and without connections.

The last thing we want is for people to feel that the country is not just ruled by the elite, but for the elite.

I am coming to think that inequality is nothing less than a major societal-wide threat for Singapore.

Social security – such as having a sense of cohesion – is as vital to our national survival as food and water security. Inequality risks disrupting that cohesion and is, in that sense, an existential threat. Just as we have faced up to the issues of terrorism, cyber security and fake news, we need to face up to the threat that inequality poses to Singapore.

We should face it, name it, and unpack what contributes to inequality, so that we can make our system more equal.

HOW MERITOCRACY CAN BREED INTELLECTUAL ELITISM

10 November 2006

I grew up in, variously, a kampung attap house, a one-room rental flat and then a three-room Housing Board flat, where my two siblings, our parents and I spent many happy, sometimes tumultuous, years cheek by jowl.

I never had my own room till I went to university overseas. In England, I had my own princely suite of bed-and-sitting-room with aged but sturdy furniture. An old classmate from Singapore visited me in my room, oohed and aahed at my new surroundings and proclaimed I had "arrived".

I raised a quizzical eyebrow, never setting much store by sentiments like these. It was only in my adult years that I learnt the many gradations of elitism and snobbery.

There is car snobbery. In my condominium carpark, every other car is a sedate establishment BMW or a Mercedes. My Japanese sedan sits among them like an upstart. I recall tales of erstwhile Cambridge students whose mothers warned them against "gold-digger" girlfriends and finally understood that the warnings were against people precisely like myself – from no illustrious "family", but whose drive and small talents propel them from their rightful obscurity into places where they rub shoulders with the "elite".

There is residential snobbery, where every Singaporean is able to peg every other Singaporean into his social pecking order by the place he lives in. When I lived in an HDB flat, I learnt the divide between "HDB" and "private" housing. Then I moved to private housing and learnt the intricate calibrations between landed, apartment and condo living. And then I learnt that there are condos and condos, and Bukit Timah is a good place for one. And then a Bukit Timah veteran told me I didn't know anything; that some stretches of Bukit Timah are more prestigious than others.

And I haven't even got round to fathoming the relative rank of Tanglin and Orchard addresses, the Ardmore Park and the like.

I have long wondered why, for such a meritocratic society, Singapore is so elitist. And then I finally understood that the two are inextricably linked: Singapore is such an elitist society precisely because of meritocracy.

For meritocracy tells us that anyone can achieve, if they have the gumption, the wherewithal, the drive, the talent, the ability. In a meritocracy, success depends on your own efforts – on merit.

And so we are led into the seduction of believing the reverse: that if you don't do well, if you drop out, there's something, well, unmeritorious about you, and so you deserve your mediocrity.

In a meritocracy, you can blame your parents only once. After that, the rest is really up to you.

If you were born into a humble family and still didn't do well in your own adult lifetime, you can't blame your social class, your wrong accent, your lousy sartorial instincts, your lack of educational opportunities.

You can't pin the blame on others, because there is no shortage of poor kids made good in Singapore to prove you wrong: They become millionaires; they become prime minister; they become materially successful. If you are not among them, you take a good, hard look and realise you can blame only yourself.

This is the uncomfortable subtext of meritocracy, which isn't much remarked upon, but which runs like a subterranean thread in our social conversations.

Singaporeans ostensibly frown on car and condo snobbery even as many aspire to those shallow symbols of "success".

But our ethos of meritocracy condones, indeed encourages, another form of snobbery: intellectual elitism. Singapore's merit-based system hinges almost entirely on the meritocracy of academic achievement. Do well in school, and there's a good chance the kid from a poverty-stricken background can break out of the poverty cycle.

When education becomes such an important social leveller and vehicle for social mobility, is it any wonder that intellectual ability becomes imbued with such positive attributes that it nearly becomes associated with a moral virtue?

Subliminally, we imbibe the message that intellectual achievement is not only a mark of mental acuity, but it is also a reflection of character, strength of purpose, dedication, of moral virtue.

This is not to say that we are so naive as to assume that those who get As are more saintly than those who fail their examinations. But I think many of us do assume that the A-getters are more disciplined, more hardworking, more driven to excel, more deserving of reward, than those who get Cs.

And so academic achievement becomes conflated with character and moral attributes.

All this is by way of explaining how bright young things in the country's elite schools may turn out to be both staunch believers of meritocracy and staunchly elitist in their perspective.

Is it any wonder they turn out so, when the ethos of Singapore society is based on the idea that academic merit helps sort people into their respective social classes? That may sound like an extremely meritocratic argument to make, but implicit in it is the idea that if you are sorted into the "lower" classes, it is because you lack academic merit – and are somehow inferior.

And so the emphasis on meritocracy and academic achievement

becomes the flip side of elitism: one justifies the other. So when talking about elitism in Singapore today, we should not run away from the uncomfortable truth that our merit-based system can breed a "smarter-than-thou" attitude of intellectual snobbery, evident in the recent blog of the 18-year-old student which attracted such attention.

What is the solution to this creeping merit-based elitism?

Clearly empathy is one response, and there is no shortage of very successful people who devote time and money to helping others.

But there is another aspect of the issue we should never forget, which is to police our meritocratic system and fix its failings.

Former senior civil servant Ngiam Tong Dow, speaking to the Oxbridge Society recently, emphasised how Singapore can refine its system of selecting the elite. I thought the entire premise of his argument extremely elitist. For surely the more pertinent issue is how to entrench fair competition in a meritocratic system, not how to improve selection among the elite?

We should ask ourselves: Are there structural impediments to poor kids making good in today's system? What can we do to remove those obstacles?

United States studies have consistently shown that the children of wealthy, middle-class parents have a better chance of doing well in school and going to college. Some nascent studies in Singapore have shown that the effects of parental background on a child's academic achievement are considerable.

Rather than assume the elitist position that Singapore's meritocratic system is so well-oiled that those who don't succeed deserve to fail, we should be taking a more rigorous look at how our much-vaunted meritocratic system may be failing those who deserve to succeed.

THE REALLY SHAMEFUL THING ABOUT POVERTY

13 March 2016

When I first started coming across commentaries a few years ago about a new school of research that linked poverty to poor behavioural patterns, my initial reaction was one of indignation.

Talk about blaming the victim, I muttered under my breath, as yet another op-ed filtered onto my computer screen suggesting this.

The theory was popularised in 2013, after the publication of the book *Scarcity: Why Having Too Little Means So Much*, by Sendhil Mullainathan and Eldar Shafir, a Harvard economist and a Princeton psychologist.

The idea is that when people are short of something – money, time, affection – their minds start to get fixated on the thing they lack. Their mind then reacts in two ways. First, it develops a hyperfocus on the thing they lack. If they lack friends, their minds zoom in on a ghost of a smile. If they lack money, their minds are better able to grasp the cost of things.

But anxiety over their scarcity also taxes their brain, leaving little "mental bandwidth" as the writers call it, to deal with decisions. They may then end up performing poorer than normal in exams, or in cognitive tests, or making bad choices.

The two writers did experiments on people, including sugarcane farmers in India before and after money from their harvests come in. They found that people made better decisions when they were flush with cash than when they needed money.

So the theory is that very poor people are so worried about having enough food, a roof over their heads and money to pay bills, that they may "neglect to weed their crops, vaccinate their children, wash their hands, treat their water, take their pills or eat properly when pregnant", as The Economist summed it up.

My initial reaction to such research was scepticism and irritation.

Many people, especially those born to poor families, are poor because of circumstances.

Saying that their poverty then hinders them from making good decisions seems like adding insult to injury. Many of us come from poor families, whose parents may be uneducated but who made many good decisions for the family.

They worked hard, they saved hard, and they nagged us to study hard. So the children studied hard, which helped them secure good jobs, and then they too worked hard and saved hard in their turn. Hundreds of thousands of Singaporeans have broken out of the poverty trap that way, and brought their parents into a comfortable retirement.

But I later understood that the writers were talking about extreme scarcity – not just families which might be in the bottom 20 per cent of households, but those who are down to their last $5, who don't know where their next meal is coming from, and who don't have money for their children's recess.

Then I could entertain the possibility that such constant mental stress can cause parents to make poor decisions for their children.

How then to help the poor?

My colleague Toh Yong Chuan wrote that it was more realistic to forget the parents and focus on helping the children. Where necessary, and where the home environment was negative, let the teenager stay in a boarding school where he will get help with schoolwork, a disciplined timetable, and a drug-free, crime-free environment.

His commentary drew a heartfelt rebuttal from sociology professor Teo You Yenn, who argues that the way we view poor people determines the kind of solutions we come out with to help them.

From her research talking to low-income households, she says, she finds that they are very much invested in their children, and try to make good choices for them.

However, when the choices have a bad outcome, they may lack resources to mitigate the consequences. She cites a real case of someone she knows: A foreign woman married a Singaporean, moved here and had a child with him. But she didn't register for the baby to be Singaporean at birth.

"Soon after, she was widowed, and several attempts to secure citizenship failed. Her daughter Jen (not her real name) has been living in Singapore for most of her life and knows no other home. Jen's mother encouraged her in her studies and she has just completed her A levels. Their limited income and Jen's lack of citizenship, however, means that she has accumulated arrears in school fees. Unless she pays, her certificate will not be released, barring her from university. The few thousand dollars owed seem insurmountable and the 'bad choice' of not applying for citizenship immediately means the vast difference between upward mobility and stasis."

You Yenn also points out that society tends to assume that poor parents are more neglectful of or abusive to their children.

As many of us from poor but loving and functioning families know, that is a patent untruth and a gross over-generalisation. You Yenn points out that "comparable actions are judged differently across class". For example, a child may be left at home alone or with a domestic worker. In both cases, the parents are working and leave the child. Yet society would treat the first as neglect, but view the second as normal.

Yet which method is better for the child's upbringing and values?

Those of us who fended for ourselves, in the long afternoons after primary school, sans maid, sans tutor, sans grandparent, learnt how to take care of our own meals and managed our time, while those with the domestic maid may grow up feeling entitled, used to having meals served on a platter – literally – and having someone else pick up after them.

I think the research on scarcity and the very poor is useful in giving us a better idea of how extreme poverty stresses people. But it should not be used as a stick with which to beat the poor.

The solution is to raise people from extreme poverty – give them enough, so they are not on the brink of starvation – into the land of the ordinary poor.

This is an easy sentence to write, but it has immense implications on our social policy. For one thing, it means having a higher Public Assistance allowance so those receiving it don't have to eat only plain rice with gravy, or live in the dark at night to save on electricity bills.

It means relooking our wage model and having what is called a "living wage" – wages of a sufficient level for people to live with dignity. Then we won't have the situation of old folks working 12 hours a day, six days a week, for $800 wages that aren't enough to pay for their rent, utilities, basic meals, and bus fare.

We have to remember that there is no shame, no stigma, and no mental deficit to being poor. But where there is extreme poverty, and people are on the brink of starvation in a very wealthy country like Singapore, it is indeed a shameful thing.

On the rest of us, and the way our society is organised.

THE STORY OF AN IMMIGRANT, THE NATION'S LIFEBLOOD

12 August 1995

Most of us have seen them around, these elderly, dialect-speaking women who have slaved a lifetime for family and children, and now sit on stone chairs and at tables in void decks, keeping an indulgent eye on young grandchildren milling around.

These women are always addressed as Ah Soh, Ah Sim or Ah Hmm, depending on the dialect. They are a ubiquitous feature of the heartscape of an average Housing Board estate.

Madam Lou was one of them, often sitting there at dusk while her grandson played with other children.

Like the others, she had a story to tell. And through her tale pulsed the lifeblood of this young immigrant nation.

It was 40 years ago that Madam Lou boarded a boat from her hometown in Shantou to embark on a one-week voyage to Nanyang, as Malaya was called then by the Chinese.

It was 1955, and she was 28. She was joining her husband, whom she had married eight years before and been separated from, when he left to make a home for them in faraway Nanyang.

Her husband was what the villagers called a returned sojourner, a voyager who had ventured to the glamorous Nanyang and returned. These were the men with derring-do and drive, who might one day make their fortunes.

Madam Lou spent two years in Kuala Lumpur, before settling in Singapore with her husband, a carpenter by trade.

As an immigrant wife, she learnt to do many things her sheltered childhood in a well-to-do family had never prepared her for. She hauled bricks for two months to help pay the rent of their first room. There was no time to do the beautiful embroidery she had enjoyed in Shantou.

Here, every stitch of the needle had to be prosaic, aimed at a specific utilitarian purpose. With her trusty steel scissors that had survived the voyage to Nanyang, she cut and sewed, and clothed her husband, herself and later the three children they would have.

The young immigrant couple's first break came when Madam Lou won $50 in a lottery. They bought a trishaw, and with it became roving hawkers.

Over the years, they would sell many different food products.

Together with her husband, she learnt how to make *popiah*, fry chestnuts, prepare pineapple cordial, cook rice dishes and noodles, and negotiate the best prices in the market for her wares. These culinary skills were not leisurely pursuits, but their means of livelihood.

They pushed their trishaw where there were crowds: around the Esplanade and the City Hall areas, the backdrop to so many important national events; the Serangoon Road area on racing days; and the Catholic church at Novena on Saturdays.

On Aug 9, 1965, Singapore's independence was declared. Madam Lou became a citizen shortly after.

Through the years, she had been sending money and clothes to her relatives in China. But letters became less frequent.

The Cultural Revolution from 1966-76 threw China into upheaval. Several relatives committed suicide. After her sister died, the last emotional tie to her homeland was severed.

Through it all, she made her living in Singapore, kept house and raised three children. Later, she sent them to English-speaking schools where they learnt about the flag of her adopted country and soon internalised its values.

I asked Madam Lou if she would return to China one day.

What for, she replied. Her family was here. She had only very distant relatives in her hometown.

As we spoke, she was cutting up old bath towels to be used as floor rags, with the very pair of scissors she had brought with her on her voyage 40 years ago. I held it almost in awe.

As she spoke, her four-year-old grandson ran up to her in agitation.

He gestured towards the red-and-white flag that hung from the balustrade outside their flat. He was almost in tears. Something was very wrong in his childish world.

I went out into the corridor. One end of the string which held up the state flag hung out for the National Day celebration had snapped. The flag now fluttered limply in the wind. I consoled him and set the flag right.

Madam Lou, my immigrant mother, had sunk roots in this tiny island state that was now her home, and mine, and would remain her grandson's.

DANGER LURKS EVERYWHERE

At wet markets, knives lie sharpened – ready to slit the throats of unwary greenhorns who are more used to the fixed prices of supermarkets

23 October 1999

They say Singapore is a very safe place. I agree.

But there is one area in Singapore I hesitate to venture into even in broad daylight, an area I step into with quaking heart, where inhabitants adopt aggressive cut-throat practices towards outsiders.

Their sharp eyes can tell at a glance how foreign I am on their territory and they adopt sharp practices to put me in my place and rip me off at the same time.

The place? The wet market, where stallholders are veterans of that arcane art the Hokkiens call "slaughtering" – or the practice of inflating prices for special categories of customers.

I recognise it because, in our time, my family did the same for all *ang moh* customers who dared order from our food stall. We have all since reformed, of course, but, for my sins, I now have the privilege of being given the same treatment by the wet-market butcher and fishmonger.

A few months ago, I went to the Lakeview wet market with our maid. We normally shop at NTUC FairPrice but wanted more varieties of fish to choose from, so we went to the market. Everything seemed expensive to me but, not being one of those housekeepers who note to the last cent the unit price of everything from *chye sim* to pomfret and vacuum-tumbled chicken wing drumette, I paid up whatever I was told.

Until we got to the butcher. A luscious-looking pig's tail hung on the hook. I asked for it. The woman butcher weighed it and quoted me a price. I recoiled in shock and asked her how much it cost per kilo. Thirteen dollars, she said.

One of the few things that had seeped into my brain from sojourns to FairPrice was that pork cost $9 to $10 per kg. So, suspecting she was a butcher in more ways than one, I said that was expensive. No, she insisted, it was the going rate.

Okay, I said, annoyed at having been given the run-around by all and sundry that morning, I would buy it now but the next time I came to the market, I would bring my mother and show her which stall had "cheated" me and she would tell all her friends.

It was petty – but it worked, because suddenly the butcher reduced her price, just like that.

Later, when I told Mother, she laughed and, naughtily, brought out an equally luscious-looking pig's tail she had bought, much more cheaply, from FairPrice. "They take one look and they know you can be cheated – young lady, obviously not used to the wet market, with a maid, so must be rich. Everybody will raise his prices for you!"

Needless to say, it was the last time I ventured into enemy territory – the Lakeview market – alone.

You could say the wet-market phenomenon is the revenge of the heartlanders on the cosmopolitans.

Or you can see it as a way to redistribute income.

I like to interpret it as a case of Third World trading practices clinging on in pockets of Singapore, which suit those used to it, like Mother – who will lose her way in an Orchard Road department store, but can stand her own among the raucous fishmongers. For the rest of us more familiar with the practice of standard pricing and good customer service, it is a case of *caveat emptor* – buyer, beware.

In the Tekka market the other day, Mother took me to a fishmonger she frequents. We picked out some fish – seabass, pomfret, *batang* – and placed them neatly in a basket. One of the helpers hovered around her, weighing the fish and quoting her a price.

Later, another helper, Worker B, helped tot up the price – but, in so doing, quoted us a different price for each type of fish. Mother complained and ticked him off, whereupon he was packed off to attend to someone else, while the fishmonger *towkay* himself, an old Teochew man, came over to attend to her personally.

If I were alone, I would have paid up whatever I had been quoted, which was some 30 per cent more than the price Mother got – and worse, there was a high chance the fish I paid for would have ended up in someone else's home, as the fishmonger warned us, because Worker B was known to clean the fish at another nearby stall and re-selling a few quietly to some other unsuspecting customer.

It begged the question of why the fishmonger should hire someone so patently unreliable, but in this wet-market world, different rules applied.

Perhaps there was a familial reason, or a debt owed someone, that resulted in him taking on this worker. I desisted from asking.

I was, after all, a novice in this wet-market world, which had different assumptions and ways of doing things. Mother, blur as *sotong* in the modern high-tech world, was the expert here, and the talisman I took with me whenever I had to venture into that nether world.

The other day, she took me to the Ang Mo Kio Central market, a place she has frequented for over 20 years. She took me to her favourite fish stall. It was run by a cheerful young man who spoke fluent Teochew and ribbed her and joked while earning her money.

He had taken over the business from his father – who happened to be from the same village in Teochew province as Mother. Mother gave me a brief run-down of his family history as she poked and pried open the fish gills.

She introduced me to him. "And this is my daughter. Take a good look, make sure you remember her face. The next time she comes without me, you make sure you don't 'slaughter' her, *hor*."

He: "Me? Slaughter? Don't know the meaning of the word."

Mother: "All you market businessmen. Everyone of you has a knife with a keen edge, all ready and sharpened (*tor buah lai lai*)."

He (in mock horror): "Ah Soh! You buy fish from us for so many years, how can you think that?"

Mother: "Yah, yah, I buy from you because your father was honest. And you, because you have the gift of the gab and can charm birds off trees."

I have not put Mother's prowess to the test, so I do not know yet if her injunction to the fishmonger would have been sufficient protection in that world. But then, there is also the vegetable seller, the pork seller and the fruit seller to reckon with.

Unfortunately, Mother lacked the necessary connections to "pull strings" for me with them.

So last week, when the food stock ran low, I bypassed the wet market and returned to the supermarket.

It lacked variety but, at least in the predictable – and air-conditioned – world of the supermarket, clear rules govern commercial behaviour, and no *tor buah lai lai* lies in wait for unsuspecting shoppers!

CAN'T SWEAT IT OUT? POLITICS IS NOT FOR YOU

19 November 2004

Over the years, I've come to know some individuals who have gone through the "tea sessions" that the People's Action Party (PAP) hosts to suss out potential candidates.

In recent weeks, as the PAP's search for candidates fans a media frenzy, I've met some of them, and asked them the usual questions: Have they been to tea? How many rounds have they gone for? And, if so, will they say "yes" if the question is popped?

The answers vary, depending on how well they know me, and how much they think they should dissemble.

Some are quite happy to be considered. Among the replies I've heard from those who say they won't stand as PAP candidates: "Business interests take me overseas"; "My kids are young"; "My organisation needs me now and I can't leave".

The most candid of all are replies which are variations on this theme: "I don't mind having a say in policy, but I don't want to go for block parties/ attend Meet-the-People Sessions/kiss babies/do grassroots work."

At one such conversation recently with several high-achieving friends, one was trying to persuade another to take up a tea invitation with the observation: "Can delegate all this work."

Not to put too fine a point on it, I'm appalled by such sentiments, yet unsurprised.

Many people want the influence that being in politics brings, without the pain of actually contesting an election.

Witness the bumper crop of 37 applicants vying for nine seats in Parliament as Nominated MPs. These are all people who care about Singapore, want a say in its development, are attracted to the august responsibility of being in the highest debating chamber in the land – but don't have the stomach for the hurly-burly of electoral politics.

This may be a fairly harmless phenomenon. After all, there are many ways to participate in the political process, and each finds his or her own niche.

(My view of the NMP scheme is that it's second-best – a viable alternative to having an electoral opposition. In the long run, however, its effects may be less benign: It absorbs a potential pool of possibly dissenting, politicised Singaporeans who may otherwise throw their hats into the electoral arena. This may work well for the incumbent PAP – but delays the progression to a more lively, viable opposition political scene. But more on that some other time.)

What I'm concerned about now is the sense of underlying disdain of the rough-and-tumble of electoral politics among the chattering classes from which potential NMPs and PAP candidates are often recruited.

There's a view that intellectual effort to craft policies is a worthwhile pursuit while sitting down for three hours listening to constituents' grouses during Meet-the-People Sessions is a waste of time.

Again, not to put too fine a point on it, therein lies the road to political perdition.

For no one should forget that in the end, policies are for and about people: All those beautifully-planned and well-argued policies that so scintillate the intellectual elite are all meant to do one thing – make for a better life for Singaporeans, to boost that hawker's earnings, or give that cleaner's daughter a leg up in her future.

I've always believed that it is close contact with the heartlanders, with the masses, that keeps a politician honest.

I don't mean honesty in the sense of probity and integrity. For that, a person's character, strict laws and party discipline play a bigger part. I mean honesty in the sense of reminding a politician just what his job is really about, and driving home to him the source of his power.

It bears repeating, in Singapore's political culture which tends to see politicians as "political leaders", that in the end an MP's job is to serve his constituents. Sometimes he serves best by "leading" them (persuading them to retrain, for example, so they can get better jobs), but his main purpose is to serve, not lead.

It also bears repeating that while it's the political party that gives him a platform from which to secure votes, it's voters who give the MP the power to enter Parliament.

It's imperative, if MPs and ministers want to remain in touch with the pulse of Singapore, for them to spend time in direct, unmediated contact with the masses: the retrenched, the single mother, the family struggling to cope, the contractor trying to marry a foreign wife.

Such contact also gives politicians the first-hand knowledge of constituents' concerns they need to make good speeches in Parliament.

During the Parliament sittings this week, I remember MP Arthur Fong telling the House about a constituent who was sent to jail for letting out his apartment to someone who turned out to be an illegal immigrant. I remember MP Ahmad Khalis, speaking from obvious knowledge, urging the Government to be flexible in considering marginal applicants for the Home Ownership Plus Education assistance scheme for lower-income families.

Many ministers make it a point to attend Meet-the-People Sessions personally. Prime Minister Lee Hsien Loong has stated that he finds them useful in getting feedback on policies: He has a system of tagging "red stickers" on cases that reveal gaps in policies that may need changing.

Without that constant contact with "the ground", it's easy for policymakers to lose touch with reality.

So when I hear people say they don't mind being in politics to shape policy but don't fancy the constituency work, I tell them: You're better off saying "no" to being a PAP candidate.

I should add: Singapore is probably better off without politicians like you.

For no one too proud to shake a fishmonger's hand and ask for her vote deserves to be in Parliament.

YOUR MP IS NOT THE CHIEF SOCIAL WORKER. HE'S SUPPOSED TO RAISE ISSUES AND MAKE LAWS

22 August 2015

————

There I was, scrunched with the latecomer reporters, at the back of the People's Action Party (PAP) branch office in Clementi.

Up front, Mr Tharman Shanmugaratnam was introducing the party's candidates for Jurong Group Representation Constituency (GRC) for the coming General Election.

Reporters who turned up an hour early got to sit right in front – cross-legged on the floor. The lucky ones got chairs. Then the photographers positioned themselves in lines. Behind them, several stood on chairs to get better angles.

And right behind the scrum – peering through the legs of those balancing themselves on chairs – were those of us who turned up later. Serves me right for not being *kiasu*.

I couldn't see the candidates' faces except on the camera screens of colleagues in front of me. I could hear, but had to strain to keep my attention from wandering.

One by one, each candidate spoke about their wish to build a more caring community in Jurong GRC. To be sure, they sounded sincere.

Mr Tharman himself, although Deputy Prime Minister and Finance Minister with matters of state to occupy the buzzing brain underneath that gleaming bald pate, spoke passionately about the "Jurong way" – "Our style in Jurong is to be on the ground all the time and to serve with our hearts. That's our style."

Helping people when no one is looking, away from the glares of the camera, day in, day out.

The incumbent candidates – Mr Tharman, Mr Desmond Lee and Mr Ang Wei Neng – highlighted some Jurong GRC initiatives: helping disadvantaged kids; giving second, third chances to ex-inmates; harnessing volunteers.

The two new candidates in the GRC – Madam Rahayu Mahzam and Dr Tan Wu Meng – were also introduced as candidates with a genuine heart for the people.

Indeed, Madam Rahayu, 35, has been a volunteer since she was 17. She has met many families in difficulty. She wants to work with disadvantaged families and youth.

Dr Tan called himself "a doctor who has a heart to serve, who's very concerned about helping make people's lives better, who's very concerned about looking after elderly residents". He spoke about a Lions Befrienders seniors activity centre at Blk 420A in Clementi to befriend vulnerable elderly, a childcare centre nearby and a special-needs early intervention centre elsewhere.

But listening to them, my mind started to drift at the litany of the social programmes in Jurong GRC.

I started wondering: Were they standing as Members of Parliament, or angling for posts as Chief Social Worker in Jurong GRC?

In Singapore, it seems MPs have to be all things to all men – and women, and children too.

We want MPs to run town councils. They have to be financially trained too, to get accounts right.

We want them to step in to sort out disputes, so they must be skilled mediators and negotiators.

We want them to listen to our problems, so they have to be counsellors. We want them to help the poor and needy and the elderly and link them up with available resources, so they have to be social workers.

We go to them to write letters of appeal to government agencies to waive fines or speed up/review/reverse a decision, so they are glorified scribes.

We want them to get government agencies to put a playground here or a bus stop there, and take away a funeral parlour and put it elsewhere, so they are political lobbyists.

But in fact, the core of an MP's role is as a legislator.

MPs make laws in Parliament that determine how a country is run. They decide on policies. They decide how much money to give to which ministry to get programmes done.

Your MP isn't your social worker, although doing social work is a good way to win hearts and minds – and votes. These programmes also make a genuine, often lasting, impact on people's lives. They are wonderful.

But your MP should also be your representative in Parliament, championing issues you believe in.

And so, from the back, blocked from view, I asked a friendly photographer standing on a chair in front of me, to raise a hand to get Mr Tharman's attention.

I just had to ask this question.

I asked each candidate to highlight one issue he or she would like to champion in Parliament. I added: "And please don't say 'caring, inclusive society', which is a catchall. Please try to be specific – one issue that might be close to Singaporeans' hearts that you want to champion in Parliament."

Mr Lee, who is Minister of State for National Development, highlighted housing for seniors and helping families live close together. He went on to speak with considerable conviction, if less than perfect syntax, about his wish to "build communities of stakeholders" such as those around Pulau Ubin and the green rail corridor: "Bringing in one cosy room, stakeholders from green groups, heritage groups, academics, musicians, artists, cyclists, educators, social anthropologists, come in together and each and everyone of them, not just having a say, not just giving a view but also actively participating in the constructive dialogue and a process that results in actual things happening on the ground both immediate and long-term."

Madam Rahayu wants to focus on issues to do with family. Dr Tan plans to focus on healthcare: to help residents have better access to healthcare nearer their homes, integrating hospital care with community care. Mr Ang will focus on education, reducing the emphasis on grades, and transport. In the last, he wants to focus on the "first and last mile connection. So whether it's the cycling path, whether it is a walkway, covered walkway – making it easy for people to connect to the transport modes".

Listening to the issues they want to champion gave me a glimpse into what matters to these candidates.

It also makes them more relatable. I found myself agreeing with Mr Lee (retaining Singapore's green spaces is important) and Mr Ang: Indeed, it is often the last mile connection that lets us down – if only there were a safe path to cycle to the MRT station so we don't have to wait for the feeder bus.

In the next few weeks before the polls, every candidate aspiring to enter Parliament will stress his willingness to serve and maintain she has a heart for the people. In many cases, this will be true. But it is not enough.

Candidates must also articulate their positions on policies, and say what they wish to retain, adapt or see changed.

This is especially critical for those on the PAP slate expected to be parachuted into office-holder positions if elected, such as Ong Ye Kung, Chee Hong Tat and Ng Chee Meng, and perhaps one or two others.

Serious-minded Singaporeans will want to know their positions on issues that have been hotly debated publicly for the last few years.

This applies too to opposition candidates. Whether from the PAP or another party, candidates shouldn't hide behind party manifestos and slogans and give up the challenge of articulating what they themselves believe in or stand for. In fact, political parties too should be clearer about their stands on issues.

Voters want to know what their representatives in Parliament will fight for.

On immigration – do they support the move to tighten the tap on foreign workers or should it be loosened? On the economy – do they agree with those who say Singapore's high-cost, high-wages growth model benefits the high-waged elite, but is a burden on the low-waged who struggle to have a dignified life in a high-cost living environment? Should SMRT, which is listed, be corporatised, and public transport become a public service provided by the state?

What do the future leaders of Singapore, whether from the PAP or the opposition, stand for?

Or are they all for the status quo? In which case, Singapore's future is dim indeed.

HDB FLATS FOR EVEN RICH KIDS' CHILDREN?

**Yes, let them remove their heads from
the bubble and breathe normal air**

28 June 2015

It's difficult for a heartland born-and-bred Singaporean like me to imagine, but there are apparently people in Singapore who have never lived in, or even stepped into, a Housing Board flat.

When I was discussing property purchases with a group of friends, one of my girlfriends confessed she would not buy an HDB flat because she wouldn't feel safe in one. She grew up in private property and her first purchase was a condominium.

I got to thinking about this issue, following reports that National Development Minister Khaw Boon Wan wants to make it easier for all couples, including high-earning ones, to own and live in an HDB Build-To-Order (BTO) flat.

In a live radio talk show on Chinese-language station Capital 95.8FM, he is reported to have said: "If you ask for my personal opinion... I generally prefer to give every Singaporean couple a chance of living in HDB. You may come from, say, an upper-income group. You do not need an HDB flat. But I feel that it's good for... almost all Singaporeans to have a chance of living in HDB for five years, and interact with the community."

He added: "It's part and parcel of the Singaporean way of life. It's just like males go for national service... If we can give them this opportunity of staying in HDB towns, I think there are more positives than negatives."

His remarks were made in the context of raising the income ceiling for HDB flats, which he said could happen by September.

Now, a married couple with a joint monthly income of up to $10,000 can buy a subsidised, new HDB flat. It was raised from $8,000 in 2011.

This isn't the first time Mr Khaw made such a comment. In an exclusive interview with The Straits Times in April 2013, he had broached the idea of scrapping the income ceiling to allow even couples with very high incomes to own HDB flats, as living in HDB flats would give people more chances to interact with others of different races and incomes. But the lower-income households would still get bigger housing grants.

Mr Khaw said then: "If a rich man's kid wants to apply for a BTO flat, provided he stays the five-year minimum occupation period, there's nothing wrong with that to me."

My reaction both times was bemusement.

For most Singaporeans, HDB living is part and parcel of being Singaporean. Most live in HDB estates. Those of us who grew up in one, and moved on to private property, will probably always hanker after the bustle of HDB life.

You see all the BMW-driving businessmen in long-sleeved shirts wiping away beads of sweat as they wolf down their *bak chor mee* or *mee goreng* at their favourite HDB coffee shop and hawker centre, and you see the looks of blissful content on the well-dressed women as they buy their cheap laundry baskets or pick up kitchen utensils at the household sundry shop, and you know you can take the boy or girl out of the HDB estate, but you can't take the HDB out of the boy or girl.

So the idea that a special policy is needed to encourage people to live in and interact with HDB residents will appear slightly surreal to some. On my Facebook, a friend commented that she felt insulted, as though HDB residents were creatures in a zoo that the rich are being encouraged to visit to see.

I empathise with that comment. It's like having a special policy to encourage those who live with a permanent bubble around their heads to take their heads out of the bubble and breathe normal air like the rest of us.

Breathing normal air is the default, and should be so. But I can see that if segments of our population have become so used to living in that bubble of air, it would take concerted policy action to persuade them to try normal air for a change.

The truth is that Singapore society is stratifying. Whereas many of today's middle-aged professionals grew up in HDB flats, it's probably the case that more of today's 20-something-year-old professionals and managers grew up in private housing. So the idea of having them live in and experience HDB life isn't a bad one. From the point of view of social cohesion, it makes sense.

In Singapore, public housing caters to the majority of the population – 80 per cent of Singapore resident households live in HDB flats. The idea is precisely that we would all grow up in mixed neighbourhoods that jumble up people of different races, different income groups, and different socioeconomic status.

So it makes sense to encourage the small minority who never had a chance to do that when they were growing up, to do so in their young adulthood.

I often wonder how many of today's young Administrative Service civil servants, and the smart youngsters who enter the banks, the legal profession, and even the media, have lived in HDB flats, and if they have empathy for the average Singaporean who does. These people are future leaders and decision-makers.

If too many of them come from privileged families, they would never have experienced poverty, or suffered from want or anxiety over money problems. But if they had a friend in school or in their neighbourhood who did, and were close enough a confidant to share vicariously in the friend's struggles, their worldview will be more rounded than the wealthy child who lives with, plays with and goes to school with only other wealthy children.

If raising the income ceiling to allow more young couples to live in HDB flats can help reduce the social gap that can exist between the privileged and the masses, then it is reason to do so.

I know some readers will argue that HDB flats should be reserved for the lower-income. Let the high-income earners who want to live in HDB estates buy flats on the resale market.

But the fact is that, with 80 per cent living in HDB estates, HDB flat owners already include the high-income. Increasingly, the subsidised HDB flat is being viewed as the birthright of every Singaporean couple. The HDB gravy train gives them a ticket to an affordable first home – and a firm step up the ladder of financial success, if they are lucky enough to make hundreds of thousands of dollars subsequently by selling it on the open market.

But opening up the floodgates this way will inevitably lead to demands from other groups to be given the same access to HDB subsidised flats. Mature couples who missed out on buying HDB flats earlier will also want to be allowed to buy subsidised flats. And singles will demand more leeway to benefit from housing subsidies too.

The arguments about the social benefits of having every Singaporean experience HDB living apply equally to them.

FROM MNC TO MAMAK SHOP: THE PAP GOES LOCAL

13 August 2015

I turned up yesterday morning at the People's Action Party (PAP)'s branch office at Block 187 Toa Payoh Central, expecting the party's press conference to introduce its first slate of candidates to be held there. Instead, I was directed to the coffee shop next door.

I had two thoughts.

The first was that the PAP is going back to its local roots, eschewing the previous style of introducing its new candidates at the party headquarters at Bedok. Is this grassroots PAP just a change in style, or substance? Time – the election campaign and the next five years – will tell.

My second, more cynical thought was: "Let's see how welcoming the stallholders are of this 'invasion' by the PAP."

I recalled stories from the past, of hawkers sullenly putting up with such events that rob them of tables and affect their business.

At the Kim San Leng coffee shop at Block 177, two coffee shop tables were set up, with microphones set up on them. Many reporters were thronged around the tables, in ringside seats. I ascertained that candidates would arrive only at 10.30am, and spent the next 30 minutes walking around the coffee shop, talking to whoever would talk to me. I got lucky.

The coffee shop's big boss, Mr Hoon Thing Leong, was there with his son, and a business partner. Someone from the merchants' association was also present. Mr Hoon and the coffee shop manager were not just okay with the PAP folks taking up one-third of the coffee shop space.

They were welcoming, not just to the PAP but also the media present. When the press conference ended and I was having *bak chor mee* for lunch, Mr Hoon walked over to my table and handed me two *otak* and said: "It will taste better with this!"

So much for cynical doubts about whether coffee shop stallholders might resent the intrusion.

Clearly, the PAP team had done the essential and prepped the ground and picked friendly territory. Throughout the hour-long press conference, residents from pre-schoolers to retirees stopped to gawk, take photos and point out their MP to one another.

A few aunties took selfies with the debonair Dr Ng Eng Hen, the lead minister in Bishan-Toa Payoh Group Representation Constituency (GRC) and the PAP's organising secretary in charge of this election.

It is clear the PAP will be fighting this election at the local level.

Introducing candidates within the constituency, not at the party HQ, is just the start. The PAP is clearly moving away from MNC-style, top-down decision-making – where a coterie of top party leaders keep cards close to their chest, leaving the rest of the party and country guessing.

Instead, it has decentralised and is giving the initiative to the equivalent of the corner *mamak* shop – the branches and candidates at the local level. And if yesterday's event is any guide, expect local connections and local plans to be highlighted, and views on national policies muted.

It was stressed yesterday that two of the new candidates – Mr Chee Hong Tat and Mr Chong Kee Hiong – live in Bishan-Toa Payoh GRC.

As Mr Chee noted: "I have a fond attachment to this place, this is my home." The man who was, until Tuesday, Second Permanent Secretary at the Trade and Industry Ministry and once served as Mr Lee Kuan Yew's principal private secretary and has helmed the Energy Market Authority, did not talk about national policies.

Instead, on his to-do list, if elected, are exercise corners for the elderly and more walkways.

And he sounded amazingly sincere, as though it is the opportunity to do these things that would persuade a high-flier to give up a steady career in the civil service for the world of politics in the "new normal", where ministers face harsh scrutiny from voters online and off, and can be in Cabinet one day and out the next.

Dr Ng explained the choice of Toa Payoh town centre as the venue to introduce candidates – because elections are about the heartland, and voters choose MPs who can take care of the estate.

At the strategic level, of course, the PAP is also affirming that it is a party connected to the ground, in touch with day-to-day realities of residents. So Dr Ng told about how he and his team worked with the Housing Board to come up with plans for 66 lifts for the four-storey shophouses that form the spine of Toa Payoh Central.

In an indirect comparison with the opposition team eyeing the ward, he added: "Bishan Toa-Payoh residents are very savvy. They have witnessed many elections since this town was built and they are not easily enamoured of, or easily gulled by, platitudes or aspirations. They vote from enlightened self-interest and that's indeed how they should. And the party that convinces the voters here that they can best take care of them will win their support."

The PAP wants to play down its top-down image, and play up its grassroots appeal.

But as Dr Ng said, voters are savvy. They are not easily enamoured of or easily gulled by platitudinous changes in style.

To win hearts and minds, the PAP has to show that in the things that matter – in policy substance, not just in grassroots political style – it is genuinely for the heartland.

PUTTING THE HEARTLAND AT THE CORE OF ITS POLICIES: HAS THE PAP DONE ENOUGH?

29 August 2015

Coffee shop politics has come to the fore. This was after the Aug 12 event when the organising secretary of the People's Action Party, Dr Ng Eng Hen, decided to hold the traditional press conference introducing new candidates at a heartland coffee shop in Toa Payoh.

The move sent the commentariat into a tizzy. Sarcastic comments flowed online about the PAP trying too hard.

Dr Ng's move in Bishan-Toa Payoh Group Representation Constituency (GRC) was followed in Tanjong Pagar GRC and West Coast GRC, with the latter two going one better and holding their press conferences in a hawker centre (Tanjong Pagar Plaza and Boon Lay Market and Food Centre, to be precise).

Those truly in touch with the heartlands know the nuance: a coffee shop is usually run by a private operator (the Toa Payoh one was run by the Kim San Leng group), where a cup of tea or coffee with milk now usually costs 90 cents or even – gasp – $1.

A hawker centre is run by the National Environment Agency, where a cup of coffee or tea with milk can still be had for 80 cents.

If you want to be really heartland, the hawker centre trumps the *kopitiam*, anytime.

Most of the other PAP teams introduced their candidates in the party's branch offices within the constituency – still local, within the heartlands, but in slightly more comfortable surroundings, more conducive for candidates to have a Q&A with the media.

One PAP member I teased about why they hadn't held their press conference in a coffee shop muttered: "Some of us are in markets and hawker centres all the time."

The Workers' Party introduced candidates at its party headquarters. In a Facebook comment, candidate Daniel Goh, a sociology lecturer, dissed the coffee shop move as "symbolic tokenism that appropriates our living space" for political profit.

He wrote: "I live in heartland spaces every day; I get introduced as a candidate at the HQ because it is a special event. My normal reality is the heartland, the heartland is not a special event for me. My life is the heartland, the heartland is not my symbolic gesture."

As I argued last week in my blog, what matters more than the venue is the actual substance of policies.

I wrote: "To win hearts and minds, the PAP has to show that in the things that matter – in policy substance, not just in grassroots political style – it is genuinely for the heartland."

A week later, on Aug 20 at the Kent Ridge Ministerial Forum, Dr Ng explained that the PAP always crafted policies for people living in the heartland and has stayed true to its roots and looked after the interest of the ordinary Singaporean.

"All our policies are about the heartland. That's our base, the strength in our political system… If we deviate from there, we will be in trouble."

How does the PAP fare when it comes to having that heartland instincts? I think many fair-minded Singaporeans will agree that the PAP's policies have been good for Singaporeans over all, including the masses. Rapid economic growth has brought the country from Third World to First, and lifted many families from working class to upper middle income in one generation, and allowed many individuals to move from portable potties in squalid huts to jacuzzi bathrooms in luxury houses in one lifetime.

But putting the heartland at the core of its policies isn't just about growth for all, and letting trickle-down economics do the rest.

To be fair to the PAP, its recent social policy shifts have been groundbreaking in catering to the heartlands in social, health, housing and education policies. In that sense, Dr Ng is right that the heartlands are square and centre at the heart of PAP government policies.

But I think I would not be alone either in arguing that the PAP also needs to shift from what has been a traditional PAP strength – the bird's eye view of policy – to the worm's eye view, learning to see things from the perspective of the ordinary person.

Having the much-vaunted helicopter vision isn't enough. As the social gap between the ruling elite and the masses grows, and social stratification hardens, it becomes more essential than ever for the PAP to have within its ranks Cabinet ministers who can walk through policies in the shoes of heartlanders, and understand how policies affect them, in a way that is visceral, and deeply held.

It's not realistic to expect every MP, every minister, to be able to do that. But it is crucial for our cohesion, that the PAP has at least a few office-holders who have that heartland instinct ingrained in them, or are prepared to hone it.

What does it mean in today's context, to have a heart for the heartlands? It means to care slightly less about government-linked companies' bottom lines, and slightly more for the impact of policies on heartlanders' purse.

Think public transport, for example. For too many years, Singapore had the odd situation of having a public transport system run by listed companies that made money for shareholders, while commuters grumbled about overcrowding, breakdowns and fares. Yes, to be fair to the PAP Government, it has been moving in the direction of caring more for commuters' purses, with changes to the rail and bus operating models, and injecting a lot more public funds into buses and train networks.

Having a heart for the masses means cross-subsidising operations where necessary, so you don't deliberately keep closed a train station when there are residents in new HDB estates nearby, or deny residents a crucial bus service, on grounds that the local demand doesn't justify the service.

The bird's eye view looks at the issue in terms of the impact on the bottom line or the overall budget, and concludes that the costs exceed the benefits of adding that marginal station or service.

The worm's eye view looks at the issue in terms of the impact on the users and the costs and benefits to them, not the operator, of not having that marginal station or service.

A leadership with truly heartland instincts would also not allow so many brand-name schools to remain put in the expensive private property enclave of Bukit Timah, while pushing out other schools like Swiss Cottage, Dunearn Secondary, Anderson Secondary, into the suburbs. Instead, they would scatter more top schools around the island.

Having a heart for the heartlands means building amenities and creating an HDB town that really works for residents.

The PAP Government has done quite well in this respect. I would put covered walkways linking HDB flats to the bus stop or MRT station as examples of town planning that has that heartland instinct. Ditto lift upgrading, and the programme to spruce up toilets and add grab bars to homes of the elderly.

As for hawker centres? The Government began building hawker centres in 1971 to house street hawkers. It stopped building new hawker centres in 1986, when street hawkers were successfully rehoused.

Hawker centres have become social places where community grows organically. For decades, they provided the less educated with a means of livelihood, and the masses with affordable, accessible, meals.

When the Government stopped building them – the private sector, which, like nature, abhors a vacuum, stepped in. Private coffee shop operators proliferated, driving up coffee shop property prices and rentals, in turn raising food prices.

For decades, MPs and residents wanted hawker centres to be built again. In 1993, Braddell Heights MP Goh Choon Kang asked for a review of the "no new hawker centre" policy. In 1997, residents at a Housing Board forum "recommended to resume building of wet markets/hawker centres to promote community bonding and strengthen local identity".

The hiatus lasted 26 years.

It was only in 2011 – after the General Election that year – that the Government relented and said it would build new centres.

A government with truly heartland instincts would have understood the importance of hawker centre food, convenience and culture to the life of the average Singaporean.

It wouldn't have stopped building hawker centres for so long, or closed its ears to repeated appeals from its own MPs and residents for over two decades.

Yes, one can give credit to the Government for changing its mind and making up for lost time. A new centre is up in Hougang, and another 19 will be built in the next 12 years.

It may be that the PAP Government is trying hard, and learning to listen better, to the cries of the heart from the heartlands. If so, that move to hold press conferences in coffee shops and hawker centres would be more than symbolic. It would represent a genuine shift in consciousness on the part of the PAP.

WHAT TREKKING 100KM IN THE RAIN TAUGHT ME ABOUT LIFE

Being the laggard in a group hike along the Camino de Santiago reminded me of what it is like to be the slow one that others have to accommodate

15 April 2018

———

I recall a class discussion on the Singapore education system years ago, when I was in school. While some classmates lamented how exam-oriented and stressful Singapore's education system was, I defended it, chirping that actually I enjoyed school, and thought the pace and level of study was fine.

I still recall my teacher's reaction. British tutor Keith Wiltshire had spent years teaching the Humanities class and was used to Singapore's ways. He turned to me, shook his head and said with a twinkly smile: "It's people like you who make the Singapore education system stressful for others."

I was taken aback and a little indignant, but did not retort.

That little exchange came back to me recently, when I had occasion to be one of the "others" who struggle while the quicker, better-endowed ones surge forward.

I've just returned from a six-day trek in Spain, where a group of five friends and I walked the well-known pilgrimage trail known as the Camino de Santiago or the Way of St James.

The entire camino or walk is a network of various trails starting in countries such as France, Portugal or Spain that converge in the city of

Santiago in north-western Spain, where the Cathedral of Santiago de Compostela is. Tradition has it that the remains of the Christian apostle James are at the cathedral. The trail we took was the last 120km section of what is called the French way, stretching from Sarria to Santiago. It traversed small towns, many hamlets and villages, mountains, riversides and plains.

We broke the trip into six days, walking about 20km each day. Urbanite Singaporeans that we are, we arranged for our bags to be transported ahead to each night's comfortable hotel and hiked with just a light day pack and walking poles.

It rained three days out of six. I had been convinced, before the walk, that my friends would decide to do the practical thing and take a cab if the heavens opened, rather than walk in the rain.

But no. These were high-achieving ex-RGS (Raffles Girls' School) girls, who brushed off a little rain, squealed in excitement when it hailed, and said "Bring it on!" when the forecast said sleet the next morning. We walked in the rain for hours, through country roads, horse manure and muddy hilly paths. Once I was stuck behind a herd of cows that dispelled discharge as they went.

The trip had begun as a bit of a lark. The group of us – schoolmates from RGS – turn 50 this year, and we wanted a trip to celebrate our birthday. Suggestions for a gourmet dining-and-spa holiday were quickly shot down. I guess the puritanical streak runs deep in RGS girls. Most of us had been to Europe, America, the major Asian capitals and the usual South-east Asian resort cities. We flirted briefly with the Holy Land and a Nordic sojourn. In the end – I can't quite recall how we got there – we settled on the Camino de Santiago; perhaps because four of us are Catholic, and we had heard about this pilgrims' trek.

We planned for the trip in typical Singaporean style – thoroughly and way in advance. One friend, who had retired from her banking job last year, did the heavy lifting, getting quotes and making the arrangements.

During the trip, she led the way, pacing our walks, navigating to our stops, and generally getting us all to stay the course.

I was the laggard, trailing at the back of the group each day, enjoying the scenery when the weather was good and the terrain smooth, but otherwise struggling to keep pace and watch out for my footing. When it rained, I got uncomfortably clammy and hot inside, and cold outside, till I borrowed my friends' superior rain gear the last few days.

Each night, even as I tucked into the hearty dinners and desserts, I had to battle the thud in my heart when I contemplated the next day's gruelling walk, groaning each time the walk description included mentions of any "steep climb".

One friend developed a swollen ankle; another had a painful heel. They downed painkillers and walked through the pain. Even with their injuries, they outwalked me. I didn't have even one blister; only aching feet and wobbly knees. My pace was simply slower; like the students who may need five years, not four, to do their O levels, I would have preferred the hike to be done in seven, not six days, and kept each day's hike to 12 to 15 km, not 15 to 25 km, which was what we did in the end.

I enjoyed the trip in the end – especially in retrospect! – but when people ask me if I learnt something spiritual, or if I could meditate on God while walking, I had to be honest and say No.

I did learn things about myself and about life. I learnt afresh that life is about endurance, and persevering through the difficult times as you wade through dirt and mud and get drenched. I learnt that when your focus is so much on your footing, maintaining your balance, and on keeping up, you find it hard to enjoy your surroundings. (That got me ruminating about what being in a less academic stream in Singapore, or being in a low-wage job in Singapore, might be like. When your time and energy is focused on just getting through, you find it hard to plan ahead, or to relax into enjoyment.)

Most of all, I learnt what it is like, for six days, to be in the group considered slow, backward and needing assistance.

I understood why Keith said, all those years ago, that people like me make education so stressful for the rest.

When things come easily to you, you tend to like challenges and take them in your stride. You forget that what you glide over effortlessly, someone else may need effort to walk through, and may cause yet another to stumble. In that casual mastery of a skill, you toss off remarks and set new standards, believing they are motivating. "Let's finish before it rains tomorrow at 2pm!" Or "Let's aim for the school to get all As for maths next year!"

They are not motivating. They are dispiriting, because they represent stretch targets some of us know we cannot achieve.

I also realised what helps the slow and weak, and what does not. Pep talks asking people to cheer up are limited in value. For the one struggling, the discipline of putting on a cheerful face over fatigue and self-doubt is a practice one does less for oneself, and more for others. Keeping determinedly positive keeps my own spirits up, but I did it this trip out of consideration for my friends, to insulate them from my occasional pall. And once I am over a mood, it is easy to be buoyed by others' high spirits.

But what really, really helps, what gets your tired sinews going, and gives your spirit a lift of hope, is empathy and presence. Walking with someone, going beyond words to acts that say, I am here with you.

One friend in the group would walk and pace me, no matter how slowly I went. With her by my side, I was freed from the pressure of having to go at a pace I could not keep up with, and could relax to enjoy the hike. The others could charge ahead, secure in the knowledge that the slowest member was walking with a robust, reliable companion.

We would walk most of the day's trail before lunch, and then stop for a bite in the early afternoon before completing the rest of the trail. I sometimes took a cab after lunch to go straight to the hotel, arrange the check-in and to rest. I could have walked those last few kilometres after lunch each day, but it would have taken me a long time as I was fatigued by then. I also wanted to free my walking mate so she could walk with the fast crowd. In the end, I walked 100km of the 120km trail, exceeding my expectations.

People walk the pilgrims' trail for different reasons, some spiritual, some physical, some recreational. I went without specific expectations, although during the trail, I did have a specific prayer request – which by the end of the trail was answered.

The walk for me was symbolic of life – a metaphor for how life brings us ups and downs, sun and rain, hail and sleet; and still, so long as health does not give out, we step on, through earth, grass, cobbles, mud, paved roads, dirt tracks, and across flower-strewn meadows, meandering rivers, picturesque towns and bridges. There are rest stops in between, and if we are blessed enough, companions of good cheer along the way.

In the weeks before my pilgrimage hike, I had been working on a compilation of my columns into a book. I grouped them into themes, and wrote new essays to introduce the themes. The one issue I found I really wanted to write on, that I felt the most strongly about, turned out to be on the class divide and inequality, on the growing gap between the haves and the have-nots.

Perhaps because my mind and my heart were so full of the issue, I found that on my walk, I was living, in a small way, the life of those who operate in the slow lane in contemporary society, those who walk on the margins.

In my work life, in my school days, in modern Singapore, I have a place, a position, social status, financial security. In Galicia in Spain, struggling to keep up in my cheap rain gear on a pilgrim's trek, I was for a brief moment a traveller in the slow lane, constantly overtaken by other walkers, including elderly ones and a small Chinese girl who looked about five or six, walking with her father. I know that feeling of being on the margin was illusory, because I was with loving friends; I was well-fed and well-shod; and we were on a luxury hike that would end each day in a plush hotel. But that awareness persisted.

If there is one thing I hope not to forget from this trek, it is that feeling of vulnerability in the slow lane.

When something is tough, I find that it helps to admit it and accept one's limits. Then, endure and persevere and try to remain positive. Next, be open to others' help and try to be humble and gracious in receiving it.

And resolve and pray that one day, when you are among the strong, you never forget the days when you were among the weak. So that you have empathy for the weak when strong. And so that sometimes, when society wants to rank you among the "best", you will choose to slow down to walk among the rest.

2

THE BRAVE
NEW WORLD
OF DISRUPTION

D isruption is a word so bandied about these days, it's easy to forget that the concept of "disruptive innovation" is relatively recent.

In 1997, Harvard Business School professor Clayton Christensen published *The Innovator's Dilemma*, where he introduced the idea of disruptive innovation. Essentially, it's about how small, simple things and ideas can challenge big incumbents and even bring them down. Disruptive technology is contrasted with sustaining technology, which typically helps big companies get better at what they are already doing.

In Singapore, disruption entered the national mainstream vocabulary with the release in 2017 of the report by the Committee on the Future Economy. It looked at how Singapore workers, companies and organisations can prepare themselves for a future marked by tremendous opportunity yet uncertainty, as disruptive technologies change the way we lead our lives. From retail to driving and to manufacturing, the rise of disruptive technologies like e-commerce, robots, artificial intelligence and algorithms that match buyer and seller directly on a smartphone is causing workers and consumers to feel the disruptive effect of different ways of doing things.

I work in the media sector, which is a sector in the more mature phase of disruption. Because of this, the insecurity and uncertainties written about in articles are real to me. Those of us working in print media experience daily the opportunities and frustrations that the disruptive technologies of social and digital media bring to our field. When anyone can write and share their article or photograph and distribute it to thousands or even millions with a tap on their keyboard or smartphone, is there still a role for a paid, professional journalist? Why would people want to pay for news and information when so much of it is free online?

But as I wrote in an article in this volume, free is never really free. Someone is paying for it. For years, we all paid for it by giving away our data and our attention. As I write this in March 2018, there are signs of a rethink on the merits of free news. We now know that social media platforms like Facebook, Instagram and Twitter were monetising our information and selling our attention to advertisers and anyone willing to pay to try to influence us.

Disruptive technologies have done great things for consumers. Think of e-commerce bringing shopping costs down; private-car hire liberating commuters from the stranglehold of high fares and poor service from taxi companies; Airbnb turning residents into mini-hoteliers and offering many tourists affordable rooms to stay; the smartphone in your hands becoming your navigator and trusty assistant. But the dark side of disruption is just beginning to cast its shadow.

The articles in this section describe the challenges of operating in a disrupted sector like print media. They also include some essays on the retail sector, written from the viewpoint of a consumer and citizen. As disruptive technologies sweep through more sectors, we can expect more people to face threats to their jobs. In the print media sector, my company Singapore Press Holdings went through a wrenching retrenchment exercise, which I observed up close and wrote about.

Despite the best efforts of company bosses and workers, I fear many other sectors in Singapore will encounter such tough times ahead. When more jobs are under threat, there is an urgent need to rethink the way social security is delivered.

In Singapore, many of our social safety nets come via work (employer-sponsored healthcare and training, for example) and the Central Provident Fund, which is again tied to work. But what if big numbers of workers go out of work and stay jobless for longer periods? Singapore has scant benefits for the unemployed and their families. We need to work faster to have a social safety net ready to catch them when their lives get disrupted by the full force of disruptive technologies.

SINGAPORE MUST LEARN SPIRIT OF COOPERATION TO SURVIVE DISRUPTION

Companies here need to overcome competitive instinct and work together. Regulators and leaders need to speak up, and help drive that integration and collaboration. Not doing so will ensure Singapore's economy dies a slow, complacent death

27 August 2017

———

Singapore is well into a new era economically, and it will have to change its ways quickly to survive in the new age.

The much-talked-about disruption is no longer out there in the future. It is very much with us. The fear is whether we are too late to respond to it. Just how urgent the situation has become was driven home for me last week with two bits of news.

The first was the sudden announcement by listed taxi company ComfortDelGro on Tuesday, after the market had closed, that it was in talks with ride-sharing app provider Uber. When a traditional business considers getting into bed with the disrupter, you know things are heading for a crisis.

The second is the news that my own company, Singapore Press Holdings (SPH), is exiting its stakes in two entities of media group Mediacorp, which in turn is turning its print tabloid Today into a digital-only news product. It's clearly a quid pro quo arrangement, with Mediacorp going back to TV, and SPH taking hold of the print space even as it pushes ahead with its forays into the multimedia digital world.

This came 17 years after Singapore's experiment with a media duopoly, with the print and broadcast companies both crossing into each other's territories.

As with other duopolistic structures created by regulators at that time, it was consistent with the ethos then, when the talk was about market liberalisation and competition.

But perhaps those structures reinforced a mindset of domestic competition that has become an obstacle to a more collaborative mindset that Singapore needs today, in a global, digital-heavy economy where domestic borders matter much less.

Today, the talk is all about global markets, consolidation and collaboration. But within Singapore, the markets for key services have become fragmented. And the habit of competing has become entrenched in Singapore business leaders' mindsets.

Just as traditional taxi and media companies now have to dialogue with the disrupter, so too do many others. As an open economy, our companies are being buffeted by disruptive changes taking place outside.

Each day brings news of more companies consolidating, selling or buying new entities to integrate their operations.

American online giant Amazon entered the Singapore retail market recently with a modest rollout of its Prime Now service, promising two-hour deliveries of groceries and a limited range of other goods. It's only a matter of time before Amazon's vast marketplace of goods opens up here.

That might be good for consumers. But in business, analysts talk about the "Amazon Effect" – the chilling impact Amazon has on retail and sometimes the real economy when it enters a market.

Chinese e-commerce giant Alibaba is already active here. It bought into South-east Asian e-commerce company Lazada and online grocer RedMart. Its bike-sharing company ofo is here, claiming over half the bike-sharing market, with more than 100,000 users clocking more than 20,000 bike journeys daily. Alipay, its e-payment system, will soon be ubiquitous.

While Singapore is used to foreign companies operating freely here, the difference is that the game these days is on a different level.

The digital economy and the use of technology and data mean that companies want touch points with customers across their lifestyles.

So Alibaba, for example, will know what you spend on, which groceries, electronics, clothes you buy, where you live and travel to on your bike. Once you have its Alipay app on your mobile phone, it can sell you more things, and gather more information on your habits, which it can then sell to advertisers.

One article in Fast Company magazine in March on innovative companies put it thus: "Hundreds of millions of Chinese consumers now depend on these all-in-one apps to do, well, everything: interact with friends; pay for cabs and utility bills; book hotels, flights, and even dentist appointments; find love; and read news."

Data is so important and potentially so valuable, it has been described as the new oil. Companies team up to get more data. Meanwhile, hundreds of small retailers, and logistics companies, risk being shut down.

I wonder if our regulators and companies sufficiently understand the new economic landscape. They can't operate under business-as-usual mode because the wave of change is already on our doorstep, and entering our homes. It will crescendo into a tsunami soon enough.

Singapore companies have to unlearn the habits of the 1990s, and pick up new mindsets, new tools for the 2020s.

First, they must set aside their natural instinct to compete domestically, and think of ways to collaborate and work together for regional impact.

It may not be easy for Singapore CEOs to get over their habit of competing, to cooperate with each other. Many Singaporean bosses are used to being chief decision-maker in our tiny little outfit, whatever it is. Collaborating means giving up total control and taking on board other interests to be as vital as your own.

We must learn to think differently. We have to think beyond fiefdom, to kingdom; beyond company, to country; beyond personal ego, to joint value.

Already, the failure to cooperate has cost us light years in e-payments. As Prime Minister Lee Hsien Loong highlighted in his National Day Rally speech last Sunday, Singapore is surprisingly backward in its adoption of cashless payments for such a high-tech, advanced society.

One bright spot after PM Lee lamented the slow take-up of cashless payments is that Singaporean entrepreneur Tan Min-Liang of gaming company Razer offered to get a team going to set up an e-payment system in 18 months. PM Lee tweeted back asking for a report. Mr Tan is taking up the challenge.

It isn't just companies that need to cooperate. The public sector too should work with the private sector and seek their expertise. So, for example, government agencies putting out a request for ideas and crowd-sourcing for solutions for cashless payments in hawker centres and heartland shops is a good step.

Working individually may be good for your own organisation, but failing to work with others can set back the entire country. Singaporeans who go to Hong Kong have long wondered why their mass transit card Octopus is so widely used in shops, whereas Singapore has the ez-link card for trains and buses, the Nets card for shopping, and the CashCard for electronic road pricing.

Which brings me to the second point: Our regulators must step up.

Companies will have their own vested interests. They may not be inclined to collaborate even when there are benefits from it, or put it off until the situation is desperate, by which time it may be too late.

That's where regulators must play a role. The Land Transport Authority could have been faster to take the lead in restructuring the public transport landscape. The Monetary Authority of Singapore could have moved faster to get banks to cooperate on one e-payment app. It was only this year that PayNow was introduced.

Regulatory agencies must understand that their role is not just to set rules for today. They must be active in facilitating conditions for tomorrow. Step up, and use your regulatory influence to encourage collaboration where necessary. If that fails, use your power to compel.

Take a leaf from the Chinese, who two weeks ago announced something that again got my Singapore-worrier antenna up.

We know that America has its Google, Facebook, Apple, Netflix and Microsoft, each trying to create a digital universe to wall in customers and their data.

China too has its Internet giants – Alibaba in e-commerce, search engine Baidu and social media behemoth Tencent (of WeChat fame). They compete ferociously in China: In 2013, Alibaba bought Yahoo China to try to rival Baidu, while in 2014, Baidu and Tencent teamed up with Dalian Wanda, a real estate group, to create an e-commerce marketplace to take on Alibaba.

Even in communist-run China, competition is vital to keep companies' instincts sharp. But they come together when there is a state interest, and when the regulator steps in.

Just two weeks ago, news broke about a consortium being formed of about a dozen companies, including Alibaba, Tencent and Baidu, insurer China Life Insurance, ride-hailing company DiDi Chuxing and Shenzhen-based Chinese technology conglomerate Kuang-Chi Group.

Their common purpose? Putting nearly US$12 billion (S$16.3 billion) of investments into state-owned China Unicom, a Shanghai telecoms company with a vast reach.

China wants to inject private capital to take its state-owned enterprises to a mixed-ownership model. In return, these investors will get seats on the board.

While there is market scepticism about whether the consortium partners were arm-twisted to accept the deal, and some confusion over the financing rollout, there is no denying that it's a good example of China Inc in action. It shows the political will of the regulator in dreaming up this deal and being willing to sacrifice control over the reformed state-owned enterprise (SOE). It also shows the willingness of fierce competitors to come together for a common good.

When an e-commerce giant, social media company, ride-sharing company and a big telco team up, what data can they unleash for their profits? China's SOE reforms will target banks and medical institutions next. We can only imagine the potential for profits and public good that can unlock. That ability to cross-fertilise functions is one reason that China is leading the world in digital technology.

I am certain that Singapore's business and public-sector leaders have seen the future and know what is at stake.

They must know that Singapore is at risk of a complacent slide that will precipitate a quick drop into economic irrelevance. We tend to operate in silos still, behave as though it's business as usual, even as foreign competitors enter our shores.

The watchmen in the tower, who know how the world is changing, must speak up about the threats to our economy. Of course, we in the media too bear a responsibility to inform our readers just how, and how fast, the world is changing. This is essential to get Singaporeans to see the big picture.

And then our leaders must reach out to companies, find common ground and get them to work together so that Singapore companies can level up to embrace the digital economy.

In fact, Singapore's political and economic structure lends itself to collaborative efforts. Its political and public-sector elites are interconnected, and via their frequent secondments to government-linked, Temasek-linked or labour movement-linked enterprises, they are also commercially influential.

Everybody more or less knows everybody important in Singapore. It should not be that difficult to reach out to work together.

As a journalist more used to writing on social or political issues than the economy, I hesitated before tackling this issue, which has been bugging me for a while.

In my job as a newspaper editor in charge of Op-Eds, I read scores of commentaries daily on a wide range of issues. Over the months, I became more aware of the widening gap between Singapore's complacent, peaceful economy – where a national task force is formed over infant milk powder – and the rapid pace of change in global businesses, where companies face extinction from disruption by digital platforms, drones and mergers.

They are here, in Singapore, amid us, disrupting our retailers, our neighbourhood stores, our drivers, our courier workers.

The future is here, and I fear we are not yet ready.

And yet, Singapore has so much going for us. We have smart people. Big, successful companies. Habits of hard work and enterprise. We need to adopt new habits of cooperation and collaboration, and have a more global mindset.

For that to happen, we need leaders in the public and private sectors, and regulators to step up. We need companies to adopt a global mindset, and we need to work together for the long haul.

HOW TO BEAT UBER, AND OTHER INSIGHTS FROM DIGITAL DISRUPTION

Businesses are externalising functions, finding ways to reduce risk while exposing themselves to innovation

2 September 2017

I wrote in The Sunday Times on Aug 27 about digital disruption and how Singapore companies and regulators had to buck up.

One point I made: businesses have to overcome their natural competitive instinct honed by decades of competing for a small domestic market, and learn to collaborate with each other. The digital economy needs scale, and local businesses have to team up to fight back.

Several people engaged me on social media with interesting responses. I'd like to share some here.

Former banker Raymond Huang, a Singaporean, shared on Facebook that he had noticed the disturbing habit of not working together even 20 years ago.

"When a Singapore bank then could not do a syndicated deal, our banks would reject instead of sharing the deal. When my former Singapore bank hired a Hong Konger to head up the Beijing office, he would call all his Hong Konger friends to give the deals to them, even our office renovation!"

Another Facebook friend lamented: "We need to abandon our small island mentality and our uptightness. The digital economy has changed the Chinese into a people who think win-win at all times. I've enjoyed working with my Chinese colleagues tremendously, as we are always looking out for one another and helping one another to excel."

On LinkedIn, Dr Tommi Chen, an Internet and telco consultant based in Malaysia, agreed with the need for collaboration and added: "Digital culture is all about cooperation, partnerships. Old culture is about internalisation (tasks mostly done in-house) while new culture adds a huge dose of externalisation (tasks carried out through partners, customers, would-be customers, public) to reduce costs but mostly to improve effectiveness."

I'm familiar with the idea of externalisation in psychology – that people tend to externalise and blame others for their own mistakes – but not in business.

So I started reading up about externalisation in business. And I hadn't realised it until this week, but my job as an Op-Ed editor has been rife with externalising, a business model very much in vogue with a digital economy.

Traditionally, businesses developed multiple functions in-house because the transaction costs of getting others to do it for you are too high. Companies then hired people full-time to produce widgets, with logistics, sales and marketing, human resources. If they had to keep finding people to do these jobs when the need arose, it would be too slow and too expensive.

The Internet's amazing ability to match people to jobs, across geographical barriers, has substantively reduced that transaction cost.

Many companies have moved to externalise functions, even core ones. Externalising is a good way for businesses to cope with uncertainty.

Global pharma company GSK has since 2008 externalised its research and development. Instead of spending huge sums to develop its own products and then betting big on the few promising ones, it works with labs and outside partners (for example, cancer centres for oncology drugs) who are specialists in their own areas. It then bets on many ventures including some with lower probability of success, but which would have a huge payoff if it succeeds. This helps it to reduce risks, while broadening its exposure to innovative breakthroughs.

Externalising makes sense in a digital economy. Transaction costs are brought down. The digital economy is in flux, with multiple new developments in your own sector. It's more cost-effective to work with others than to hire resources to do it all within your own organisation.

B2B and now B2C externalising

There are degrees of externalising.

The first might be to outsource a function, and pay for someone else to do the service. In my line of work, this would be the equivalent of a newspaper outsourcing, say, its printing and newspaper delivery service.

The second might be to externalise by using contracted services-as-needed. This would be the equivalent of engaging a freelance videographer, say, to produce a video of an important news event overseas. Or – in my case – paying a university professor who is an expert in healthcare a fee to write a commentary on our healthcare system.

Previous Op-Ed editors in The Straits Times had the luxury – or burden, depending on your point of view – of managing a team of half a dozen or more full-time writers employed by The Straits Times. The headcount costs must have been astronomical.

These days, I have one deputy (associate Opinion editor Lydia Lim) and zero staff writers. Instead, we work with colleagues across The Straits Times newsroom to incubate commentary ideas to fruition.

We collaborate with many external partners too. Most of my time is spent working collaboratively with contributors from Singapore and around the world.

When the US presidential election trickled in last November and it was clear Mr Donald Trump was heading for a shock victory, I was on my e-mail within minutes, reaching out to academics around the world who could make sense of this for our readers.

When the US navy ship USS John S. McCain collided with an oil tanker in the Malacca Straits, I contacted a US navy commander who wrote a useful piece on how the navy might deal with such incidents. I don't think anyone in my organisation could have offered that perspective.

There are many news developments each day. The range of expertise required to give an insightful perspective on each of them is so broad, no news organisation will be able to afford to have so many experts on their payroll. In any case, they would not remain experts in their field – say, augmented reality – for long if they remained full-time writers!

As technology and geopolitical changes advance at supersonic speeds, news organisations too have to adapt.

In The Straits Times, one way we have done so is to tap on partnerships and collaborations to broaden and deepen our content. In addition to working with individual contributors, we are also part of the Asia News Network, a network of over 20 newspapers in the region that have content-sharing agreements.

Every business organisation these days has to work collaboratively with partners.

The two types of externalising I mentioned earlier both have to do with B2B – business-to-business – externalising. Whether outsourcing to an external company, or engaging a freelancer for a specific service, it's essentially one business externalising its functions to another business.

The next wave of externalising is B2C – from business to consumer.

You see this happening already. DIY payment kiosks, self-ordering menus using iPads, creating chatbots to help customers troubleshoot their own devices, are all examples of B2C costs externalising – when a business transfers its costs to consumers.

Consumers don't seem to mind too much. Witness the alacrity with which we took to online banking or iPad menu ordering.

Other examples of B2C externalising are citizen journalism, peer reviews on TripAdvisor, Airbnb, and any number of product comparison websites that cleverly make use of this useful B2C externalising tool.

To tap such crowdsourced content productively, you would first have to create a platform that makes it easy for people to upload their content, share it, and rate it.

Nurture your competitors

Large digital companies understand the need to externalise. The smart ones don't just outsource operations or work with partners. They work with competitors to turn them into collaborators. Some even nurture competitors.

Chinese ride-sharing giant Didi Chuxing is headed by Ms Jean Liu, whose father is the founder of Lenovo. She studied in Beijing and Harvard, then spent 12 years at Goldman Sachs in Hong Kong before she was recruited to join Didi Dache. When she entered the market, Didi Dache was head-to-head with rival Kuaidi Dache. She managed to merge the two into one consolidated whole – just in time for when Uber entered the China market.

Competing with Uber was bruising, with both reportedly spending US$1 billion (S$1.4 billion) each to subsidise rides to gain market share. Uber finally bowed out of China. It sold its China operations in return for a 20 per cent stake in Didi. The deal was presented as a win-win option – essentially to save face for Uber.

Ms Liu also mentors competitors.

A report on the Quartz online news portal noted: "Liu's egalitarian approach isn't limited to Uber. She mentors, rather than tries to crush, her competitors. Take her approach towards Grab, a dominant force in ride-sharing in South-east Asia. Grab's founder Anthony Tan has praised the sense of camaraderie and advice he receives from Liu.

"'There's this sense of brotherhood, that we're in this battle together, let's show them the power of Asia. It's so inspirational,' he told a conference in Kuala Lumpur."

In this world of ongoing digital disruption, smart business leaders know they have to externalise, cooperate and collaborate.

Put aside the instinct to compete and kill your domestic competitor. Team up with him and get bigger together.

The alternative is to have a huge digital company enter your shores and gobble up your business.

FUTURE ECONOMY NEEDS FUTURE-READY SOCIAL SAFETY NET

**As job insecurity looms in a world of churn,
we need to attend to the well-being of citizens too**

26 February 2017

As a consumer, I love start-ups. Airbnb, Uber and car-sharing apps transformed my vacation experiences, opening up cheaper – and more interesting – accommodation and transport options. You can live in someone's lovely house, get to know them and their family, drive a neighbour's car, order food in when you feel like it, and even make new friends instantly via social meet-ups.

In Singapore, I use Uber, Grab and food-delivery platforms. I order food in restaurants from iPads. (Smartphone QR code ordering should be next.) I console myself that when my job is taken over by a robot one day, I can make extra income from renting out my car and extra room in my apartment.

As a shopper, I like cheap goods whose unit production costs have been brought down by automated manufacturing, and whose delivery costs are now negligible, because logistics is being streamlined, with robots taking over warehouses, and eventually, driverless vehicles and drones making deliveries.

As a journalist who likes new ideas to write about, I find it exciting to live in a world of churn, where technology and automation are disrupting jobs, enriching our consumer experience, and challenging existing social orders, all at once.

But as a worker, and a frail human being, I find the trends towards automation, and looming massive job losses, rather disturbing.

In a word, they add up to a feeling of job insecurity.

Experts point to looming, massive job losses. Forrester, a market research firm, predicts that robots will eliminate 6 per cent of jobs in the United States by 2021, including customer service representatives, and truck and taxi drivers.

Professor Moshe Vardi, a computational engineering don at Rice University in the United States, predicted last February that robots will take over at least 50 per cent of jobs in 30 years.

Singapore is fully aware of the trends. This is why the report of the Committee on the Future Economy (CFE) tries so hard to say what Singapore must do to prepare itself for that tumultuous future.

There was a lot in the CFE report about industry transformation, scaling up our enterprises, going global, and reskilling workers.

But there isn't enough about how to help workers adapt. For example, what about social safety nets?

As former civil servant turned academic Donald Low wrote: "The CFE missed an opportunity to discuss how Singapore's social security and regulatory systems might be adapted for what is widely referred to as the 'sharing economy'."

I too feel there is a huge gap in the conversations we are having about the future economy, and it has the changing employment status of workers and the gnawing, invidious sense of job insecurity that will affect many.

While 50 per cent unemployment rates may still be one or two or three decades away (one hopes), today, more work is already being done ad hoc, not via full-time, permanent paid employment.

In Europe, half of new jobs created since the global financial crisis were offered through temporary contracts. In a 2015 report, the McKinsey Global Institute found that 162 million people in Europe and the United

States – 20 to 30 per cent of the working-age population – were doing some kind of independent work.

Singapore lacks data on the number of workers in such casual work, although the Ministry of Manpower tracks part-time employees and own account (self-employed) workers. The latter include taxi drivers and private-hire car drivers.

Without permanent work, people could suffer an acute sense of job insecurity that erodes their dignity.

No government can protect citizens from the forces of disruption. It can't guarantee everyone full-time, permanent, meaningful work with a comfortable salary that lets them plan for their future. It can, however, make sure existing social provision programmes are future-ready.

Last year's widespread discussion in some countries of a universal basic income – an allowance doled out to all, regardless of work – is one such attempt to give financial security to citizens.

In Singapore, we need not think of such a radical measure yet. But we can certainly do a lot more to assess if our social security systems are adequate for a world where many people don't have work, or work part-time, or do micro-jobs for micro-pay for many different people.

Professor Laura Tyson, who chaired the President's Council of Economic Advisers under the Bill Clinton administration, has argued that there is some consensus on what kind of social security benefits would work in a gig economy:

"They should be portable, attached to individual workers rather than to their employers. They should be universal, applying to all workers and all forms of employment. And they should be pro-rated, linking employer benefit contributions to time worked, jobs completed, or income earned."

Singapore is fortunate in that our Central Provident Fund (CPF) system is already portable and universal, as is our MediShield Life. Can CPF also be pro-rated?

Under current laws, those who employ part-time workers need to pay CPF. But not if the workers are deemed contract or freelance workers, or own account workers.

Can a system be devised to have pro-rated CPF payments? I don't see why not.

MP Tan Wu Meng in a commentary last November suggested: "What if a minimum employer CPF contribution were specified, for each hour worked or each unit of labour?"

Once you set a unit CPF payment for each hour or dollar of work performed, you can then develop a system where workers can get multiple CPF micro-payments from employers, or companies that buy their services.

The Uber or Grab driver, part-time house cleaner, honestbee grocery shopper, or TaskRabbit worker, will get his fee, plus an X per cent more to his CPF from the employer or buyer of his service, that can be used for his future housing, healthcare and retirement needs.

Beyond the CPF system, there is also the question of whether the protections employees take for granted are available to gig economy workers. Examples are annual leave, medical leave, maternity leave, defraying of medical bills, and workers' compensation under workplace safety and health regulations.

Even our much-vaunted CPF system has a serious drawback in a disrupted economy of the future: It works only when you have a job.

In fact, most of Singapore's social security measures are funnelled, via employers, to employed workers. The CPF system assumes you have an employer who tops up your fund. Many medical benefits are given by employers. The Workfare Income Supplement tops up your income – if you have a job.

If you are jobless, all the above benefits disappear. Singapore does not have unemployment insurance. For those with low savings, a few months of joblessness could leave them and their family in penury.

The labour market has been tight for decades and jobs are aplenty. But in the disrupted future economy, we can't rely on that. Already, the younger, more tech-savvy Uber driver is disrupting the livelihoods of many taxi uncles, some of whom will find it hard to get other jobs.

The prospect of joblessness, or job insecurity, is looking very real.

As a nation, we should be paying as much attention to the future of citizens' well-being, as to the future of the economy. For what is the point of having a vibrant future economy, if hundreds of thousands of our citizens suffer acute anxiety from joblessness, or job insecurity, and without adequate social safety nets?

WHY THE DEBATE ON UNCONDITIONAL BASIC INCOME IS RELEVANT FOR SINGAPORE

Technological disruption is expected to cause massive job losses – which is why some European states are debating giving citizens a basic income that can see them through such changes. This may sound extreme to Singaporeans, but the debate highlights the need for social welfare systems to move away from being too dependent on employment

7 June 2016

On Sunday, the Swiss voted against a proposal to give every citizen a basic income, regardless of their wealth or whether they are working.

The proposal was to give a monthly income of 2,500 Swiss francs (S$3,500) to each adult and 625 Swiss francs to each child. The plan was defeated, with 77 per cent opposed to it and 23 per cent backing it.

Despite its defeat, the significance of the referendum – and the idea of a universal basic income (UBI) for all – reverberated across developed countries.

In fact, the Swiss aren't the only ones considering such a universal basic income. The Financial Times (FT) reported: "In countries as diverse as Brazil, Canada, Finland, the Netherlands and India, local and national governments are experimenting with the idea of introducing some form of basic income as they struggle to overhaul inefficient welfare states and manage the social disruption caused by technological change."

The thinking goes like this: Robots and tech disrupters will cause jobs to disappear by the millions. Meanwhile, the number of people lucky enough to get full-time paid work that comes with several weeks of vacation leave and medical benefits is likely to diminish. This is because disintermediation platforms like Uber and TaskRabbit, as well as sites that match labour to jobs, see more employers and workers give up full-time work contracts for short-term work on demand.

The rise of this so-called gig economy can be said to be good for workers in that it offers more of them more flexible work hours.

But it is terrible from a financial and employment security point of view. Such gigs usually don't come with medical leave or healthcare benefits, paid vacation leave or retirement plans. Workers will become more vulnerable, exposed to the vagaries of long spells of joblessness, or illness, and could be left financially desolate in old age. It is against the backdrop of such fears that the idea of an unconditional or universal basic income has arisen.

The Economist, The New York Times and the FT have all reported on this in lengthy features in recent weeks, and traced the intellectual arguments underpinning this seemingly radical idea.

One recent advocate is Mr Robert Reich, a labour secretary in the Clinton administration who teaches at the University of California, Berkeley. The FT reported him as saying the digital revolution was increasing economic insecurity and inequality. The development of car-hailing apps, such as Uber and Lyft, had brought great convenience for consumers but was also creating a "spot auction market" for labour.

The FT report continued: "This insecurity was also fuelling a crisis of aggregate demand in the economy... A more equal division of the fruits of the technological revolution would revive that demand while providing a broader social good. The aim of all rich societies, Mr Reich said, should be to provide a basic level of subsistence, enabling people to do more of what they wanted and less of what they did not want to do. For all these reasons, he said: I think that UBI is inevitable."

Just as the birth of the industrialised society eventually led governments to create the welfare state, with disability, unemployment and health insurance that protects workers when they can't work, so the birth of today's post-industrial society is seeding debate on how social welfare systems need to change.

Cheaper than welfare?

UBI is emerging as a possible system to augment or even replace the welfare state.

In Finland, the social insurance body will pilot a scheme next year, giving up to 180,000 Finns a basic income of €500 to €700 (S$770 to S$1,000) a month – less than the average Finnish income of €2,700.

European cities which have generous welfare systems are keen to try out these pilot schemes to see how people respond to a basic income, and to test if it does not need monitoring and might end up cheaper than a complex conditional system that needs constant monitoring.

We may think that giving a UBI will remove the work ethic. But will it? After all, those on conditional welfare may lose their benefits if they work and start to earn above a certain sum, so they may choose to shun work. But someone with UBI who chooses to work gets to keep all his salary, plus his basic income.

So the effect of a UBI on work motivation is unclear.

In the Netherlands, a complex experiment will begin in Utrecht and several other cities to test out these questions. One group of benefit recipients will remain on the old workfare regime, under which people who live alone get €972.70 and couples €1,389.57.

Another group gets the benefits with no conditions. A third group gets an extra bonus if they do volunteer work. Yet another group is allowed to find work and keep the extra income. How people behave under each scheme is what the authorities want to know.

Opponents say such a UBI will be horrendously expensive. Switzerland's proposed model will cost one-third of GDP, about 13 percentage points more than the 19.4 per cent of GDP it now spends on welfare.

An analysis in The Economist estimates that "a basic income of 15 per cent of average income would require tax revenues of 15 per cent of national income dedicated to it. That is a lot of tax for not much basic income (about US$8,000 in America, in this example)."

How about Singapore?

I read the reports on this issue with great interest, because it signposts the kind of issues we in Singapore will have to grapple with.

To be sure, the idea of a UBI for all citizens sounds rather extreme to me. Most of us who are working don't need it, and may prefer state funds to be concentrated on those who need the help.

But the impetus behind this whole debate is important for Singapore.

Already, the gig economy is upon us. Many people are turning to Uber and similar part-time, freelance, portfolio work, rather than going for full-time employment.

As Singapore restructures its economy and embraces robots, autonomous vehicles, Big Data analytics and any number of tech disrupters, the potential for changes to employment is immense. Many people will find themselves out of jobs.

Yet our social security system remains so dependent on full-time employment. The Central Provident Fund system assumes you have an employer who pays his share of contributions. Many medical benefits are given by employers, which means workers lose them when they most need them – when they are middle-aged or old, and lose their jobs.

Even the Workfare Income Supplement for low-wage workers presupposes you have a job before it can augment your wages.

In Singapore, if you are jobless for a month or two, hopefully your savings or family or friends can tide you over. You can also get some short-term assistance.

If you are jobless for a year or two years, there is no real safety net for you, beyond that offered by subsidies for retraining. You're lucky if you have a working spouse meanwhile; otherwise you may end up having to think about drastic measures like selling your home and downsizing.

While jobless, you can't get Workfare. Your CPF payments stop. And Singapore has no unemployment benefits.

In Europe, the discussion has advanced to a point where they're talking about a basic income for everyone regardless of need.

Over here in Singapore, we need to start talking, fast, about how to rework our social security systems to protect workers better from the churn and turn of the gig economy.

WHEN TECH FOUNDERS WARN OF SOCIAL MEDIA FATIGUE, IT'S TIME TO LISTEN

16 December 2017

The year is slipping to a close and one of the things I've learnt this year is both how important social media is, and how insignificant it really is.

For a few months earlier this year, I was a social media junkie. WhatsApp, Facebook and LinkedIn were the last things I checked at night; the first things I looked up when I woke up. I took part, intermittently, in a poetry-writing group exercise in April where people write short lines to various prompts.

When I sent each missive into cyberspace, I would check my status updates to see how many "Likes" I got. After weeks of being borderline Facebook-addicted, I spent one evening offline. Of course I had to declare my offline intention on Facebook. I wrote: "Only 9pm. Nothing urgent to fix at work. (Touch wood!) No dinner to attend. No family member to entertain. Resisting Netflix. Gonna go offline and curl up with a nice book – a real book book. Bliss for a couple of hours. Then sleep."

When I went back online the next day, I was chuffed that the simple post had gotten 64 likes.

As I chugged along through the year, it occurred to me that I was getting a bit too fond of my social media interactions. I was getting to like all those positive strokes of Likes and Comments. Soon, I was checking several social media and messaging apps throughout the day.

Then I decided to spend some time in Australia. I've been in Melbourne for the past month or so; on leave and then telecommuting. (I'm lucky to have a job that lets me work from outside Singapore so long as there is a secure VPN connection.) Social media becomes a way to remain in touch with friends; but I stopped obsessively checking my accounts. Ethereal things of the digital world faded away.

Here, the weather reigns supreme. In the weeks I've been here, the temperature has ranged from 35 deg C sweltering heat one day, to 10 deg C the next. One weekend, the entire state of Victoria was on high alert for massive floods touted to be a once-in-a-century event; I cancelled all travel plans that weekend and stayed indoors.

In the end, the worst of the floods did not materialise but there was sporadic flooding across Victoria. People took it in their stride, so inured are they to extreme weather. On previous visits, I'd been hit by thunderstorms that led to massive power failures, and by shrieking winds that can literally blow you off your feet unless you grab on to a lamp post, and rock your car side to side.

When life confronts you with its sheer physicality, your first resort is not to social media. It is to survival and getting shelter, somewhere safe. Facebook updates won't help you cope with lashing rains or winds; in fact, it won't even survive a power outage or a breakdown of your Wi-Fi connection. You may take to Facebook to share photos or to rant; but an extreme weather event reminds you that life is real, it happens in the here and now, and it assaults your five senses.

Social media is a mere repository of life, not life itself.

So this morning, while mulling over what to write in my weekly blog, I prepared for the article not by checking what people are saying on social media. Instead, I spent a pleasant hour in the garden, pruning the rose bushes, and then snipping a few bunches of blossoms to put into vases.

Then it was time to water the garden. I never knew until recently, just how therapeutic it is to water plants. Armed with a hose and nozzle, I walked around in a placid trance, watering each bush. Roses need a lot of sun and a lot of water. Watering each bush takes a few minutes. To mark time, I said a few Hail Marys per bush. There are about a dozen rose bushes in the garden, so watering them all, and the other shrubs, takes quite a long time.

The summer sun beat down, but I was well protected with sunscreen, hat, gloves and a long-sleeved top. The air was cool, the bees hummed, and, after a while, time stood still.

The hour slipped by. I have no photos to remember it by; no smart status update to post; only a memory of a lovely hour, and a deep sense of gratitude for life. I could still post about this – come to think of it, I will be posting about it when I share this article on my Facebook page – but for those few moments, that time was special, because it was just time happening; just time spent watering the garden, with no expectation and no pressure; meaning nothing more than what it was – time spent watering the garden.

Life happens, and sometimes we want to share them with others on social media. Sometimes we don't. That is the proper order.

It should not be: Let's do things so I can talk about and share them on Insta, Snapchat, Facebook.

I was wondering if the sense of social media fatigue I experienced was just me; but it turns out, it's not.

Signs of social media fatigue are cropping up.

Twitter's monthly average user subscriber growth was flat in the second quarter of 2017.

Facebook's user base is growing, and its monthly average user exceeds two billion, as more people across the world flock to it. It is, however, losing ground among teenagers and millennials.

Statistics show that Facebook's organic reach has been declining since 2013. Engagement with each post sent out by brands and marketeers has gone down 20 per cent in 2017. (Reach refers to the number of people who see your post; engagement refers to how many Like or Comment or Share it).

Those of us who are active on Facebook might have noticed that our news feeds are looking distinctly less interesting these days. Gone are the article shares or news videos by friends; instead, I get a lot more photos of their activities and personal lives. These are nice, but less interesting.

These shifts are in part due to Facebook's own tinkering with its algorithm that now privileges your friends' personal posts over posts from brands or news organisations. If this continues, Facebook will resemble more of what it started out as – a space for college mates to hang around and share goofy photos – than what it was reaching to be, which is a global community for people to share ideas and experiences.

A thorough survey by Deloitte of consumer mobile use trends suggests that heavy usage of smartphones and devices – which are often used to check social media – is plateauing.

People check their phones 47 times a day – which is high, but no higher than in past years. More than 80 per cent reach for their phones within an hour of sleeping or waking; nearly half check it in the middle of the night.

The report noted: "The number of times we look at our phones each day has not increased over the past three years, and the urgency with which we reach for our phones has plateaued as well... Even the number of apps consumers download and install on their devices has more or less plateaued. The average number of apps installed has increased only marginally to 23, from last year's 22. Asked for their reasons for not installing more apps, 57 per cent of respondents said they didn't see the need for them, while 25 per cent maintained they did not have enough space on their phones for more."

Some thought they were using their smartphones too much, noted the report.

"And which age group expresses the highest levels of concern? Seventy-five per cent of those ages 25 to 34, and 72 per cent of those ages 18 to 24 report that they "definitely" or "probably" use their phone too much... Almost half (47 per cent) of all ages said they try to reduce or limit their smartphone use. Again, that trend is led predominantly by the two youngest age groups."

It isn't just users who show signs of social media fatigue. A few social media founders are turning into jeremiads warning about overuse of the platforms they created.

YouTube's co-founder and former chief executive Chad Hurley said in January that excessive checking of social media was unproductive. He predicted: "I think there's going to be a sense over the next few years, that there's going to be a social [media] fatigue that sets in. There's so much information that is being produced, that people start tuning out."

Microsoft founder Bill Gates didn't let his kids use smartphones till they were 14; Apple's Steve Jobs didn't let his play with the iPads he invented.

In November, Sean Parker, one of the co-founders of Facebook, was reported as saying that he thinks social media is damaging the health of humans' brains. "It literally changes your relationship with society, with each other... It probably interferes with productivity in weird ways. God only knows what it's doing to our children's brains."

He admitted that Facebook and its successors were deliberately designed to consume as much time and attention as possible from their users, to create "a social-validation feedback loop" and that the exercise was all about "exploiting a vulnerability in human psychology".

As many psychologists have noted, social media is designed around psychological theories about rewards and behaviour. For example, the practice of having people click Like or Share does two things: It gives a series of quick, immediate positive rewards to the person putting out the original post; and it engages the person who clicks Like or Share, turning a casual, bystander reader into a participant. Over time, such practices lock users into the social media ecosystem and users get addicted to the rewards (number of Likes) in it.

When we look back on this decade, we would probably think of the smartphone and social media as key inventions that changed our lives. But it is even odds whether we will say it enhanced our lives, or made it more stressful and less satisfying.

Meanwhile, there is an easy fix if you find yourself checking your phone for your social media updates too often. Stop and smell the roses. Or at least take a walk. No, Pokemon hunting while in the park doesn't count.

HOW TO FUTURE-PROOF YOUR JOB: TIPS FROM A GEN X WHO LEARNT FROM A MILLENNIAL

Re-skill by requesting to move to the disrupting department.
It's about future-proofing yourself – making yourself relevant
and keeping abreast of developments and technology

6 May 2017

What do you do when you fear robots may take your job? And when you work in an industry like mine – print media – going through technological disruption that is upending traditional business models, and changing the way we work each day?

You can get out of the game. You can stay but resist change. Or you can join the fight. And for news media, the fight is to go digital.

I spent a week recently attached to the Digital section of my newspaper. My colleagues who work on The Straits Times' online and mobile content sit in the large newsroom with all the rest of us working on the print paper. But their timelines and instincts are different. Print folks work to daily deadlines, while they operate under minute pressure. Those who write and edit the Breaking News section can't even take pee breaks without having someone else cover for them, in case, you know, the North Korean leader chooses to do something dramatic in those few minutes.

In print, many of us still think in words and sentences. Some of us like subtle. Online, you think in pictures, and videos, and lists, and short bursts of text that grab the reader by the eyeball and yank her into a story.

I had a great time learning from my Digital colleagues. I learnt how to use our content management system so I can edit headlines and rearrange the flow of articles on our Opinion page website myself, without having to send out irritating e-mails to already over-taxed Digital sub-editors.

I spent enjoyable hours fiddling with controls, downloading pictures, piecing together a short, very straightforward video. It took me six hours to make one short 30-second video. It isn't even very good, but I felt proud of it the way a mother loves her ugly baby. When I needed help, I sat down beside my colleague Tay Hong Yi, a 20-year-old intern, who clicked and moused and pressed a few buttons to show me how to add credits, edit captions, move frames, and rip videos. I had to ask him to please slow down so I could observe and take notes. That was a lovely Gen X-meets-Millennial moment.

That week with Digital was one of the highlights of my career, right up there with the thrill of covering elections. In part, it's because, after over 25 years of writing and editing for print, I'm a bit jaded. Nearly every issue I come across in my news feeds – apart from the remarkable phenomenon called Donald Trump, which is truly eye-opening for this generation – is something I've read or written about some time in the last two decades. Even disruption – technological advancements changing business models and lifestyle, threatening jobs – is an issue that has been much analysed. So I enjoyed the feeling of my synapses firing up as I struggled with learning a new content management system, learning about Facebook analytics, seeing how data can be converted into tables that tell a story, and learning different ways of telling a story.

The Straits Times has put our print paper online since the late 1990s. But we truly began to merge our news operations and develop a digital DNA only in the last five years or so. Our reporters now routinely file for online, then develop a fuller version for the print edition. Print editors have to think digitally. As Opinion editor in charge of op-eds, I'm constantly online, sifting through not just legacy wire feeds of news, but also online sites, blogs, and even my own Facebook news feed, for fresh perspectives. I also write a regular blog, write Facebook blurbs, and rewrite print headlines for digital. Next: repackage serious commentaries into bite-sized morsels that can be easily consumed by social media users; and turn some into short, snappy videos.

Unlike some writers who like being *cheem* (deep), I have always taken pride in trying to write simply and clearly as a journalist. When I was a writer (and not an editor who spends most of her time working on other people's copy), I relished the challenge of processing hundreds of pages of reading and hours of interviews, and distilling the essence of all that information into an article of 1,000 words – or 1,500 if you are very very lucky. It's fun to take a serious topic, digest it, give it both the bird's eye and worm's eye perspective, and spew it out in the form of a snappy article that people want to read.

Digital extends the reach of good writing, so we journalists love online, and the way social media lets our stories get liked, commented on and shared. And unlike some editors who think it's dumbing down to churn a listicle out of a serious commentary, I see such efforts as ways to reach new audiences. If I can "trick" some readers into reading articles they would normally not pay attention to, I would feel like I'm doing something good – good for the reader, for the author of the article, and good for all of us as a society, since we should all be reading beyond our filter bubbles, right?

But whatever I'm trying to do to save my job from robots will only work for a while. Already, artificial intelligence bots have been able to generate news articles for a few years now. Narrative Science and Automated Insights are two tech companies that have language-generating platforms. They can write news articles on sports, market reports and election results. And if you think robot-generated articles are robotic, you're wrong. The later iterations of bot-writers can weave in analysis and context.

The Washington Post reported a congressional election this way:

"Republicans retained control of the House and lost only a handful of seats from their commanding majority, a stunning reversal of fortune after many GOP leaders feared double-digit losses." This was a report on how Republican Steve King beat off Democratic challenger Kim Weaver in the race for Iowa's 4th congressional district seat in November 2016.

As Wired magazine reported in February: "The dispatch came with the clarity and verve for which Post reporters are known, with one key difference: It was generated by Heliograf, a bot that made its debut on the Post's website last year and marked the most sophisticated use of artificial intelligence in journalism to date."

When bots can write political analysis, what's next? Bot editors, that's what. Already, algorithms can rearrange the flow of stories on a web page or choose pictures or headlines to maximise audience reach. They can do so faster and more accurately than human editors. Sure, such bots will need some human interface or human editor to make some decisions. But instead of 10 editors, future news websites may need just one.

What's happening in the media industry is replicated across industries. Retail is up-ended by e-commerce as people shop online. Manufacturing is handed over to robots. Automated vehicles send drivers out of jobs. Avatars and animation whisk jobs from actors.

So you see, joining the fight was all about job security.

How to future-proof your job? Okay, that was a trickster headline to lure you in. But seriously, ask yourself: "Where's the fight in your industry?" Figure it out, then take action.

If you're an SME boss, understand digital, sign up for a Google or other digital marketing course. A worker in a fast-changing industry? Watch a TED video, keep up to date with online news in your area. Re-skill. Ask for a move to the disrupting department.

Actually, it's not about future-proofing your job. It's about future-proofing yourself, making yourself relevant, and up to date, and engaged.

The key is to embrace change, before change knocks you off your feet.

LEARNING TO SHOUT ABOVE THE DIN

**There's market failure in the marketplace of ideas.
The Internet is crowding out traditional media and
the latter has to shout to get attention online**

13 May 2017

When the marketplace of ideas fails, what happens? Traditional media need to shout louder to get attention, that's what.

Historian Timothy Garton Ash spoke about this at the St Gallen Symposium. A functioning democracy, he argued, needs a credible, responsible, and free media – one that offers factual information and a range of views so citizens can make informed decisions.

But the Internet is now polarising views and many netizens live and read within bubbles that don't expose them to others' views.

Meanwhile, the Internet's penchant for encouraging extreme, anonymous content means even staid media producers now need to shout louder – and get more sensational – to compete. Result: declining quality of discussion, which is bad for democracies.

He said: "Very simply the Internet is destroying the business model of newspapers. For at least two centuries we have had a public good – news, the information we need for democracy – delivered by private means. A newspaper was a means of delivering the public good of news by private means."

That model worked for 200 years because people paid to get a newspaper and advertisers paid to advertise in them. Not anymore: "The Internet has just knocked away both these pillars. So the newspapers produce the information. Facebook and Google get the profit."

What happens to traditional media companies with their struggling finances?

"This has a very negative effect on the newspapers on which we have relied for our news. First of all, what do you do if you're drowning? Well, you wave and you shout. So all our newspapers are becoming more sensational, more partisan, more celebrity; more sensationalism, more 'if it bleeds, it leads, if it roars, it scores'. The desperate competition for the clickstream, clickbait. The amount of serious news, investigative journalism and foreign reporting is going down because that's expensive. This is a real problem for the journalism we need for democracy. What we have here is potentially a market failure in the marketplace of ideas."

Professor Ash suggested two remedies to help media producers continue to invest in the kind of information-gathering that's good for democracies. "I think public service media is part of the answer – foundations funding serious news, investigative reporting and foreign news are an important part of the answer because that means you don't have to go to the state for it."

The other remedy is to resort to the craft of journalism. Establishing facts is relatively easy. "The challenge for journalism is to get those facts and that evidence into the echo chambers of the populace and to get them to readers and viewers who don't particularly even want to hear them because they'd much rather have the warming solidarity of simplistic indignation."

In other words, journalists need to get good information and diverse viewpoints into the social media feeds, onto the smartphones, and tablets, of large swathes of the population who may otherwise never get to read those articles.

How do you do this? Shout louder? Sometimes, you need to get slightly creative.

This week, for example, we turned a serious commentary on

intellectual property (IP) as a source of competitive advantage into a quiz. The IP quiz reached as many people on Facebook as the long, serious article did. I hope some readers who clicked through to the quiz learnt a few things about IP they would normally not have bothered to read about.

We distilled a long piece by Bilahari Kausikan analysing the limits of the United States' "military options" for North Korea into a listicle of four "Hard Truths from a Hard-Nosed Diplomat". If you're a bit hazy about the North Korea issue, I recommend reading that cheat sheet listicle. It's all about learning to shout above the din that is the messy, riotous, noisy, glorious Internet.

FREE CAN BE FATAL, ESPECIALLY WHEN IT COMES TO NEWS

Consumers pay for 'free' information online with the loss of their privacy. Media companies pay with lost revenues. Big Tech companies are finally wising up to the fact that free can be fatal

8 October 2017

———

I grew up with Chinese immigrant parents whose life ethos manifested the notion that you work hard for what you need, because nothing is free in this world.

In my adult life, I still tend to look a gift horse in the mouth and am suspicious of freebies and too generous offers. If a deal seems too good to be true, it probably is just that. Stay away.

But like many other modern citizens of a rich, industrialised, interconnected world, I've been seduced by the flood of freebies I get on the Internet. Information is free. Entertainment in the form of countless articles and videos is free. Search is free.

Google puts the wealth of centuries of research and knowledge literally at my fingertips, condensed into bite-sized, graphical and relevant information. I expect Google to read my mind when I key in a few words and to know precisely what about "big tech safe harbour" or "singlit poetry wrestling" I need to know to edit or write an article.

I expect its algorithms and bots to trawl through millions of web pages and sites to deliver the handful of pithy, relevant articles I need to read to get up to speed on a subject. I expect the information delivered in three seconds, and I expect it free.

But as some have warned, and many of the rest of us are just discovering, nothing is really free. Not even information or search results. We use Google to search for information we want online. We use Facebook, Twitter and Instagram to connect with friends and share photos and updates. It's all free.

But when something is free, often someone, somewhere, is paying the price. And in a roundabout way, the price often comes back to us.

Let's talk about search results. Who is paying the price of that free search?

We all are – by handing over our browsing history and personal information. Google tracks each site you visit; it may also have your contacts and your credit card details. Each of us becomes a potential customer for an ad that Google sells to advertisers.

If a shampoo-seller wants to advertise a hair product for women who want more lustrous hair, Google might notice that I'd been searching "what to do with thinning hair" or "how to style my hair so it looks fuller" and serve me up as a customer for that shampoo-seller.

That shampoo ad might pop up the next time I open my browser to search for something unrelated, like "best omakase meal in Singapore under $50". (That search would of course be noted and Google would be serving me restaurant ads next.)

Internet users are in effect handing over their personal information and preferences, and allowing sites such as Google and Facebook to monetise their Internet-browsing habits.

How about the information that goes into those search results?

Who's spending time researching, and writing, about "big tech safe harbour" laws, for example? Or "income inequality and impact on economic growth"? Or "when is the next season of Billions coming out"?

Who are the ones spending money to produce videos, graphics and stories on, say, the Las Vegas shooting, the Catalonia independence vote, or even the reserved presidential election?

One big group of people involved in producing high-quality, credible information are journalists in newsrooms worldwide. Getting smart, energetic, ambitious people to devote their careers to gathering news and interpreting it is expensive. Media organisations know it and have traditionally expected people to pay for that information produced.

The Internet has broken that business model by serving up a lot of news and information for free.

The result has affected the financial bottom line of mainstream media organisations (including Singapore Press Holdings, which publishes this newspaper) which now find their traditional revenue streams of subscriptions and print-based advertising hit. Predictably, some media companies have scaled down on journalism resources; just as predictably, over time, the information vacuum left behind has become filled by clickbait news sites while the proportion of in-depth, verifiable, credible information available in the digiverse has declined.

This explains why the issue of "fake news" or false information masquerading as news has become so prevalent in the last year. Bad information is driving out good.

Things have got to such a state that even Google and Facebook, which benefited from serving up free news for their users, are now coming to see that there is merit to helping media organisations stay viable to produce good news and information.

Otherwise, the quality of Google's own search results will deteriorate, if they are populated by public relations spin from commercial companies and fake news content from websites created just to channel traffic there for advertising revenue.

Just last week, Google changed a key policy towards news publishers. It ended its decade-old "first click free" policy that makes news publishers give away stories for free each day, in exchange for high search rankings. Those that don't want to give away their content free and who keep stories behind a paywall, as the Wall Street Journal did, would rank low in Google search results. When WSJ bowed out of "first click free" this year, its traffic from Google fell 38 per cent and year-on-year referrals from Google News were down 89 per cent in August.

Google's vice-president of news Richard Gingras last week said the tech company will go for "a flexible sampling model where publishers will decide how many, if any, free articles they want to provide to potential subscribers based on their own business strategies".

Google went one step further, saying it will help news publishers convert casual news readers into subscribers.

A New York Times article said of the Google move: "One of the company's goals, Mr Gingras said, is to help 'take the friction out of the purchase process' by using its own technological capabilities, as well as the information it has on users – including e-mail address and credit cards – to make subscribing simpler."

Mr Gingras said Google expected to begin rolling out its suite of subscription support services in the first half of next year. "We're not suggesting this is a magic bullet for growing subscription revenue," he said. "We'll continue to collaborate – this is a journey."

Facebook has also announced plans to help publishers gain paid subscriptions.

The move to recognise that news has to be paid for has been welcomed by publishers worldwide, especially as it comes from the two big tech behemoths that together gobble up nearly all the growth in digital ad revenue each year.

At the heart of the change in direction is a growing recognition that there is no such thing as free news or information. Free comes at a cost: to consumers, who surrender their private information and preferences, and pay in the currency of their attention; to media companies and journalists whose hard work is devalued when it is forced to be made free; and ultimately, to all of us who use the Internet, as the cybersphere becomes awash in untrustworthy information.

Meanwhile, the platform companies such as Google and Facebook, which have access to all the data analytics, will of course continue to monetise their information about us.

In the arc of things, the pendulum that says information wants to be free is slowly swinging back to a more median position where information has a price, and where we all decide collectively we are prepared to pay a reasonable price for it.

Hence, rampant digital piracy is already giving way to millions of paid subscriptions to streaming services. Already, many people are finding that it's worth their while to pay about $10 a month to subscribe to a library of music or TV shows or movies they can watch anytime rather than to engage in illegal downloading of such content and risk falling afoul of the law, and risk their computers being infected with malware and, for some perhaps, risk living with the moral stigma of becoming a thief who steals from the content producer.

I hope more of the rest of us ordinary consumers of news and information realise that there is a cost to things that are free.

As a journalist who writes for a living, I am aware that my argument can be seen as self-serving, and indeed it is. But it is no less in the public interest. As an increasing number of commentators have argued, quality journalism is a public good that is for building stable democracies and as a watchdog on power.

For the Singapore media, the challenge is for us to step up, going beyond our traditional consensus-building role, to provide more incisive journalism that does not duck difficult issues. Otherwise, without quality information, what might be the long-term effect of mindlessly imbibing low-grade content and digital ads doled out to us?

In a brilliant article in the Washington Post, reprinted in last week's Sunday Times, Franklin Foer, the author of *World Without Mind: The Existential Threat Of Big Tech*, warned about succumbing to the lure of Big Tech.

"We've spent too long marvelling. The time has come to consider the consequences of these monopolies, to reassert our role in determining the human path. Once we cross certain thresholds – once we remake institutions such as media and publishing, once we abandon privacy – there's no turning back, no restoring our lost individuality."

He drew a parallel with the growth of convenience and processed foods about 50 years ago which delighted a generation that was freed from onerous cooking. It took decades to understand the price paid for convenience and efficiency.

"Yes, processed foods were feats of engineering, but they were engineered to make us fat. Their delectable taste required huge amounts of sodium and sizeable stockpiles of sugar, which happened to reset our palates and made it harder to sate hunger.

"A whole new system of industrial farming emerged, with penny-conscious conglomerates cramming chickens into faeces-covered pens and stuffing them with antibiotics.

"By the time we came to understand the consequences of our revised patterns of consumption, the damage had been done to our waistlines, longevity, souls and planet."

He added: "Something like the mid-century food revolution is now reordering the production and consumption of knowledge. Our intellectual habits are being scrambled by the dominant companies."

His key thesis is that "as with the food giants, the tech behemoths have given rise to a new science that aims to construct products that pander to their consumers".

In traditional media, high-minded and "snobbish" elite editors decide on what's news to shape public opinion for the better, as Foer noted. Today's infosphere is dominated by Silicon Valley executives who use science, data and algorithms to, as he put it, "exploit the public's worst tendencies, its tribalism and paranoia" and target them to serve up content and advertising.

He added: "The proliferation of falsehoods and conspiracies through social media, the dissipation of our common basis for fact, is creating conditions ripe for authoritarianism."

Even if you don't agree with his political worldview and warning of Armageddon, think about the core of his warning: that the information we are all getting for free today has a price tag – and we will pay one day.

Unless we take steps to remedy the situation today.

THE OPPOSITE OF RETRENCHMENT IS RESILIENCE

There is no good way to retrench people. But as I found out, the opposite of Retrenchment is Resilience

21 October 2017

The past week has been emotional for many of us in Singapore Press Holdings (SPH), especially in The Straits Times (ST) where I work.

The retrenchment of over 30 of our colleagues in the ST newsroom, part of the 130 retrenched from across the SPH company, has sent many into a tailspin of emotions.

This was the first retrenchment exercise I observed up close. Here are my takeaways:

There is no good way to retrench people

No matter what senior managers do, how well they plan the exercise, the impact on those affected will be largely negative. For SPH's case, unions and management negotiated what is widely considered a generous package: one month's pay per year of service, capped at 25 months, plus notice pay (one month for bargainable staff, three months for more senior staff). We had career coaches and counsellors on standby and a database of job openings.

My bosses made it plain that people were being retrenched because their jobs were no longer relevant, or the number of positions for a particular skill-set had shrunk. Performance was not the issue. But no matter how it is portrayed, the stigma of retrenchment remains. It stings.

And for those who had been happy at work, the trauma of instant separation must be hard to bear. You come in one day as an employee of a company. Before the day is over, you are told you have to leave; you pack your things and you hand in your pass. SPH gave those retrenched leeway to come back the next day or over the quiet weekend to pack – but separation is separation, even if some of your worldly artefacts linger on in a former abode.

For my company, one big boo-boo took place when some staff found out they were retrenched the hard way – when they couldn't log into their computer system after they came to work. It wasn't meant to be thus, but it happened. SPH bosses apologised for the error.

When you scale down, you also need to boost up

Retrenchments take place in companies facing challenges.

For SPH, whose stronghold was in newspaper publishing, the decline of print media is structural. Our media profits have been falling. Everyone knows that. While the company remains profitable, an increasing share of those profits come from non-core businesses in property and healthcare.

The core media business is dwindling, as print advertisement revenue dries up, and digital ad revenue has yet to flood in. The retrenching of editorial staff should come as no surprise.

But even as print media declines, the promise of digital media is ripe. Digital ad spending is on the rise worldwide.

As SPH moves from print to digital, we will need fewer of some skill-sets, and more of others. We need more videographers, fewer print photographers, for example. We need more interactive graphic designers, fewer print illustrators. So even as SPH retrenches staff, it also needs to grow, and expand, and join the war for digital talent.

And even as a company retrenches, its leaders must be able to rally the rest to believe in a future.

This is why SPH chiefs spoke about having to retrench in one breath, and the need to expand its media operations in the next. The Straits Times, for example, is expanding its regional coverage and is hiring experienced journalists to report on the region.

Boosting morale and rallying the troops to believe in a bright future is the flip side of retrenchment.

After all, you trim to get the body corporate into fit fighting shape for battle.

Think with the brain, feel with the heart

Retrenching is wrenching, but it may be necessary.

Retrench with the head – and then execute and empathise with the heart.

I had the privilege – or discomfiting position – of being in middle-management through this exercise.

Rationally, I can understand the reasons for retrenchment.

When a business is declining, you have to streamline operations and reduce costs. You can't forever have, say, the same 100 people producing work that generates three-quarters of the revenue of what was generated 10 years ago, as is the case for the core media business in SPH. Even if other parts of the company are still profitable, you don't really want to carry on with that cost structure of 100 people producing stuff with declining revenue.

But emotionally, you feel the impact of seeing colleagues devastated by the retrenchment.

I decided to compartmentalise the two parts. Accept the fact of retrenchment rationally. Then try to be there emotionally for those affected.

There are three groups of those affected.

First, those retrenched.

For this group, the rest of us can just be empathetic and supportive. Listen and sympathise. Help pack up or drive their belongings home, if that's needed. Have a cup of coffee with your colleagues in the canteen. Match your ex-colleagues with job openings that you know of. I have a wide range of very nice friends and contacts. I asked around for job openings. Other editors did likewise. We helped funnel job openings to those looking for new opportunities. Research has shown that weak ties – such as friends of friends – are often the best sources for job openings.

The second worst hit emotionally, in my view, are the bosses who made the decision on where the axe should fall.

The editors I know in SPH are decent, good people. One of them said at a townhall meeting that this was the most difficult decision he had to make in his career of over 25 years. Another boss felt "physically sick" from the long sessions and difficult decisions.

It is therapeutic for people to point the finger upwards and blame bosses. But now that I am in middle-management and see their point of view, I can't do so with a good conscience.

No matter how they decide, bosses will face criticism for their call; worst of all, they will feel the moral burden of deciding whose job should go. I don't think many people bear such burdens lightly. I was appreciative that my boss, a key decision-maker in the exercise, told us middle-managers that if there was any "opprobrium" from staff, it should be directed at him.

At the same time, the leaders who made the decision must remain emotionally engaged with those retrenched, and those who remain, and make time to let staff talk through their feelings.

The third group affected are the rest who remain.

They may feel anxiety and sadness for those affected. There will be feelings of vicarious indignation for those retrenched, and empathy. Inter-washed among the maelstrom of feelings will be some relief – or disappointment in some cases from those who wanted the payout – of being spared this time round.

Engulfed with heavy feelings, a colleague and I left the newsroom that

Thursday for an early dinner. We both had the same uneasy feeling – a sentiment akin to survivor's privilege or even survivor's guilt – why them, not us?

There is a time to be a cog in a company wheel. There is a time to be a person. When someone has lost his or her job, it is time to be the latter.

The opposite of retrenchment is resilience

Some of the colleagues I spoke to remained upbeat and positive.

D-Day, Thursday (Oct 12), was a shock for some. But it was all systems go from The Day After.

I had breakfast with a young colleague on Saturday. On Monday morning, she was meeting a prospective employer. In the afternoon, she was discussing a freelance assignment.

Another colleague I was bugging to finish up her CV, told me she had to finish a last article for The Straits Times. My heart choked at that point – such loyalty from this young reporter, to an employer who had just dispensed of her service. I decided to be a friend first, an employee second. Forget ST, I said. Do your CV first. (The company in question was looking for people urgently.)

Another colleague told me the other team members she had worked with for years in ST had rallied round her. She is staying hopeful, looking ahead.

One colleague organised a farewell tea inviting ex-colleagues who had just been retrenched. This is one small way to aim for closure.

Resilience means accepting the inevitable, dealing with the hurt, and then doing one's best to cope by remaining hopeful of new openings.

CITIZENS GAIN WHEN CONTENT IS KING AGAIN

As news publishers compete for subscribers, the local media has to produce richer, more robust content to stave off competition for local audiences

29 October 2017

A recent slew of news and developments coming out from the global media industry offers hope for news publishers like Singapore Press Holdings (SPH), which publishes The Straits Times. Even as SPH retrenched staff nearly three weeks ago, it is also mindful of the bright spots in the media industry. Let me count the ways in which the news business is looking hopeful again.

People are moving away from clickbait information, and gravitating towards credible news

This has been noticeable in the United States following what the New York Times calls the "Trump bump". This was a surge in media subscriptions from people keen to get in-depth White House coverage after the shock election of Mr Donald Trump as President.

The rise of fake news and the exposure of websites with seemingly high traffic generated by bots, not human readers, have also led mass readers to go back to mainstream media publishers.

The NYTimes' second-quarter earnings announced in July saw digital revenues from advertising and subscriptions offset declines in print advertising.

NYTimes has been pivoting to a subscription-based revenue model. Chief executive Mark Thompson said: "We believe that the demand for quality, in-depth journalism is growing, not only in the US but across the globe... We believe that more and more people are prepared to pay for access to this kind of journalism. This is the foundation of our strategy."

Mainstream media companies like the NYTimes in America, the Guardian in Britain, and The Straits Times in Singapore, have been active in transforming themselves from traditional print newspapers into digital media news publishers. Already, all these publishers distribute content across digital platforms.

The Straits Times, for example, is going for a "first to digital" strategy, putting out news reports online instantly, and curating a print edition for the next day.

This move to credible news has been apparent for months now. What has given added hope to news publishers are reports that more people are prepared to pay for news.

Free is so yesterday. Paying for what you use is the new norm

Some uplifting news last week came from the Reuters Institute's Digital News Report. In the United States, millennials are flocking to subscribe to mainstream media publishers in large numbers. A range of media publishers report strong growth, typically 70 to 100 per cent, in subscriptions from those aged 18 to 34. This was the case for NYTimes, the Washington Post, the serious, high-brow Atlantic, and the business-oriented Wall Street Journal.

One reason for this? Millennials are used to paying a flat fee per month to consume music via streaming services like Spotify, and for movies via Netflix. As they come of political age, curious about the world, they are forking out money to subscribe to quality journalism.

This is a marked difference from the Internet mantra of years ago that "information wants to be free".

There is increasing realisation that "free can be fatal, especially when it comes to news", as I wrote in an Oct 8 article in this space. If you don't pay $1 a day for news, you pay for it in attention devoted every day to ads and soft-sell content conditioned to get you to click to buy things you don't really need or want. Meanwhile, the quality of information and journalism, starved of revenue, declines overall.

I am hopeful that the media sector in Singapore and the region will also see a boost in digital subscriptions in the coming years. For this to happen, however, content has to become the centre of our strategy to widen readership and audiences.

Content is king again

How does one make money on the Internet? It was Microsoft co-founder Bill Gates who in 1996 wrote an influential essay titled "Content is King" on the company's website.

He wrote: "Content is where I expect much of the real money will be made on the Internet, just as it was in broadcasting.

"The television revolution that began half a century ago spawned a number of industries, including the manufacturing of TV sets, but the long-term winners were those who used the medium to deliver information and entertainment. When it comes to an interactive network such as the Internet, the definition of 'content' becomes very wide.

"For example, computer software is a form of content – an extremely important one, and the one for Microsoft will remain by far the most important. But the broad opportunities for most companies involve supplying information or entertainment. No company is too small to participate."

The Internet industry has gone through various cycles. The latest ad-driven cycle was fuelled by the rise of tech platform companies, such as Google and Facebook, which use content others provide to get eyeballs and clicks which they then monetise to marketeers to sell to advertisers.

In that transaction, content providers like news publishers get a raw deal as they have little share of the digital ad revenue and are not paid fairly for the content they produce.

There are some signs that the model is shifting. Google announced on its blog early this month that it would work with news publishers to help convert casual readers of news articles, in search results, into paid subscribers.

As content moves to premier position again, news publishers skilled in generating compelling content with text, image, audio, video and interactive elements will have a fighting chance to compete in that territory.

For Singapore media, the fight for audiences rests on the robustness and richness of our content

Global trends in the media sector, and rapid tech developments, will all affect the media scene here.

While Singapore can ring-fence print media production to some extent via licensing and newspaper printing laws, it can't ring-fence users from exposure to news, information and entertainment available online, streamed into homes, and onto tablets and mobile devices.

Citizens here are lapping up the rich engagement experiences online. A younger generation raised in the no-holds-barred arena of Internet discourse becomes acclimatised to free debate and expects to engage in similar discussions on local issues.

The local media risks losing these audiences for good if it does not broaden the parameters for such discussion on its platforms.

The Singapore Government should continue to encourage, and enforce, legal and social norms in public discussion, such as enforcing strictures against incitement to violence or hatred, and protecting individuals from harassment.

Local media publishers are also responsible companies that will hew to the public interest and can help build a national consensus on important issues.

But the state cannot and must not hold back mainstream media companies from engaging fully with the competition for attention and subscription dollars that is reaching our shores. To do so is to hobble the local media even before the fight begins.

The NYTimes this month announced that it has opened a sales office in Singapore for the South-east Asian market. It is gunning for 10 million subscriptions, up from about three million print and digital subscribers now.

Nor is it just NYTimes that wants to eat our lunch. ST editor Warren Fernandez, who is also editor-in-chief of SPH's English/Malay/Tamil Media Group, met executives of Quartz and Wall Street Journal during a recent trip to America and found them upfront about their bid for Singapore audiences. As he wrote last week: "The competition in the media industry is now increasingly digital, increasingly social, and increasingly global."

The challenges facing the local media do not apply only to The Straits Times, but across titles and companies.

At The Straits Times, one of our strategies to face the competition is to boost our content to raise digital subscriptions locally and in the region. This is why the paper wants to hire more "foreign correspondents", which refers to correspondents reporting on an overseas region for a media company, not to foreign journalists.

As for Singapore coverage, The Straits Times as Singapore's news publisher for 172 years knows Singapore best. We must report on it honestly and unflinchingly. To do so, we need creative, capable and courageous journalists and editors.

Journalistic standards must be kept high, but editors should not be viewed primarily as gatekeepers. Instead, their role is to marshal resources to produce compelling content that resonates with readers in

Singapore and beyond, and to drive reader engagement. Good examples of such content that The Straits Times produces regularly now are the profiles of people who succeed against the odds by my colleague Wong Kim Hoh and stories of resilience among ordinary folk from Theresa Tan.

Singapore benefits if it has a local media staffed with journalists and editors who are able, willing and given the room to push the boundaries.

We want readers who understand Singapore's unique constraints yet demand we raise our standards, thus keeping us on our toes. We also need a relationship with stakeholders that allows such robust content to be created, and a state that does not use its considerable influence, resources and enforcement powers to box the local media into a corner.

A timid local media will fight a losing battle to gain readers' respect and their subscription dollar. The result will be a gradual fragmentation of the national consensus, as more and more young Singaporeans turn to foreign media outlets to get their news and information.

Can a local media publisher compete with global titans and win? For an answer, look to the prestigious Editor and Publisher EPPY Award 2017, which last week announced that the best website infographic award goes to The Straits Times for its Anatomy of Cancer infographic. It features 3D human models which can be rotated on screen, allowing viewers to click on body parts to zoom in on information on the top 10 cancers in Singapore. Not bad for a newspaper company rapidly transforming itself to be a regional digital news publisher.

When it comes to the future of local media, I think the interests of citizens as readers, the commercial interests of the media publishers, and the interests of the government are aligned.

If they are not, they should be.

Each group should strive for richer, more robust content that is compelling to local and regional audiences.

DISRUPTION IN THE HDB HEARTLAND

HDB shops become hipster cafes, and a wet market business goes digital, as a new generation takes over traditional businesses

23 September 2017

Did you read about the fishmonger in Beo Crescent who's gone fishing online? It's about a couple who took over the family's fish business.

DishTheFish has a wet market stall in Beo Crescent, and an e-commerce platform. It's run by Jeffrey Tan, 32, and his wife Angeline Ong, 29. Jeffrey used to help his father cut fish as a teenager.

They plan to open another outlet in a mall, where they will have space for a demo corner to teach customers how to steam a fish or sous vide it to perfection. They use tech and data analytics to figure out what fish to buy, track users' preferences, and handle inventory, accounting and human resources.

That story of millennials taking a heartland business digital was my favourite news article of the week.

I've always had a soft spot for heartland businesses. I think in part because my parents were also small business folks – they made a living selling drinks or snacks and in my growing up years, they ran a char kway teow stall at a hawker centre. I also grew up in HDB flats.

Back in the days before the Internet, I used to write a column called Heartlanders. It was about, well, life in the HDB heartland.

It was former minister George Yeo who popularised the term "heartland" to refer to our Housing Board estates. Once derided as vertical cemeteries of the soul, they became "Singapore's heartland".

The term "heartland" in America's cultural lexicon refers to the vast land in between the two oceans.

Depending on the era and your own sensibility, it can refer to ranches, vast plains, or mountainous areas.

"Heartland" was also used to describe a certain ethic around the working class – hardworking, honest, no-nonsense. The salt of the earth type of community.

The term "heartland" as a way to refer to our own public housing estates caught on.

Many of us embraced the identity in the 1990s and after. It was a badge of honour. To be a heartlander was to be a person plugged into Singapore's tradition, a speck in the continuum of our history that reaches back to the hardworking, frugal, self-denying, sacrificing pioneers.

I always think you can take a heartlander out of the HDB heartland, but you can't take the heartland out of a true blue heartlander.

Even today, when I've shopped all over the world and Orchard Road is a short dash away, I enter a wonderful, wordless, weirdly content zone when I wander aimlessly in and out of shops in HDB town centres.

Even today, after I've lived in private condos with pools, landed housing with gardens, and in heritage stone buildings overseas at college, my dream retirement home is an HDB flat.

I can just see myself living happily in a mature estate that has an MRT station, a wet market, a town centre with shops and a mall or two nearby, all within walking distances or a short bus ride away.

Having a seniors' activity centre nearby where I can do group exercises, and maybe volunteer at a small residents' library managed entirely by seniors, with books for neighbourhood kids we can read to, would enhance the quality of my life.

If there's a hipster cafe nearby where I can enjoy my soy latte and Eggs Benedict, all the better.

My generation – born in the 1960s and 1970s – is at home in both the old HDB estates and the new hipster enclaves sprouting up all over the island. I enjoy most the HDB estates that have both.

Think Tiong Bahru. Ghim Moh/Holland Village. The Sunset area in Clementi. Tanjong Pagar. Dakota Crescent. Toa Payoh Lorong 1.

Every time I see a shop in an HDB estate taken over by a hipster cafe with its minimalist/rustic/industrial chic decor, I make a mental note to check it out one day.

It helps that I have a millennial niece with a nose for such things. So I've gone to places near my office like 51 fiveone degrees (the orange chiffon cake is a hit wherever I bring it), Creamier (love the waffle), the Daily Press and the quaintly-named froyo (frozen yoghurt) shop Frozen by a Thousand Blessings.

One afternoon a couple of years back, she bundled me into my car and we set the GPS for a cafe in Jalan Bukit Ho Swee. How hipster can a cafe there get? I thought to myself. I know the area for its rental flats and poor working-class neighbourhood.

She knew it for Sin Lee Foods, a former coffee shop that got a new lease of life when a young couple took it over. Where once Sin Lee would have sounded *ulu*, they embraced the name, making good on their promise to the third-generation owner to retain the signboard for the original Sin Lee Hup Kee coffee shop. The cafe's Facebook page indicates the cafe has closed and it is scouting for a new location. I hope it keeps its heartland hipster vibe in its new home.

It's a sign of Singaporeans' self-confidence that we embrace our humble working-class roots, branding hipster cafes under dialect names (think Chye Seng Huat Hardware which despite its name is a coffee joint) and turning common daily items from our past – like colourful enamel ware, cockerel design bowls, red vacuum flasks and the ubiquitous white cotton Good Morning towels used in most homes – into iconic cultural markers. A new generation of Singaporeans is rejuvenating our HDB neighbourhoods, turning some hipster, and others digital.

As a consumer, I enjoy the way they expand and enhance my buying and eating experience. As a heartlander, I'm glad to see the neighbourhoods get a new lease of life, the shops get new tenants, and to see the way a new generation of Singaporeans enjoy life in the heartland, in a way that is refreshingly different from my generation, but no less valid.

Disruption is in the heartland – in a good way.

SMES NEED SOME START-UP ENERGY AND TALENT

25 March 2017

I love living in Singapore, a start-up city that just got ranked No. 1 when it comes to having start-up talent globally.

It's a city where enterprising young people are trying out different business ideas, creating novel services to make life more interesting and convenient and designing new products that consumers didn't know they need until they see a prototype of it.

In the last couple of months, I've signed up for a food delivery service that sends me frozen dinners. I order in packs of 14, and they get delivered in microwaveable containers.

It's not gourmet, but tastes rather good. It claims to be healthy, with a calorie count of about 500. I've been eating these meals for a few weeks now, and all I can say is that I don't miss the MSG-laden, oily economic rice or *hor fun* that I would tend to grab for dinner in the past.

Fitness Ration is run by a group of young people aged 21 to 27. The managing director is 24, according to the website.

Then, the other day, I saw an article in my Facebook feed about a stand that you put on your desk to hold your computer, which can zoom up so you can work standing at your workstation.

Right now, I use Muji storage boxes, tissue paper boxes and stacks of books to raise my computer and keyboard when I want to work standing at my desk.

The idea of having that handsome-looking contraption on my desk which I can raise with a press of a button was tempting. It comes with an app – of course it does! – that you can set to prompt reminders to stand or sit, and that helps you track calories burnt.

I fell for it. I signed up and am expecting delivery of the Altizen desk in April.

Call me a start-up sucker, but I like supporting these initiatives by enterprising young people.

When I click Buy, I'm not just buying a meal delivery service – I'm supporting the start-up dream of a bunch of young folks out to change the world, one frozen meal or standing desk at a time.

At the same time, I'm mindful of the fact that each start-up that takes off might spell the end of one, or two, or five, traditional small business.

The new healthy food delivery service is just a new twist to the traditional *tingkat*, where you get packs of rice, soup and three dishes delivered daily to your home. I think *tingkat* will be around for a while yet in Singapore, as it offers Chinese or Asian-style staples, and is much cheaper than most of the online-based services – a *tingkat* meal costs about $5 per person, while the healthy food option tends to be double that at least.

But if some of the food delivery services take off, would traditional *tingkat* caterers lose market share?

Sometimes, it seems to me that start-ups benefit from being on the right side of history. There are many government grants for them. Consumers like me are willing to support them to try new products and services.

In contrast, many of our small and medium enterprises, especially those in the heartlands, are facing problems, squeezed by rising rentals and manpower shortages, and falling demand.

As a consumer who grew up with HDB shops and still frequent them, I don't want them to fade off and close shop. I still like traditional *kopi* at the coffee shop more than any Starbucks brew in a cafe. When I need something for the house like a laundry basket or S hooks, I head to the

HDB household goods sundry store, not department stores.

My hope is that start-ups and traditional businesses learn from each other and adopt each other's best practices.

I'd love a food delivery service that sends me healthy, nutritious, flash-frozen, easy-to-reheat Chinese meals. I'd love to go to a HDB photo-printing shop that can convert my printed analog photos into a digital format and lay them out into a nice photobook, without me having to spend hours choosing templates online and designing them myself.

I got to thinking about traditional shops and start-ups, after reading an article about what the Canadian city of Quebec is doing to help small businesses survive.

Among the many articles I read in the last two weeks as part of my job picking what to reprint in The Straits Times, that was one that stood out and remained in my mind.

In the article, authors Sandrine Rastello and Frederic Tomesco say that small businesses create many jobs, but many are run by baby-boomers nearing retirement. In Quebec, almost 60 per cent of Quebec's small firms are expected to change hands in the next decade, but only 10 per cent have a formal leadership plan.

"Up to 10,000 entrepreneurs, or about 6 per cent of the total, were at risk of closing their companies by 2023 for a lack of succession plan, jeopardising as many 139,000 jobs, according to a 2014 Chamber of Commerce of Metropolitan Montreal report," said the article.

Enter the city's planners, working with universities and businesses to facilitate "transfers" – as the process of business changeover is called. Young people (some offspring of the original owners) are identified and trained to take over small businesses. There are tax incentives for "transfers" of businesses within families.

Transfer agencies or companies also work to help match buyers and sellers of business, including some that operate online, letting people post their business profile and expectations to find buyers. One boss of a transfer company said it takes about three to five years to work out a smooth transfer of business.

At the top level, the business of transfers gets strong support. According to the article, "Canada's second-largest public pension fund manager recently unveiled a plan to invest C$250 million (S$262 million) in mid-size companies that are planning a transfer".

On the ground, the agencies that do the matching describe a process that is highly personalised and time-consuming to match business sellers with new buyers.

One woman training to take over her parents' shop observed: "Everybody is talking about starting their own company," she said. "There are lots of amazing companies already started."

The article struck a chord with me because I could see that Singapore has a similar problem as Quebec. Both are rapidly ageing cities with a large pool of small companies headed by ageing bosses who don't have anyone to take over their business.

The difference is that in Singapore, we talk about disruption, which is a polite way of saying, let the market decide, and let the old businesses just die out.

The problem of course is that each business that closes may cause 10 workers to lose their jobs.

Quebec isn't giving up on their small businesses. I wonder if we should do more too, learn from Quebec and work actively to match energetic young people to some of these ageing businesses.

THE GUILT OF SHOPPING AT AMAZON

By going online to shop for groceries and household goods, am I aiding in the killing of Singapore's retail icons like NTUC FairPrice, Cold Storage, Sheng Siong and HDB shops?

29 July 2017

———

I like going to supermarkets, browsing the aisles in pleasurable anticipation of the delectable meals that can be fixed, or the crunchy snacks I can munch on. I've never seen the point of shopping for groceries online.

Then, on Thursday (July 27), Amazon announced its foray into Singapore, the beachhead of its entry into South-east Asia, with the launch of a two-hour delivery service.

When the news flashed across my computer screen, it was lunchtime. I needed a break. I downloaded the Amazon Prime Now app. Within minutes, I was scrolling through the easy-to-use app and clicking. Before I knew it, I had a cart full of items. Ads promised a 10 per cent discount. I applied the promo code and got my discount. I keyed in my Amazon account information and up popped my credit card details and delivery address. It was so seamless, I ended up making my first grocery online purchase with little effort.

Then, the questioning and guilt set in. What had I done? Was I aiding a foreign e-commerce company to kill off local retailers?

In the days before Uber and Airbnb disrupted businesses, I was a happy online shopper and Internet user. These days, I know better.

The big tech companies are platform companies, providing a

marketplace that matches sellers to buyers of goods. This can be immensely empowering – think the low-income women in Third World countries weaving crafts that can be sold to First World corporate customers, for example; or the millions of migrants who can't find jobs in their host countries but can suddenly become Uber drivers, or the socially awkward geek who can't hold down an office job but can sell his computing skills online. In the early days, disintermediation was a good thing – it got rid of go-between companies and matched vendors to buyers.

But that was the age of innocence.

These days, we know that platform companies disrupt businesses in a big way, and can cause massive losses of jobs. Uber is driving taxi companies out of business – and taxi-drivers' livelihoods are threatened. In fact, Uber itself has said self-driving cars is its aim, which means the work lifespan of Uber drivers is also limited.

Social media platforms like Facebook and Twitter bring the tools of publishing straight into the hands of citizens, disrupting the mass media business, and putting tens of thousands of journalists, sub-editors, type-setters, newspaper vendors, out of jobs. Those of us in the media business live with the reality of disruption each day. We know the anxieties it brings, as well as its potential to unleash creative ways of redoing our core business, which is reporting and analysing the news and telling stories of people.

Retail is now facing that tsunami.

As a shopper, I want to use my grocery dollar wisely.

I don't want to support Amazon, or Alibaba and RedMart, and inadvertently cause the death of the local retailers I like. I like supermarkets. I have a steady, long-term relationship with NTUC FairPrice. I get tired of it sometimes and grouch that it takes me for granted. Then I seek out my on-off flirtation with Cold Storage and bask in its courtship. I'd actually hate for either to close down.

I also want to support our local HDB stores. I have a favourite fruit man whose tattooed arms pick out cherries, grapes and peaches that are invariably juicy and sweet. I point, he picks, I never bargain. I also enjoy going to the HDB estate near my apartment to browse the amazing array of wares in the ubiquitous household goods stores. So many colourful containers of all shapes and sizes; every kitchen utensil I never knew I would have a use for; all manner of brooms, brushes, laundry baskets, cleaning tools. I have spent many pleasant evenings lost in those aisles, emerging happily an hour later to pay for some item I will hardly use.

Now that I've discovered the convenience of online grocery shopping, will I push these stores to extinction faster?

That was my topmost guilty question.

Next, if I am to shop online for groceries, should I go with Amazon or Alibaba and its online grocer partner RedMart?

As a consumer, I feel a little like Singapore, caught between the two big superpowers China and the United States. Like Singapore, I don't want to be forced to take sides between American Amazon and Chinese Alibaba. I want to be friends with both. I want both to be around, so that they can push local companies to improve, and can compete with each other, and improve consumer choice and customer experience.

The two e-commerce giants have different business models. Both are big conglomerates whose remit goes far beyond e-commerce to e-payments (Alibaba) and cloud servers (Amazon). But for its e-commerce operations, Alibaba is mainly a marketplace for third-party sellers. It takes a cut from these sales. Amazon's core e-commerce business is to sell products directly through its online portals. It started with books and music, and now sells household goods, electronics and groceries. It has even developed its own house brand, Amazon Basics.

When I buy something from Alibaba, some small China company might be the one making the product and making a profit. When I buy something from Amazon, most times, the profit goes mainly to Amazon.

According to a very interesting article in TechinAsia that compares the two business models, "Amazon earns $1 in revenue for every $2.30 in merchandise it sells, while Alibaba has to sell $28.10 in merchandise to earn that same dollar."

Should I be backing Alibaba's model that at least lets many small businesses make a profit? But then many of those companies making profits are from China. While Alibaba's boss Jack Ma says its marketplace is inclusive, and spins its logistics hub in Malaysia as a gateway for Southeast Asian merchants to sell to China customers, it's more likely that the flow of goods and benefits will be the reverse.

Even as I write this, however, I know the part I play as a consumer in this phenomenon is miniscule, and I know the end game will not be pretty for retail.

Amazon Prime Now in Singapore started modestly, with about 20,000 products from food to beauty products to household goods. The average supermarket stocks about 50,000 items. Even with such a modest inventory of items, demand overwhelmed its ability to deliver within the promised two-hour window. I had to opt for next-day delivery.

Singapore supermarket shares fell on Amazon's launch. The Business Times reported that shares of Sheng Siong slid 4.5 per cent on Thursday to S$0.95. Shares of Dairy Farm International, which operates Cold Storage, Giant, 7-Eleven and Guardian stores here, fell 0.4 per cent to US$8.14.

The Financial Times had a chilling article this month saying that some analysts see retail as the "next big short".

With online shopping sounding the death knell for retail, mall developers, supermarkets, shops and every other associated business, analysts are predicting that share prices of these companies will drop, and some are betting on it, in the same way that some hedge funds made a lot of money betting that the US housing market would fall with sub-prime mortgages.

The article said: "The relentless rise of online shopping is posing a huge challenge for US shopping malls, developers and investors who own shares and bonds in household names. The core problem is a dramatic overbuilding of stores, coupled with the rise of e-commerce, Richard Hayne, Urban Outfitters' chief executive, told analysts on a conference call earlier this year. 'This created a bubble, and like housing, that bubble has now burst,' Mr Hayne said. 'We are seeing the results: Doors shuttering and rents retreating. This trend will continue for the foreseeable future and may even accelerate.'"

Analysts are nearly unanimous in saying that shopping in future will entail a mix of online and brick and mortar experiences. Many of us still like to be able to see and touch what we buy. The future of retail malls probably lies in offering experiential and different concepts of shopping.

My ideal supermarket would be one with a stripped-down range of goods. The space freed up will be filled with large activity areas with cooking, slicing, stir-frying cooking demos, and lots and lots of free food tasting with drinks. I won't need to drag a trolley around. I'd saunter in, scan my membership card, and click Yes when it asks me if I want to replenish my usual orders.

Then I'd head over to the food tasting stations and snack my way through the options, before deciding which new products I want to buy. All my orders will be consolidated when I check out and pay. If I want to self-collect my goods, I just key in my car park lot number and a robot will deliver it to my car. Otherwise, I'll pick a home delivery time before heading off to my next appointment.

IF A NEW PLAYER DISRUPTS THE RULES, MAYBE IT'S THE RULES THAT NEED TO CHANGE

The regulator's job is to look at the potential for good in a new player

10 January 2016

Pity the regulator today.

He inherited a system at the peak of its success, with rules carefully thought out. He thought his role was to implement and enforce rules.

Then things change. Disruptive technologies change the industry and new players enter the market. Unhappy incumbents want to deny the new players access to funding or infrastructure they had paid to build, and hold the regulator to the rule-book.

Meanwhile, consumers clamour for choice and diversity at ever declining prices. Citizens who once trusted the state to preserve a stable status quo now question its impartiality and ask whose side it is on.

Across different sectors, the chaps in government whose job is to come up with rules for industry are facing a hard time.

In transport, the entry of Uber and other car-sharing apps turns owners of private cars into chauffeurs for a fee. Taxi companies are unhappy, but consumers are delighted – they get a chauffeured private car service for a fee about equivalent to or less than for taxis.

The Land Transport Authority is now looking at these issues.

Next, consider the infocomms sector. The three telcos – Singtel, StarHub and M1 – have settled into a cosy equilibrium, and some say they act like a cartel.

The entry of new broadband players had shaken up that industry. Why not open the mobile market to new players too? This was the thinking behind the call for a fourth mobile operator.

Last July, the Infocomm Development Authority (IDA) came up with a novel proposal: It would set aside mobile spectrum at a heavily discounted rate to attract a fourth telco operator. It called for public feedback on its proposal.

At least two companies – MyRepublic and OMGTel – expressed interest. But the three incumbents objected. They said a fourth player would lead to congested airwaves which would be bad for consumers. They questioned IDA's rationale for subsidising the newcomer.

IDA hasn't firmed up its decision.

The cases illustrate the conflicting demands that today's regulator must take into account. Regulation has never been easy, but is especially complicated when technology is changing so fast, and disrupting markets in such unexpected ways.

Regulators should be guided as always by a clear-headed assessment that balances different objectives: protect investors; protect consumers; promote competition; and promote efficiency. It's clear from even a cursory look that the objectives are conflicting – protecting investors for example can be very bad for consumers.

To do their jobs well, regulators have to shift from thinking of regulation as setting rules, to thinking of managing risks.

Rules will still be needed of course – but should be construed not as something that prevents bad things from happening but as something that allows good things to happen.

Transport regulators, for example, shouldn't be thinking of rules to box Uber in or how to make sure it doesn't harm consumers or the market. They should be thinking of rules that can help unlock the tremendous potential of car-sharing apps to improve our transport system, in a way that is good for consumers and fair to incumbents.

I am fairly sanguine that when it comes to industry and economic issues, Singapore's regulators will be able to shift from rules to risk, and will tend towards decisions that promote competition and efficiency. The pro-enterprise, open-minded DNA runs deep in the public sector's economic agencies.

It will be a greater challenge for our social regulators, brought up in decades of parsimony, to rethink their role. They shouldn't see themselves only as guardians of the public purse. Instead, those who control social funding should develop the instinct of venture capitalists looking to support deserving social innovation.

Take the Ministry of Health's (MOH's) refusal to give subsidy funding for a nursing home for dementia patients. The Jade Circle project by Peacehaven, the Lien Foundation and Khoo Chwee Neo Foundation wanted to offer dementia patients a different kind of setting. Instead of living in dormitory-style wards with six to eight beds each, patients would live in single or twin-bed rooms with attached bathrooms, clustered around a living room. Medical research shows that dementia patients are less disoriented and happier in settings that resemble a family home, than in an institutionalised, regimented setting.

MOH, however, declined to provide subsidies for such beds, saying: "As a matter of policy, it will be difficult for MOH to provide ongoing subsidies for patients staying in wards that are designed to proxy private or A-class ward configurations such as single or double-bedded rooms only. Such parameters will be hard to scale or to be financially sustainable, if applied to the rest of the aged care sector."

The decision seems to spring from a reflex that subsidies should be used for the indigent or the very poor. This very stringent view of what merits subsidies is outdated, even by Singapore's own tight-fisted standards. Public housing subsidies extend even to high-income young couples who can fork out $1 million for a unit in executive condominiums that come with swimming pools. Healthcare subsidies for intermediate and home care cover households that earn more than the median income.

I find it perverse in the extreme that the ministry would deny an operator subsidies for offering a higher level of healthcare. Imagine the Ministry of Education telling independent schools that since they offer "premium" education, it will withdraw the subsidy it gives to every student's education.

Rather than say No Subsidy to the new entrant, MOH should take the opportunity to relook its entire financing model of allocating subsidy levels by the class of hospital ward.

Does such a system encourage over-usage of subsidies by those who can afford to pay non-subsidised rates? My colleague Salma Khalik reported last July that more patients are choosing subsidised wards.

In 2000, 26 per cent of all public hospital patients opted for C class wards, which enjoy subsidies of 65 to 80 per cent. In 2014, 46 per cent did so. It might be time to tweak a system that results in such skewed behaviour.

Then there is MOH's argument that subsidising single or twin-bed rooms isn't scaleable and is hard to justify financially.

Contrast this with the Ministry of Social and Family Development's (MSF's) position on group homes for seniors. MSF set up senior group homes in 2012 to let the frail elderly age in place – in Housing Board rental blocks.

Each HDB flat is shared by two to three frail seniors – which means each room has one or two beds. Five to eight such flats form a cluster. For these clusters, voluntary welfare organisations funded by MSF will coordinate and monitor services for the seniors such as home care, rehabilitation services and social activities.

Unlike MOH, MSF chooses to allocate subsidies to the needy person who needs it, not the place or room where he is receiving care. It is also not afraid to experiment with new care models. And what can be more scaleable and sustainable than letting people age in their own homes, with some support? Surely not the building of massive institutionalised nursing homes with large dormitory rooms.

As for financial justification, if IDA is prepared to subsidise a telco's entry into a market worth hundreds of millions a year, it is hard to understand MOH's reluctance to give subsidies to a new entrant in the nursing home market trying out a new model of care.

Bear in mind that the new home isn't asking for additional subsidies. It is merely requesting the same level of subsidies for its needy patients as the nursing home that packs the elderly 20 into a room.

Bear in mind too that global research suggests this new care model would be good for patients – and hence good for the healthcare system, if patients remain well and avoid the need for acute care.

Whether it's LTA, IDA or MOH, the regulator's job isn't to protect the current model or the big incumbents. Nor is it to impose rules to limit the harm that a new entrant may bring. Instead, the regulator should look at the potential for good in the new player. And if existing rules don't fit, maybe the problem is with the rules, not the new player.

3

GOING ROUND ON A CAROUSEL: POLITICS IN SINGAPORE

C overing politics as a journalist in Singapore requires a set of skills akin to those of a circus performer.

As a reporter, you learn the discipline of rigorous accuracy. When you write a news article, you strip your words of emotion and colour. When you quote newsmakers, especially important ones, you quote their every word, wrong grammar and all, adding perhaps a *sic* to indicate that you're merely transcribing their poor English, not condoning it. When you paraphrase them, you pick the words carefully, to make sure they convey what was said, in the tone in which it was said, without embellishment. Every choice of word in a paraphrase is a tell. Like a performer on a pole act, you learn to be precise, careful, controlled in every (linguistic) movement.

As a political commentator, however, you learn a very different art. You traverse balance and nuance. You learn to walk the tightrope between intellectual candour on one side, and political over-reaction on the other. You avoid trespassing on rules against defamation, racial and religious disharmony.

Unusually in my industry, where most people get their first bylines for a news article, I got my first byline for a commentary. I joined The Straits Times in 1991, in the heat of a debate on Shared Values. I was a brand new reporter and my editors hesitated to give me anything substantive to work on. Bored, I thumped out an essay giving my views on the debate. It was published that weekend. Thus began my career as a political columnist.

I've since written hundreds of commentaries on politics and policies in Singapore. I sometimes agree much with what the Government is doing, and will say so. I sometimes disagree vehemently, and will also say so. In the days before the Internet took off, when criticism of the Government was scant, I tended to write articles that were more critical of policies. Then, as I began to write more, I was mindful not to come across as a loose cannon firing too often on things I disagreed with.

I developed an internal rubric: I would write one pro-government article, one neutral, and then reserve my bile for the third. I have some pet targets. The arrogance of the People's Action Party (PAP) Government is one, including its tendency to ride roughshod over voters. The transition to a pay formula for ministers and senior civil servants explicitly pegged to the winners of a capitalist society – a handful of top income earners in each profession – was another. Over the years, I wrote about these periodically. Some earned my bosses irate phone calls from government leaders. My former editor-in-chief Cheong Yip Seng recounted one such incident over a column I wrote questioning the use of the upgrading-for-votes strategy in 2006 in his memoir *OB Markers: My Straits Times Story*.

As the Internet took off and the trickle of criticism became a veritable flood, then tsunami, I changed tack slightly. I've always had an instinct to defend the underdog, and the Singapore Government was becoming one online, the target of much unfair and sometimes unnecessarily vicious criticism. I would sometimes write articles in its defence. More of my articles were supportive of government policy. In part, this was due to life-cycle changes too; from being a young reporter pushing the boundaries, I had become a middle-aged established editor with institutional memory who would sometimes defend the status quo. I soon found myself being viewed with scepticism and mistrust by both sides – government leaders who might have remembered my past criticisms were wary of my views, and critical netizens viewed me as a government lackey for my pro-government articles. Some readers who viewed me as pro-government would express surprise when they came across a commentary that was more critical. Some surmised that I had "soured" on the state, after years of sucking up and getting nowhere – still remaining a lowly journalist. Conversely, I've had government leaders ask if I feel the need to land a punch on the state now and then to win brownie points in the eyes of readers.

In truth, there is no such dynamic. Being a political columnist means you never please everyone, so I long ago stopped obsessing over whom I may offend. Over the years, I've veered from being critical to being supportive of the Government for a very simple reason: I agree with some policies and object to others. Among the wide array of issues that surrounds political and public life in Singapore, there will be many issues on which I close ranks with the Government, and many others on which I have different views. I pick which of these to write about, and when.

In that sense, a political columnist learns how to balance on the beam and be a master acrobat, agile with words and nuance, choosing sometimes to perform a somersault on stage, and at other times to seize the trapeze to swing high above the audience. If that constant mental acrobatics means my views defy being pigeonholed into the "pro-government" or "anti-government" box, that is just the way it is.

But in fact, those who have read my columns over the years will know I make no bones about my own political and social positions. I am a social progressive, and tend to be sympathetic to issues like gay rights, more benefits for single mothers, and greater state engagement with civil society activists. On fiscal matters, I am rather conservative and support the Government's general stance on Budgets – save as much as we can today, because the future is uncertain and scary. In fact, I sometimes think I am even more of a fiscal conservative than the PAP Government. I have lamented the use of interest income from past reserves for annual Budgets, and fretted about the move to tap long-term borrowing for critical national infrastructure projects.

In politics, I tend towards a liberal bent. I believe Singapore would be much better off with more democracy, a freer media, and fewer attempts overall to control the political environment. I dislike the ruling party when it is arrogant, and hate the way it has bullied and intimidated its political opponents. But I also acknowledge it has had a very good track record as a government in raising Singapore from Third World to First. I belong to the group of disappointed Singaporeans who think the country's political system is in a state of arrested adolescent development, as my former colleague Cherian George put it in the sub-title to his book, *Singapore, Incomplete: Reflections On A First World Nation's Arrested Political Development*.

When I was conceptualising the theme for my own volume of articles at the end of 2017, I had in mind the title *Singapore, Interrupted*, a throwback to the memoir and movie, *Girl, Interrupted*, by Susanna Kaysen, about her arrested adolescence as she was hospitalised for mental illness. Like that girl, Singapore's political development trajectory is thwarted. From there, I came up with the title *Singapore, Disrupted*. It is a play on the theme of technological disruption, and on the idea of Singapore's development being thrown into disarray, or disrupted.

As I wrote in the preface to this book, Singapore is at a crossroads. We can continue as we have for 52 years – with a dominant know-it-all state that instils a system of strong political and social controls – or we can renegotiate the relationship between people and government into one where citizens are respected and trusted. I believe that Singapore's future will depend on which path we take.

After 27 years as a political commentator, I have come to see that in politics, the glass is one-quarter full.

There are some signs of positive change. One very good change in the recent decade or so is in the way elections are conducted. As I mention in some essays in this collection, the PAP has played fairer in recent elections, tending to stay away from too blatant gerrymandering, all-out personal attacks on political opponents, and the use of votes-for-upgrading. It may be that the political landscape has shifted so much that those sledgehammer tactics so common throughout the 1990s will never be brought back into the arena. Or they may still have a role to play when there is a change in the PAP leadership. Only time will tell.

Another positive development is the shift in social policy stance. From a very minimalist, residual welfare state that confines help to the long-term disabled or frail elderly, Singapore has become much more generous in recent years when it comes to helping citizens cope with the usual risks of life, such as illness and disability. Subsidies once confined to the bottom 20 per cent or so of households are now given to median-income households. I've been in the business long enough to understand the import of such shifts.

In the 1990s and early 2000s, I wrote several impassioned commentaries arguing for more state support for early childhood education. The usual answer then was that there was not enough evidence to show that preschool education significantly increases a child's chance of success in later life. Today, generous government subsidies pay for preschool. A family earning up to $3,000 a month pays about $6 a month for full-day childcare. The change was in part a response to more studies worldwide showing that quality preschool does make a difference; but more likely it was just part of a general shift towards higher income redistribution after the 2011 election delivered a sobering lesson to the PAP.

After my own experience with breast cancer in 2002 and becoming uninsurable, I wrote several commentaries lambasting the gaping holes in the state-run health insurance programme MediShield. Around that time, MediShield stopped covering people after 92; limited annual claims to $70,000 and lifetime claims to $300,000; and did not cover people with pre-existing illnesses. For a universal health insurance plan, it was a very "holey" one. In 2015, MediShield Life was introduced. It covers everyone for life, including those with pre-existing conditions. It limits annual claims to $100,000 but did away with lifelong limits. Overnight, much anxiety over high hospitalisation costs was assuaged.

The moral leadership shown by the Government in instituting social policy reforms like MediShield Life led me to hope for the same in the political arena. But sadly, there are few signs of such sweeping reform in the political arena. Perhaps it is early days yet.

On ministerial salaries, for example, there is no sign that the Government will do away with the move to peg the salaries of ministers to those of top earners in the private sector. As I wrote in 2007, the formula alters the relationship between people and government, from one based on the idea of moral and ethical leadership to a transactional one. The criteria used to decide how much bonuses to pay out have been tweaked over the years. The incentive structure is substantively changed, so that GDP growth is no longer a main criterion. Instead, new indicators also look at unemployment rate, and real wage growth of median- and lower-income households. These are certainly improvements.

A glass that is one-quarter full is, of course, also three-quarters empty. When it comes to the way government leaders deal with its critics, not much has changed. This was seen clearly in the debate that erupted on Singapore's foreign policy options between two former permanent secretaries of the Foreign Affairs Ministry, Kishore Mahbubani and Bilahari Kausikan, over the former's commentary saying Singapore as a small state should be more prudent in its conduct of foreign policy.

The way PAP ministers and MPs engage with the opposition and other political challengers also harks back to the 1990s. One example was when PAP members and Workers' Party (WP) members crossed verbal swords in Parliament over the goods and services tax (GST) hike in March 2018. Several PAP members rose in turn to chide the WP's Sylvia Lim for suggesting that the Government had intended to raise the GST soon but delayed the hike after public responses. They recounted a series of government statements that showed various leaders having spoken about the need to raise GST – not immediately, but in the next term of government – and said this showed the Government had not changed its mind on the timing of the hike. They accused her of dishonesty, wrongly accusing the Government, and demanded an apology. Ms Lim stood her ground, saying she was doing her job in raising concerns, although she accepted that her suspicions about a change in timing might have been wrong.

The PAP may have won an argument in the House – but lost the war in the hearts and minds of many people watching PAP leaders "gang up" to verbally rake Ms Lim over the coals. As a political reporter in the 1990s and early 2000s, I had had to report on the ways opposition candidates like Tang Liang Hong, James Gomez and others were attacked verbally by government ministers during election campaigns. Mr Lee Kuan Yew's combative style still prevailed during elections then. Watching a similar play enacted in Parliament in 2018, by a new generation of younger PAP leaders, was dispiriting, giving truth to the old saying about old wine in new bottles.

At its core, the incivility in political discussion stems from a lopsided power relationship between state and citizens. The state has all the power; citizens much less. A more equal power balance would require citizens to be more responsible, and the state to be more responsive. But there are few signs that the state is willing to cede power by trusting citizens more.

Its *modus operandi* in dealing with activist groups remains that of patron and client. Activist groups lobby and plead; the state considers and dispenses. In dealing with the media, the same tendency towards control and reining in prevails. The use of the Official Secrets Act against a Straits Times journalist in 2017 for asking questions about an HDB (Housing and Development Board) portal before it was launched was a clear use of brute power by the state directed at the media and civil service. That case also reminded civil servants all down the line of the importance of keeping official information secret. The journalist was let off with a stern warning, while the HDB official who had given her the information was fined $2,000.

The prosecution of young dissenters who blog, produce YouTube videos or mount protests signals the Singapore Government's resolve to continue with its model of social and political controls, and shows its unwillingness to brook dissent from a younger, bolder generation of critics. Again, old wine, new bottles.

In fact, the era of terrorism and fake news has given renewed justification to the strengthening of state apparatuses and legislation that abridge civil rights for the sake of national security. I should add here that I generally favour the state erring on the side of control and public order when it comes to such equations. I would want a legitimately elected government to protect public order in Singapore, rather than leave it to profit-seeking Western tech companies making mealy-mouthed statements about building users' trust and upholding community standards to do so. But there must continue to be recourse to judicial review or parliamentary oversight of such executive decisions. And apart from emergency situations, laws should be scripted narrowly, not over-broadly to permit unfettered ministerial discretion.

For decades, citizens wielded power at the ballot box. These days, social media has an equalising effect, giving citizens not only the last word, but also multiple, daily, incessant rights of reply and commentary. This is empowering to citizens, but sadly, the power is not always wielded responsibly, and the level of discussion is sometimes low, and often unnecessarily vitriolic. But one must put the blame where it is deserved: A citizenry unused to having open, fair-minded discussions is flexing its muscle as keyboard warriors, and may just be mimicking the dismissive, blunderbuss approach it has seen the powers-that-be adopt towards critics.

Singapore is well engulfed now in an era of greater contestation with more vocal activists and a more questioning, querulous electorate. Both state and citizenry have to learn the art of disagreeing agreeably – and learn it fast.

Amidst the flurry of daily news, constant legislative updates and appointing of new committees, there is a temptation to see activity as advancement. But when you parse those changes, you realise that the activity occurs on a carousel: well-dressed horses daintily tripping up and down, simulating the trot or even the gallop, but they all go round and round on a well-defined roundabout. All that motion, those lights, that music – the carousel is pretty, and draws our eyes – but in the end, the horses go nowhere. There is no advancement, only motion. So it is with politics in Singapore.

For now, midway into the electoral term, the glass is one-quarter full. Meanwhile, the carousel continues its merry-go-ground.

It took the 2011 General Election for the PAP to shift its social policy. The 2015 General Election saw voters return to the embrace of the ruling party, giving it a 70 per cent mandate on the heels of nostalgia over the country's 50th anniversary celebration and the death of its founding prime minister Lee Kuan Yew. The PAP may have interpreted that result as approval for its course of action – cede money, but not power: that is to say, social reforms via income redistribution are fine, but political reforms are not needed.

The next election, due around 2020, will be decisive in shaping how the PAP responds to voters, which will in turn determine how the nation ventures into the future.

By then, the much-touted 4G (fourth-generation) political leaders will be very much in charge. Will they prove to be more old wine in new bottles, resorting to the tactics of the 1990s in dealing with political contest and opposition, or will they be more in sync with a new generation of voters, more confident, more collaborative, more collegial?

I don't know. I hope it's the latter. The optimist in me – one needs to be an optimist to continue as a political journalist in Singapore – says it is early days yet.

BASIS OF GOVERNMENT-PEOPLE TIES SHIFTING – FROM MORAL TO TRANSACTIONAL?

13 April 2007

Heard the one about Senator Hillary Clinton giving up her presidential bid in America? She's coming to Singapore – because the pay is better.

This joke, and similar ones about White House officials angling for jobs at the Istana, circulated this week, as Parliament debated a move to raise salaries of civil servants and ministers.

Jokes provide an avenue for the body politic to let off steam. Unpack their hidden meaning, and a wealth of latent sentiments emerges.

As the three-day parliamentary debate on pay showed, there is a growing sense in the Singapore body politic that public service is a misnomer: With pay packets explicitly pegged to that of top private-sector executives, ministers are performing less a public "service", or even a public "duty", than just another job.

Having watched debate on the issue since 1994, I was struck by the way so many MPs in this debate argued that it was unreasonable to expect ministers to make big financial sacrifices to take up public office.

This was the majority viewpoint in the People's Action Party (PAP), forcefully articulated by its ministers and MPs. Only a minority of MPs (mostly opposition and Nominated MPs) warned about the erosion of the sense of public service if pay was pegged to head honchos' salaries – a point of view the PAP leadership disagreed with.

Certainly there is no simplistic, linear relationship between pay forgone and level of moral authority. A lowly paid incompetent or dishonest official has no claim to moral standing.

But as I have noted in a previous commentary, to claim the compensation pegged to the most successful in the market, and yet expect the moral adulation of citizens for performing a highly paid job, is to want to have one's cake and to eat it too.

Even Prime Minister Lee Hsien Loong thinks that forgoing his own salary increases for five years and donating the money to charity raises his moral standing to explain the pay hikes to the people.

Changing social compact

The debate over ministers' pay this year shows Singapore at the cusp of change: transiting from a more traditional, hierarchical society which views its leaders as moral superiors making a sacrifice for the nation, to a more transactional relationship where political leaders are expected to be held to account for their performance in return for market-based pay.

To use terms from political philosophy, the social compact is changing.

Those who subscribe to the first feel outraged, even betrayed, at the thought of ministers who may think a $1 million pay packet isn't enough and want $2 million. Many Singaporeans, especially among the pre-Independence generation accustomed to viewing political leaders as their betters, belong to this group.

For this group, the pay issue will always fester: a reminder that society, and its norms, and notions of service and duty, have changed.

I may be over-generalising, but I think the post-Independence generation, to which I belong, views the relationship between government and governed less in moral terms, and more from a "rational-legal" point of view (to use sociologist Max Weber's characterisation) where governing authority is based on law and resides in the will of the people expressed in elections. The foundation of the relationship between government and people is shifting: from a moral one between a superior parent figure and a child, to a more transactional, contractual relationship.

Moral philosopher John Rawls' influential *A Theory Of Justice* describes three stages of moral development. The first is the "morality of authority", when children who lack independent reasoning or means, are subject to the legitimate, loving authority of parents. The parent has the duty to provide care, make good decisions on the child's behalf and behave in a way worthy of the child's love and admiration. From the child, "the prized virtues are obedience, humility and fidelity to authority".

When a child grows up, he learns the "morality of association", forming attachments to peers and groups, and agreeing to live by their rules. At this stage, he is expected to honour obligations and duties, and expects others to behave likewise.

If I may be allowed a conceit in applying this to Singapore, the electorate today is like a maturing child, outgrowing the confines of the first morality based on authority, to accepting one based on association. In this second phase, reciprocity is a key value. Voters pay taxes which fund the government. In return, they expect paid officials to perform, and to be sanctioned if they do not.

When we understand Singapore society in this transition, then we are not surprised at the lexicon used in this week's debate on pay issues, when MPs spoke of publishing key performance indicators and making public how ministers have performed.

In Rawls' rubric, there is a third phase, the "morality of principles", when people strive to do what is right and good for their own sake, not because authority or peers encourage them to. This group includes normal people with consciences who strive to do the right thing, and a separate category of superior moral beings. The morality for the latter group – "the saint and the hero" – includes virtues of "benevolence, a heightened sensitivity to the feelings and wants of others, and a proper humility and unconcern with self".

The Old Guard typified this. But as PAP ministers and MPs noted expressly in this week's debate, it is unrealistic to expect ministers to be such "saints" nowadays.

Nor does my generation have such expectations.

Different expectations

We understand that those who enter political office have done their sums. They weigh the loss of privacy and the opportunity cost of their time, against the psychic satisfaction of doing good and the attraction of power and prestige. The $2 million salary helps remove pay out of the equation, so it is neither an obstacle nor inducement to be in public office.

Having made his calculations, he takes the plunge and gets a top market-based wage. Having paid top dollar, citizens demand top-notch performance. It's a quid pro quo arrangement. Talk of sacrifice on $2-million-a-year salaries rings hollow to many.

If he does not perform, no amount of talk about sacrifice will endear him to taxpayers. If he does perform, he earns the respect due to any top-performing executive in his job. But the kind of reverence and moral authority the Old Guard got from our parents' generation? That's only for "saints" who demonstrate a superior kind of selfless morality in public service.

The social compact is changing, and a younger generation has different expectations of those in public office.

FORGET POLITICS-AS-PRIESTHOOD. POLITICS IS NOW A CAREER OPTION

15 August 2015

The new normal of politics in Singapore comes with a revolving door. People enter politics, lose, try again. Some enter politics, win, become ministers, then quit.

Despite the uncertainty, there is a line of others outside to get in. They give up their successful careers in the civil service, the military or government-linked companies. And for what? The political race, which they may lose. Even if they win it and get a Cabinet post, there is no guarantee of a long-term career. It makes for uncertain personal careers.

Worse, it can change the face of government. If those in power today fear being out tomorrow, will they make decisions with an eye to their own future? This is not just fear-mongering.

Just listen to Mr Lui Tuck Yew, who this week said he was stepping down from politics. Mr Lui, 54 this month, has been Transport Minister for five years. In that time, the train and bus network has expanded, but train breakdowns have also been regular, with 12 disruptions of over 30 minutes in 2014, more than the 11 in 2011, when public transport became a political issue in the May General Election.

What's next for him? He has no idea. He told reporters: "No thoughts, no whatever of what's to come yet. That's for much later. In any case I'm in no hurry. I don't have the financial needs. My lifestyle is a simple one. So none of those financial worries or things like that that require me to really look very quickly into something else."

In an earlier interview with Chinese daily Lianhe Zaobao, he had put it more starkly: "I don't want my mind to be cluttered with transitions, what's to come... The last thing you want is for decisions to be second-guessed, for people to say, 'Oh, you were planning to go to this company, that firm, that whatever, so did you make your last decisions supporting them, favouring them, or anything like that?' That's the worst way to do things."

Might future ministers, who know too well the vagaries of politics in the new normal, make decisions flawed by self-interest? This was not such a worrying issue in the past. Entering People's Action Party (PAP) politics and getting a Cabinet post was like entering a priesthood, with job security virtually for life. Iron rice bowl, critics will sniff. Proponents say it allows for stable government and long-term policymaking.

Whatever one's view of its pros and cons, that era is over.

It was of course the 2011 election that changed things. In that election, Foreign Minister George Yeo lost his seat, and hence his Cabinet post.

Within two weeks, five more ministers left the Cabinet in a radical reshuffle by the Prime Minister: Messrs Lee Kuan Yew, Goh Chok Tong, Wong Kan Seng, Mah Bow Tan and Raymond Lim. Mr Lui took over from Mr Lim then, as Transport Minister, but he has lasted only one term.

Meanwhile, this time round, waiting in the wings are a new batch of candidates likely to make it to Cabinet if elected in the coming election expected in September 2015.

They are Mr Ong Ye Kung, Mr Chee Hong Tat and Lieutenant-General Ng Chee Meng. The first two were from the elite Administrative Service, while LG Ng was chief of defence force. All have had to leave their public service careers for a chance in politics.

In the past, men with such pedigreed careers would be assured of a parliamentary seat and a Cabinet post. These days, nothing is assured, as Mr Ong knows. In 2011, he was the newbie in an Aljunied Group Representation Constituency (GRC) team that lost to the Workers' Party.

Of the five candidates who lost there, Mr Ong, the youngest, is the only one vying to make a comeback. He remained as grassroots adviser in the Kaki Bukit division of Aljunied GRC until last September, when he became more active in Sembawang GRC where he will be contesting this time round, in a ward considered "safe" for the PAP. After the civil service, he had joined the labour movement, then left after 2011 and plunged into the private sector in Keppel.

Yesterday, he described losing Aljunied GRC as a setback which helped make him a better person. Politics is binary, he said. There are winners and losers. Setbacks are common, people fail exams, break up in a relationship, or do badly at work. He lost an election. But "no setback is a waste", he added.

For decades, Singapore has been insulated from the more unsavoury aspects of revolving door politics, a term that refers to the entry and exit of people who are in the government as regulators one day, and out in the private sector the next.

The opportunities to trade in information and favours and capitalise on networks are many, and the temptations, real. In contrast, when ministers know they are in it for the long term, they get assurance of career and income which is vital for their family's well-being. In return, citizens get continuity in policies and long-term thinking.

What does revolving door politics in Singapore mean? For now, it just means that those entering politics jousting for political office need a Plan B in case they lose. Those who are already in Cabinet understand that their seats are not assured. Longer term, I think the revolving door will have a bigger impact on politics and policymaking here.

Human nature being what it is, the temptation to make biased decisions to safeguard one's future cannot be wished away.

It becomes more important than ever, in such a climate, to make sure that those who aspire to a post in Cabinet are not motivated by profit or power, but by a sense of purpose and a desire to make good policy for the people.

A DEBATE THAT WON'T GO AWAY – BUT HAS MOVED ON

18 January 2012

In 1994, I sat in Parliament listening to former prime minister Lee Kuan Yew explain why Singapore needed to pay its ministers top dollar, and why the proposal to peg ministers' pay to top private-sector individuals was necessary. In 2000, I heard then Prime Minister Goh Chok Tong use hard numbers to argue that a good minister makes a critical difference to Singaporeans' lives.

The cost of the Cabinet then was $34 million a year – $11 per citizen.

The price of bad government could have been $9.5 billion, if the economy had shrunk by 5 per cent during the economic crisis, or $3,166 per Singaporean, said Mr Goh. This was during a debate on pay hikes in the public sector, which also doubled from 24 to 48 the number of top earners that ministers' pay was pegged to.

In 2007, ministers' pay was debated again. This time, another PM, Mr Lee Hsien Loong, asked the House and Singaporeans to support pay increases for ministers, as the gap between their pay and top private-sector earners had widened. Raising the pay would make it easier for him to seek political talent, he said.

Three bruising debates and three PMs later, the issue of ministers' salaries still sparks heated debate in and out of the House. Among Singaporeans, the issue still has considerable traction in cyberspace and on the cocktail and *kopitiam* circuits, eight months after PM Lee announced last May that a committee would be set up to review ministers' pay.

Yesterday's debate in Parliament was no different, with 11 MPs, including the PM, speaking on the motion to endorse the report of the committee to review ministerial salaries.

This report proposes pegging ministers' pay to 60 per cent of the median income of the top 1,000 earners. This would cut salaries from current levels by more than one-third.

Listening to round four of the debate on ministers' pay over 18 years gave me both a sense of deja vu and some hope that common ground has been forged.

This issue has dominated public and parliamentary attention so often, the risk of debate fatigue – not just among political columnists – is very real. And yet it should not be, because this issue goes to the heart of just what kind of government Singaporeans want for their country.

Do Singaporeans expect their politicians to be saintly paupers?

Three debates later, I think the answer is "no". Even the Workers' Party's (WP) Mr Yee Jenn Jong noted this: "Singaporeans do not expect politicians to lead a spartan life with a religious calling."

It was notable that even the alternative formula proposed by the WP – peg salaries to the monthly pay of senior civil servants outside the elite Administrative Service, such as the MX9 grade in the Management Executive Scheme – is justified partly by its alignment to market conditions.

As the WP's Mr Muhamad Faisal Abdul Manap (Aljunied Group Representation Constituency) noted, civil service salaries are based on "general market conditions of the job". So the WP proposal means political salaries "will go up and down based on the condition of the market experienced by the people, not based on the 1,000 top earners".

There is widespread acceptance today of the idea that public-sector and political salaries should be pegged to the private sector. Indeed, it bears reminding that it wasn't so long ago that the notion of market-based salaries for the public sector seemed distasteful.

PM Lee himself admitted arguing against raising soldiers' pay by about 20 per cent in the 1980s to keep pace with private-sector salaries, because he "thought it was too much, too fast. There was no need to be so generous and perhaps to change the spirit of the service".

His perspective, he acknowledged, had changed over the years, especially after he had to persuade people to enter politics. "I don't believe that salaries was a make-or-break issue for any of them who have come in, but I have no doubt that proper salaries have made it easier for me to build the team which I have today and to provide the best service which we can to Singaporeans to govern the country."

No one will say pay is an issue, but as PM Lee observed: "For some of them, it must have been a consideration, especially the younger ones with young families and young children, and when they say, 'I don't mind but my husband is not keen or my wife is not keen', well, we know how to interpret what it means because even if they don't worry for themselves, they must think about the financial impact on their spouse and children."

In that sense, the debate has moved on beyond philosophy, and Singaporeans accept that political leaders deserve just compensation. Many Singaporeans may admire the founding generation who served the country at great personal peril and considerable financial sacrifice. But that era and that generation are no more.

The debate has even moved beyond the million-dollar figure. The committee's ballpark figure of a monthly salary of $55,000, which works out to a package worth $1.1 million for a good-performing minister, has not drawn as much flak as would have been expected. The WP's own formula would also yield a salary of $55,000 a month, although it proposes a less generous bonus payout: a maximum of five months plus 13 months basic, making for a total of $990,000.

To be sure, there are still grumbles online and in the coffee shops about million-dollar salaries, but among professionals and the middle class, there is growing acceptance of ministerial salaries in that range.

Instead, what is most contentious now is the technical issue of what formula or benchmark is used. Many have criticised it for pegging pay to the top 1,000 earners, saying this is elitist. Even the People's Action Party's own MP, Mr Lim Biow Chuan, suggested removing the peg and using a fixed salary point, to be reviewed by an independent panel every five years.

Whatever formula is eventually adopted, one thing is for sure: The issue of ministerial salaries will continue to draw heated disagreement. The formula will be tweaked again, and a future PM will have to stand up in Parliament to seek the support of MPs and Singaporeans for yet another round of changes.

But if there is less vitriol and more common understanding in each round of the debate, then the exercise is worthwhile. In any case, there is always a new generation to be convinced.

THREE DIFFERENT STYLES IN PAP CAMPAIGN

Amid the cacophony that was GE 2006, three distinct strains can be heard

8 May 2006

The other day, someone came up to me and said: "It's kind of a weird campaign, isn't it? A bit confusing, almost like an orchestra that can't figure out what it wants to play."

A confused orchestra. There were certainly times when the campaign in General Election 2006 appeared to have been playing out to different beats.

Amid the cacophony that was GE 2006, three distinct strains can be discerned. And on Saturday, voters gave their verdicts on what they thought of each.

The first discernible beat was one voters have become familiar with: the upgrading carrot-and-stick approach.

This was used particularly in the opposition wards of Potong Pasir and Hougang, ageing estates denied government funds for estate improvement in the 22 years and 15 years respectively that they have been in opposition hands.

Senior Minister Goh Chok Tong warned voters that Hougang could end up being a slum if there were no serious effort to upgrade the estate.

People's Action Party (PAP) candidates for the two wards unveiled upgrading plans worth $80 million for Potong Pasir and $100 million for Hougang if elected.

It was Mr Goh who first used the upgrading carrot to good effect in previous polls. In the 1997 GE, votes-for-upgrading was a central plank in the PAP strategy. It got 65 per cent of the vote – the highest since 1984.

As this election unfolded, the votes-for-upgrading issue was a barely discernible beat, until SM Goh and the PAP candidates made much of it in Hougang and Potong Pasir.

The result? Contrary to PAP expectations that voters might bite, voters rejected this carrot convincingly. Mr Low Thia Khiang got his best ever result in Hougang with 62.7 per cent. Mr Chiam See Tong increased his margin in Potong Pasir, getting 55.8 per cent. A triumphant Mr Chiam declared that "Potong Pasir residents cannot be bought".

At the post-results press conference held by the PAP, Prime Minister Lee Hsien Loong said a review of the electoral strategy in the two opposition wards was in order. Dislodging the opposition MPs would involve "not just offering them something better, but overcoming this natural loyalty" voters had to their MP, he said.

Is the upgrading carrot turning into a poisoned apple for the PAP? Will continued use of this strategy end up being rejected by voters again? Only the next election can tell.

Another beat that the campaign of GE 2006 appeared to be following was the hard percussion one of hammering political opponents – a familiar beat by now to Singaporeans who have observed past election campaigns.

It intensified as the furore over Workers' Party (WP) candidate for Aljunied Group Representation Constituency (GRC) James Gomez's missing minority certificate got bigger.

One PAP leader after another accused Mr Gomez of lying and conspiring to frame the Elections Department, using footage from surveillance cameras and audio recordings as evidence. A conversation Mr Gomez had with PAP candidate Inderjit Singh was used as evidence, as Mr Gomez had apparently said the whole episode was a "*wayang*" (Malay for play-acting).

Some observers noted that the PAP response appeared reminiscent of Minister Mentor Lee Kuan Yew's inimitable combative style.

MM Lee himself said at one point that he was taking a back seat in the campaign until he got uneasy over the Gomez incident and "chased up" Home Affairs Minister Wong Kan Seng to find out the truth.

The surveillance cameras, taping of phone calls and sworn statements caused a ripple of unease among some Singaporeans. Is Singapore a police state as alleged by its critics? Are private conversations fodder which can be used as evidence against one?

Even the PAP acknowledged that some thought its response was "overkill". On Day 7 of the campaign, it decided to "refocus" the campaign back to national issues and move on from the Gomez issue for the time being.

Voters' verdict? Aljunied GRC voters gave the PAP a comfortable 56.1 per cent of the vote. Foreign Minister George Yeo interpreted the result as one where "the voters of Aljunied gave a clear stand" on the Gomez issue.

But the other interpretation is equally possible: that some voters were turned off by what they might view as excessively harsh treatment of an opposition candidate. After all, the PAP's performance in Aljunied GRC is its weakest in the seven contested GRCs.

The Gomez issue may also have had an impact on Ang Mo Kio GRC, PM Lee's own ward. Many had expected the popular PM to get a result in the 70s against a young WP team. Instead, the team got 66.1 per cent, a notch below the national average of 66.6 per cent.

Mr Singh, part of the PAP team there, said: "The James Gomez issue might have affected us a little... with votes against the leaders and myself for bringing the issue up."

Voters' verdict on this issue isn't as clear as their rejection of the upgrading-carrot strategy. But a case can be made that some voters are tiring of the old PAP tactics of excessive force in countering the opposition.

If at times the PAP campaign for GE 2006 appeared disjointed, it could be that there were different conductors for different segments: SM Goh over the upgrading-carrot strategy and hints of MM Lee in the Gomez issue.

But through these two strains, one strong, underlying melody could be discerned through the campaign.

Some may not agree with me, but I consider this campaign to have been gentler and fairer than the last few.

Enough has been said about the way the PAP gave more time to the opposition, the fact that electoral boundaries remained largely intact, and the fact that the PAP did not threaten to withdraw upgrading or other services from opposition wards.

The more gentlemanly streak in both the PAP and opposition can best be seen when the results of the May 6 polls streamed in.

Gracious in victory, Mr Low Thia Khiang credited PAP opponent Eric Low for having done his part for Hougang and hoped "he will continue to do so".

Gracious in defeat, the PAP's overall leader PM Lee said the results in the two opposition wards showed that voters wanted a credible, strong opposition.

Even Mr Low himself acknowledged: "I think the Prime Minister has been gentlemanly in this contest," referring to the way PM Lee and his team engaged the WP team in Ang Mo Kio GRC.

Instead of resorting to negative comments, the refrain from PAP leaders yesterday, a day after the polls, is that opposition voters are also "pro-Singapore" and that a more credible opposition represented by the new WP is good for the country.

In the post-results PAP press conference, a tired but calm-looking PM Lee delivered a strong message consistent with his constant refrain of wanting to build an "inclusive" society: "Whichever party you voted for, let's close ranks and, in the words of our slogan, stay together and move ahead. Singapore is our land. We can make it special for us and for our children."

These were healing words from the prime minister of a nation, not the divisive rhetoric of the chief of a partisan political party.

The voters' verdict on the fairer, more inclusive strain represented by PM Lee can be interpreted from the overall result. The PAP's win of 66.6 per cent is its best showing since 1984 (if you exclude the outlier 2001 showing of 75.3 per cent amid fears of terrorism and a recession).

The figure is all the more remarkable for having been achieved on the back of a cleaner, fairer fight. Despite denying itself some traditional incumbency advantages (such as surprise), the PAP managed to improve on its 65 per cent from GE 1997.

While many things about the electoral process still bug critics, GE 2006 will be remembered for the way the PAP under a new PM tried to play the game more fairly by existing rules.

So, yes, the PAP campaign for GE 2006 appeared confused sometimes, with at least three different styles.

When the dust settles, will the PAP take a good hard look at voters' verdicts on each, and adjust its strategy accordingly?

Only GE 2010 will tell.

WHY PARTISAN UPGRADING STRATEGY SHOULD GO

16 June 2006

Recent comments over the votes-for-upgrading issue from government leaders are confusing to voters, but suggest there is more ambivalence to the issue. It's not surprising that the signals have been so mixed, because it is one issue which is politically beneficial to the ruling party from a party-political point of view, but which is pretty indefensible on any other grounds.

The issue throws into sharp relief the dilemma the People's Action Party (PAP) Government faces: between its desire as a political party to engage in partisan moves that help assure it of political longevity, and its desire to be a government for all that aims to be "inclusive", bringing non-partisan elements to advance the country together.

Those who read political tea leaves think they discern different strands of thought on this issue among PAP leaders.

Some espy in Prime Minister Lee Hsien Loong glimpses of a potential "reformer" or at least change agent.

Minister Mentor Lee Kuan Yew is viewed as someone steeped in party battles of the past, who would not allow the PAP to embark on a path that may weaken its grip on power.

Senior Minister Goh Chok Tong is known as a master tactician. He was, after all, the one who implemented the votes-for-upgrading strategy which helped the PAP stave off the slide of votes to the opposition for a decade.

In the recent election, he and PAP candidates revived the strategy for Hougang and Potong Pasir, promising $180 million of upgrading projects if voters tossed out the opposition there and voted in the PAP. Voters did not bite the carrot offered.

But while individual PAP leaders may appear to have slightly different, nuanced, positions on this issue, the truth is more likely to be that they were all in broad agreement over the votes-for-upgrading strategy in the 1997 and 2001 elections.

And if General Election 2006 was anything to go by, probably some top PAP leaders are by now ambivalent about the strategy.

PM Lee said after the election the PAP had to review its strategy in opposition wards and rethink how to win them back.

SM Goh praised Hougang and Potong Pasir voters for loyally sticking with their opposition incumbent MPs rather than "chasing after every goodie which we offer them".

Has the votes-for-upgrading strategy come to the end of its time?

The strategy has attracted controversy since it was first announced in 1992. This was when then Prime Minister Goh Chok Tong served notice that wards which supported the PAP would be given priority for the then highly popular programme to upgrade, or improve, Housing Board estates using government funds.

The announcement met with a negative response, and died down. In the 1997 General Election, however, it was revived and became a central plank of the PAP strategy. Vote for the PAP, and your constituency will get ahead in the upgrading queue – was the message to voters. On the eve of Polling Day in 1997, Mr Goh went one step further, saying the Government would look at voting patterns by precincts (each precinct is a cluster of about 10 to 20 HDB blocks) in deciding which neighbourhoods to upgrade first.

The votes-for-upgrading strategy was used in the 1997 and 2001 elections, helping the PAP romp home with 65 and 75 per cent of the votes respectively.

Never popular, it has drawn more intense criticism this time round.

As Workers' Party chairman Sylvia Lim notes, reflecting the view of critics of the policy, the Government is using taxpayers' money for partisan purposes.

Another writer to The Straits Times Forum page this week argued that the Government is mixing up its fiduciary duty as a government to all citizens, with its interest as a political party.

Criticism of the strategy can be summed up thus: It's unfair as it deprives opposition voters of benefits from government funds which should be available to all; and it's partisan as the Government is using taxpayers' money for party-political ends.

The PAP's argument has been to retreat to realpolitik. The line from a succession of national development ministers, including Mr Mah Bow Tan in an interview with The Straits Times last week, has been consistent: Funds are limited; allocation has to be on some criteria; support for the PAP's programme has to be one such criterion.

As MM Lee said in April during a television forum with young journalists when the issue was discussed: "Look, ask yourself – does any government help the opposition to displace itself? You mean to tell me in America or Britain they gave benefits to all constituencies equally? At the same time or, worse, favour the opposition? No, you favour your supporters because you want to retain them as your supporters."

The issue has arisen again, after Mr Mah's statement last week that all wards will get their lifts upgraded by 2015 – but that PAP wards will still go first.

MPs new and old have also spoken up on the issue, defending the PAP's line that resources have to be allocated, and there is nothing wrong with allocating resources by partisan means.

But if you take this line of reasoning to its logical conclusion, Singapore will become a truly horrific country indeed.

After all, all government resources are finite. Will the PAP Government one day decide to ration, say, healthcare or education, on the basis of support for the PAP?

Imagine the arguments thus: The health budget is finite. Resources to build new hospitals have to be allocated, and will be given to PAP wards first henceforth.

Or for education: New schools will be built in PAP wards first, and opposition wards will be last in the queue. (Question: Has any new school been built in Hougang in the last 15 years, or in Potong Pasir in the last 22, since they fell to opposition hands?)

Or maybe the arguments will go down to the micro level: Hospital beds are finite in number, and PAP supporters will get priority. You can just imagine the howls of outrage and cries of "unfair!" from voters.

I'm not for one moment suggesting the PAP will go down that road any time soon, or even ever. I raise these extreme examples to make the point that it's necessary to go back to first principles to debunk the votes-for-upgrading strategy.

In other words, the PAP Government should stop using this as an election strategy, not because it no longer works in winning votes – but because it is based on an unsound principle in the first place, and sets a dangerous precedent for allocating government resources.

In reviewing the votes-for-upgrading tactic, the PAP has to think less as a political party, and more as a national government.

The strategy may have been helpful to PAP the political party through the 1990s and early 2000s. But the upgrading strategy, like the creative redrawings of election boundaries in the past, has aroused some cynicism among younger voters about the electoral process.

Word has it the PAP is spending the next six months in party huddles to post-mortem GE 2006 and lay the groundwork for its strategies for GE 2011. When it does so, it would be wise to rise above its partisan interest as a political party, to consider the impact of its decisions on the nation as a whole.

WHEN LEADERS SHOULD SAY 'SORRY'

A heartfelt, well-timed apology goes a long way towards healing rifts

21 October 2010

A series of heartfelt apologies last week has gone some way towards mending the hurts that emerged after a mistake by coach and team manager Ang Peng Siong disqualified Singapore's swimming team at the recent Commonwealth Games in New Delhi.

Mr Ang had cut it fine in Delhi's traffic and turned up too late to register the 4x200m freestyle relay team for the final. He apologised to the team and their parents immediately after the incident.

Singapore Swimming Association (SSA) president Jeffrey Leow, however, later described the mistake as "trivial", saying the team was not expected to win a medal anyway.

This remark provoked much unhappiness. The SSA sought a meeting with Mr Ang, the swimmers and their parents. At the end of it, SSA issued a formal apology.

Mr Leow himself said: "I regret that my poor choice of words... has caused offence and compounded our mistake. I am truly sorry."

Mr Ang also apologised again for his mistake. One father said "the sincere apologies from them are heartening to hear". One swimmer said the mistake was hard to accept, "but people make mistakes".

It appears that the string of "sorrys" has removed the sting from the incident, although the affair is by no means over as the SSA is investigating the incident so as to learn from the fiasco.

In public life, a well-meant, well-timed "sorry" goes a long way towards healing rifts and helping people move on.

When something goes wrong, the worst possible response from leaders is to justify themselves or explain away the problem. Witness the *beh song* (Hokkien for disgruntled) feeling at Mr Leow's initial comments.

In Singapore, there is a perception that not many public leaders will apologise readily when things go wrong. "Sorry", some say, seems to be the hardest word for People's Action Party (PAP) ministers to say.

Netizens in Singapore, especially, had this impression in the wake of floods that damaged property and inconvenienced many recently. The absence of an apology, even for a natural disaster that could not have been avoided, was interpreted as a sign of the Government's inability to climb down from its "government-knows-best" attitude. Worse, it was interpreted as a sign of the Government not being accountable to the public.

In fact, a look back shows that PAP ministers do say "sorry". Known for his candour, Minister Mentor Lee Kuan Yew has apologised for remarks he made on immigration in Australia (1988), the crime situation in Johor (1997), and the Chinese in Malaysia (2006). Prime Minister Lee Hsien Loong too has had occasion to apologise to Singaporeans. He apologised for using the phrase "no-brainer" to a teacher, for Singaporeans, unfamiliar with the American term meaning "it's obvious", thought he was calling her names. In 2006, he apologised for saying "fix" the opposition.

A more recent example from the PAP ranks is Minister for Community Development, Youth and Sports Vivian Balakrishnan, who faced flak over hiccups in the organisation of the Youth Olympic Games (YOG).

He apologised last month when certificates of appreciation were sent out to volunteers with the wrong signatures. In Parliament, quizzed on the YOG busting its budget, he admitted the ministry got the initial estimates wrong.

He accepted ministerial responsibility for the mistakes made by those he had oversight over and apologised for them. I, for one, thought the better of him for stepping up simply and plainly. Words alone are not enough, of course, but acknowledging mistakes (by the individual or institution) is an important first step in change.

When is an apology called for? A 2006 article by Harvard University leadership professor Barbara Kellerman parses the art of the apology. In "When Should A Leader Apologise", she writes that a public apology can be considered if it serves one of these purposes: individual, institutional, intergroup, or moral.

The apologies of Singaporean leaders served these purposes. As leaders of government, they understood that the mistakes could embarrass the institution, and that an apology would limit the damage. MM Lee's apologies to foreign countries also served an intergroup purpose: soothing hurt feelings in the offended country, mending bilateral relations and safeguarding Singapore's larger national interest.

Psychologists Gary Chapman and Jennifer Thomas say in *The Five Languages Of Apology* that an apology should admit a mistake (take responsibility), express regret, make amends (restitution), promise change (repentance) and request forgiveness. The most crucial part of an apology is admitting wrongdoing. But the leader is not always the best person to do that, if he was not personally at fault, argues Prof Kellerman. For example, it makes no sense for a government leader to apologise for a natural disaster or acts of God – for example, floods. An apology may be called for if the response to the disaster was poor, exacerbating injury or death, but that is another matter.

Instead, a leader should apologise if there is a critical issue at stake, and if he or she is the only person who can set it right. When DBS Bank's ATM and banking services broke down for seven hours in July, DBS chief executive Piyush Gupta thought the scale of the disruption warranted a personal response. He took personal and institutional responsibility for the mistake, and promised change. Three months later, the incident is hardly talked about.

As Prof Kellerman wrote, apologies serve a larger social purpose. "When leaders apologise publicly, whether to or on behalf of their followers, they are engaging in... a 'secular rite of expiation' which cannot be understood merely in terms of expediency. The attempt to come clean is more than an explanation and more than an admission: It is an exchange in which leaders and their listeners engage in order to move on. It is in turn this transition, from the past to the future, that enables the course correction that mistakes and wrongdoing require."

"Rite of expiation".

There is a Hokkien way of saying the same thing. A "sorry" helps remove that *beh song* feeling, allowing the aggrieved to say: "*Swarh la*!" – forget it, let's move on.

STABILITY. ENDORSEMENT. CHANGE.

What voters were saying with the key results of GE 2011

8 May 2011

The people have spoken, and what a message they sent.

Initial extreme scenarios of a big upset or a clean sweep did not materialise.

Instead, Singaporean voters – a rational, hard-headed lot – delivered a result nicely poised between stability and change.

Three sets of figures say it all. 60.1 per cent. 69.3 per cent. And 46.6 per cent.

What were the messages?

1. We want stability with a People's Action Party (PAP) government.

   Voters gave the PAP 81 seats to the Workers' Party's (WP) six. This was a tad down from the 82-2 score the PAP had in the last House, but it was a good result given the strong showing by the opposition.

   The vote share of 60.1 per cent was down from 66.1 per cent in 2006, but within the range of many observers' expectations, given that this was the most contested election since 1963, with the largest-ever electorate of over two million voters, and it was held amid simmering discontent over rising costs, housing prices and immigration.

   As they had for over 50 years, Singaporeans ultimately cast a vote for stability of the kind the PAP delivers.

   Prime Minister Lee Hsien Loong considered this a "clear mandate" and thanked Singaporeans for the confidence and strong support.

2. The second figure that matters is 69.3 per cent, with Ang Mo Kio Group Representation Constituency (GRC) voters giving a ringing endorsement to PM Lee and his team. Mr Lee's win was an improvement from last election's 66.1 per cent. This time, he outdid the national average by a wide margin of 9.2 percentage points.

   The Ang Mo Kio GRC result was no doubt due in part to the team contesting against him – a low-key team from the Reform Party.

   Still, the result, together with the PAP maintaining the vote share above the psychological threshold of 60 per cent, can be seen as a clear endorsement of Mr Lee's campaign style: fairer, with less gerrymandering, and eschewing the votes-for-upgrading carrot.

   Voters also appear to have liked what they saw of the more humble PAP in the last three days of the campaign, which saw the PM personally apologise to the people of Singapore for mistakes his government had made. He also promised that the Government would learn from mistakes and improve.

   He repeated this message at a 20-minute post-election press conference at about 3.20am, when he referred to dissatisfaction with policies and the PAP's approach to government, and said: "We hear all your voices, whether it's expressed in person or over the Internet. The PAP will analyse the results of the elections, learn from what has emerged in this General Election, put right what is wrong, improve what can be made better, and also improve ourselves to serve Singaporeans better."

   He promised that this would be "at the top of our minds".

   His good showing in Ang Mo Kio GRC will be a boost for him in attempts to bring the PAP together for some serious soul-searching.

3. The third message from voters: We want an elected opposition, not just also-rans. And when a party is credible and has good candidates, we are prepared to exact a high price for it, even at the cost of removing

two PAP ministers, a potential office-holder and a potential Speaker of Parliament.

Aljunied GRC, deemed too close to call, in the end went to the WP with a comfortable 54.7 per cent. Incumbents included Foreign Minister George Yeo; Minister in the Prime Minister's Office and Second Minister for Finance and Transport Lim Hwee Hua; new candidate Ong Ye Kung; and Senior Minister of State for Foreign Affairs Zainul Abidin Rasheed.

Mr Yeo, who had fought a valiant battle, was gracious in defeat, calling the election a new chapter in Singapore, while WP chief Low Thia Khiang said the iconic capture of a GRC by the opposition signalled the maturing of political democracy in Singapore.

Mr Yeo had characterised the Aljunied battle as one for the soul of Singapore. Law Minister K. Shanmugam described this election as one for the soul of democracy in Singapore. These are different terms which mean similar things.

At stake in Aljunied was the PAP's political vision, where the PAP itself remained the dominant single party in Parliament, with opposition voices confined to Non-Constituency and Nominated MP positions.

PAP leaders unanimously told voters that they could vote for PAP candidates knowing that the top losers could go into Parliament anyway as NCMPs.

The WP fought on a diametrically different platform of a First World Parliament. The PAP is right in saying no one – probably not even the WP – can say with certainty what a First World Parliament is. But what it forgot is that many Singaporeans understand intuitively what it is not: 82-2 is not a First or even Second World Parliament.

In the end, that is the most important message sent by voters. Faced with the best slate of opposition candidates in at least 30 years, voters rewarded the opposition with nearly 40 per cent of the national vote and six seats in Parliament – the best showing for the opposition in at least 30 years. The WP, with its better organisation and candidates, scored 46.6 per cent of the vote in seats it contested.

Post-mortems and surveys will uncover more precise reasons why so many voters chose the opposition. But for now, it is interesting to surmise what the results say about how the battle for the soul of Singapore's democracy turned out.

If you take the percentage figures of 60.1, and 69.3, and 46.6, I think the message from the two million voters reads something like this: We want a PAP government. We like the PAP's move to fight fairer, and we want to nudge PM along that path.

But we also want an elected opposition. Quite many of us don't really buy into the PAP's vision of a single-party Parliament with opposition confined to NCMPs and NMPs. In fact, in our ideal world, the best way to Secure Our Future Together is by having some kind of First World Parliament. Just what that Parliament will turn out to be, we don't quite know yet. But we think 81-6 is a good place to start.

GOOD POLICIES HAMPERED BY BAD POLITICS

15 June 2014

A Member of Parliament said this recently in Parliament, urging fellow politicians to work together to build a positive political culture: "Politicians must be aware of what political culture we are building through our style of political engagement as well as our actions.

"If you support a political party which believes in overthrowing the government by taking mass political action against the government regardless of the laws and proper channels to change things, you are building a culture of lawlessness.

"If you support a political party conducting its political engagement with a habit of playing racial politics and mudslinging and launching personal attacks on its political opponents, you are building a thug political culture. If you support a political party with the habit of fixing its opponents, you are breeding a political culture of fear.

"While all politicians play a role in building a political culture through political engagement, the government is the dominant player of politics in Singapore, and plays a significant role."

All of this forms a point of view that responsible party leaders – and voters – would likely agree with. It would surely form part of what the Government wants to see in "constructive politics", which at its heart is about having a political system that will elect men and women of good character who can work together to come up with policies that are good for the people in the long term.

And yet, after that speech in Parliament, Workers' Party (WP) leader

Low Thia Khiang – yes, he made those comments – was drawn into a heated exchange with the Prime Minister on constructive politics.

Mr Low's point was that a country's political culture matters. And what shapes that culture? The conduct of politicians, and from his viewpoint, especially government leaders.

In addition to that onslaught above, Mr Low interspersed his speech with further volleys: "If the people continue to support a government party that uses high-handed tactics against its political opponents, we are endorsing a bullying political culture.

"If the people support a governing party that uses governmental resources, including civil servants, to serve its partisan goals, we are condoning the abuse of political power as an acceptable culture. If you support a political party with the habit of fixing its opponents, you are breeding a political culture of fear.

"Using differentiating measures in policies to punish people who voted for the opposition breeds a culture of divisive politics.

"It also used to be said that the political incumbent has no obligation to level the playing field, that might is right, and that the political incumbent has the right to use all legal means to remain in power because everyone will do it if they are the incumbent. This is building a self-serving political culture."

The People's Action Party (PAP) will surely dismiss all of this as typical opposition politicking that is all sound and fury, but there will be those who will view Mr Low's comments – made during last month's debate on the Presidential Address – as depicting the PAP style of politics.

And therein lies the cognitive dissonance in the whole debate on constructive politics.

The PAP tries to take the moral high ground in this debate, depicting the opposition, especially the WP, as one that flip-flops on policy positions, or is disingenuous in ignoring difficult policy trade-offs.

The opposition – and a good segment of voters, I would venture –

looks at the PAP's political tactics past and present, and wonders if those have any part to play in the constructive politics it is now calling for.

Those above the age of 30 will remember the votes-for-upgrading strategy which some see as examples of divisive, partisan politics, and the concerted attacks on opposition candidates' character at elections as examples of bullying.

By using such tactics in past elections, the PAP risked failing to connect with a generation of voters. Many of those in their 30s and 40s today who might have become keen supporters of the establishment status quo and a solid PAP-voting bloc may have instead become disenchanted by the political process as they came of age. They witnessed one too many one-sided political battles.

Memories of the PAP's past tactics could be one factor continuing to fuel the rage that can be felt online against the Government today, when ironically it is trying so hard to win back support.

Pent-up anger when unleashed is hard to channel into logical debate.

In the same way that the PAP's digs at the WP for its policy flip-flops strike home, the WP's description of the prevailing political culture in Singapore draws blood.

Two weeks ago, I wrote in this space that the WP should "grow up" to develop its positions on policy, as this would help it mature as a party – which would be good for Singapore. After all, if the WP develops its policy-thinking capability, and blossoms into a credible alternative party, Singapore's political future will be less worrisome.

Just as the WP seems flat-footed in policy proposals, so the PAP similarly seems clumsy in the art of politics. One commentator, consultant Devadas Krishnadas, summed it up pithily in a recent Facebook post, which The Straits Times ran an extract of: "While the Government emphasises policy thrusts, the public is focused on political trust."

Just as the WP's inability to engage seriously on policies keeps the opposition in its infancy, so too the PAP's inability to engage seriously on political change hinders the country's political maturation.

The Government has tried to set the agenda with its notion of "constructive politics". Aside from its supporters, others want to hear more of that – from the Government.

Will the PAP in the next election still try its votes-for-upgrading strategy and continue its creative redrawing of electoral boundaries?

Should there be constitutional changes to the political system? Is the Nominated MP system still relevant in the face of rising contestation? Should the bar be set even higher for presidential candidates?

On an even more serious note, how prepared is Singapore for a change in government, whether by design or accident? What does the Constitution say about coalition governments?

Of course, the Government may choose to busy itself with policy changes. And there are issues aplenty, beyond those of housing, transport and healthcare that already seize the Government: Should the Government continue to be the arbiter of morals in the arts? Why should housing and social policies be privileged towards married couples? Is it time to rethink the media regulatory model?

But the question is whether good policies can make up for bad politics – or the absence of any meaningful discussion of it.

The Government can ignore the topic of political change and talk about constructive politics. But that would be like ignoring the elephant in the room – but everyone can still see, hear and smell the elephant.

GE 2015: A MORE SPORTING PAP THIS ELECTION?

1 September 2015

———

Two moments grabbed my attention this morning during Nomination Day. I was in the office, monitoring the live streaming reports filed by my colleagues from The Straits Times at nine nomination centres across Singapore.

One photo of the People's Action Party's (PAP's) S. Iswaran pointing out something to Reform Party (RP) leader Kenneth Jeyaretnam caught my eye. He looked like he was pointing out a mistake. The posture was also revealing: Mr Iswaran was friendly, smiling, and Mr Jeyaretnam, back to camera, looked like he was paying close attention.

Intrigued by the possible back story, I rang a party contact from West Coast Group Representation Constituency (GRC), where both Mr Iswaran and Mr Jeyaretnam were candidates. Within minutes, I was on the phone with Mr Iswaran, who told me a member of the PAP team had noticed that the RP hadn't indicated whether the members were contesting as independents or as a party. The form had already been signed by the Commissioner for Oaths.

The PAP team promptly pointed out the mistake to RP, which managed to get the form properly filled in, and to have the Commissioner for Oaths at the centre approve it. As nomination forms are sworn documents under oath, it wasn't just a matter of correcting the form. It meant getting it endorsed and signed under oath. There was time pressure too, as nominations open at 11am and close at noon. The RP team got the form fixed in time.

Mr Iswaran said: "It was grounds for disqualification. But we felt it was important to point this out and give them opportunity to rectify the mistake in good time. We are not looking to win by default on a technicality – we want a fair fight."

Another PAP contact told me a similar thing happened in another constituency: The PAP team saw that the opposition team's form had omitted the name of the constituency being contested. This was pointed out and fixed.

Is the PAP going into this General Election in a more sporting mood, I wondered.

Another moment that caught my attention was a video of Bishan-Toa Payoh GRC candidate Ng Eng Hen speaking to supporters after nominations had closed and candidates were confirmed. This was at Raffles Institution, where a large group of Workers' Party supporters was present to support WP candidates contesting Aljunied GRC and Sengkang West single member constituency.

Dr Ng had to raise his voice above the jeers of the WP crowd. He not only raised his voice, he also rose to their taunts and directly addressed them, angling his body to face them, and punching his hand in the air for emphasis.

"Year by year, we will improve your lives. Even if you jeer against us, we will improve your lives! And the more you jeer, the more we will improve even more – because we believe in Singapore. We will educate your children, we will find you good jobs, we will take care of you when you are old. Because this is what PAP promises – for all Singaporeans!"

For those of us old enough to have covered past elections, the sight of a PAP minister promising to work even harder to care for opposition supporters was a slightly surreal one. The tone was combative, but the words reassuring.

Is this the same PAP who threatened – then carried out the threats – of putting opposition wards at the back of the queue for estate upgrading?

Who used withdrawal of municipal facilities to try to coerce voters?

If we take Dr Ng, Mr Iswaran and the other PAP teams that reportedly helped opposition candidates get their forms right, at face value, then this might be an electoral contest more based on fair play, with candidates trying to ensure everyone is lined up at the starting line before the gun goes off.

The way the PAP announced candidates in advance, and avoided surprises, also suggests the era of ambush politics is over – at least for this election.

An electoral contest based on more sporting principles of fair play would certainly be welcomed by voters.

It also got me wondering if this election will sound the official death knell of the policy of denying opposition wards access to services.

This has long been a plank of PAP strategy during elections. After the 1991 election, the PAP embarked on a policy of treating opposition wards differently. It scaled down kindergarten services provided by its charity arm. It put opposition wards at the back of the queue for multi-million-dollar estate upgrading programme for Housing Board estates.

This votes-for-upgrading strategy was used to good effect in 1997 and 2001, helping to boost the PAP vote share to 65 and 75 per cent respectively – but it also created simmering anger at the PAP's unfair politics. By 2006, PM Lee Hsien Loong said there was a need for a rethink on how to win back opposition voters.

This time round, when I asked the PAP's Nee Soon GRC candidate K. Shanmugam at a press conference what would happen to the many constituency plans being announced, if a ward fell to opposition hands, he was quick to explain that government plans for the constituencies would likely go on as planned, no matter which party's candidates were elected. No more threats to deny government plans to constituencies that choose the opposition.

But the MP of an area can "fight" for plans and influence their implementation, he added. The ability to do so, and the extent of the MP's influence, would depend on the relationship he or she has with government and other agencies carrying out the project.

The PAP has moved away from its hardball stance of denying opposition wards access to municipal improvements and facilities. It is instead going into active wooing mode.

It is now telling voters, especially opposition supporters: "Look, we want a contest. We will even help the opposition candidates so they don't mess up their forms, so there is a contest. And you can jeer against us if you will. The PAP will be here to stay, and it intends to improve your lives."

Corny? A little. Fairer? Rather.

Let's hope the hustings too will be fairer, devoid of threats directed either at voters or opponents, and stripped of egregious personal attacks from both sides.

HOPES FOR GE 2020

PAP and opposition can learn from GE 2015 to create a politically more mature environment

20 September 2015

One week after the momentous result of the 2015 General Election, I have just two wishes for the future political direction of our country.

For the People's Action Party (PAP), I hope the resounding win gives it confidence to go beyond policy shifts, to substantive political change.

For the opposition, I hope the result makes opposition politicians wake up from their slumber to realise that voters now want more from opposition candidates than a reasonable CV, good speaking skills and a friendly social media presence.

First, my hopes of the PAP.

Its strong mandate on Sept 11 should deepen its resolve to move towards more friendly social policies. As many people have remarked, its shift to the left fiscally, in the form of large subsidies in healthcare, eldercare, childcare and the Pioneer Generation Package, has clearly won over many voters.

At the same time, many have voiced their concern, online and in private, about whether the PAP will go back to its rather top-down, authoritarian approach to people management.

PAP leaders have taken pains to call on all its candidates to be humble in victory, and several, like Prime Minister Lee Hsien Loong and Education Minister Heng Swee Keat, who helmed the Our Singapore Conversation series of dialogues, have pledged to consult often, and widely, on policies.

But as an image that went viral last week shows, there is a latent fear of the PAP going back to its bad old ways. It shows a couple of men in a slave galley ship, shackled at the feet, pulling away. One of them tells the other, who is presumably complaining: "Oh shuddup! You voted for it!" To which the complainant whines: "But he said that it's a cruise ship!"

Have voters given their vote to a captain who promised a cruise ship experience, but will use its passengers and crew as galley slaves? The answer to that is, of course, no.

The strong mandate should instead be an opportunity for the PAP to seize the moral and political imperative, to institute reforms to the political process.

This view was voiced by many, including a foreign observer, University of Chicago professor Dan Slater. He remarked in an article on the East Asia Forum: "These latest election results might well lead the PAP to conclude that its combination of open-handed spending and strong-armed social control remains an invincible one.

"But its popularity comes from how much it does for Singapore's people, not from how much it intimidates them.

"If the PAP is a 'philanthropic ogre', as poet Octavio Paz once dubbed Mexico's ruling party, why not just preserve the philanthropy and ditch the ogre routine?"

Prof Slater hoped this will be the PAP's "last authoritarian election" and urged the party to introduce reforms to tilt the playing field to be more even.

I agree with the thrust of these calls. Having secured its strongest mandate in over a decade, at a time when many expected it to suffer further setbacks at the polls, the PAP can use this opportunity to strengthen trust with citizens, by fixing what many critics view as a flawed, even biased, political process.

To be sure, Singapore's elections are clean, hardly influenced by money politics. In this election, PM Lee and his team fought a studiously fair and clean campaign, in that there was little of the blatant gerrymandering or character assassination of yore. But the way the election is structured gives rise to charges of bias: The PM decides on the timing, and electoral boundary changes are done behind closed doors by a small group of civil servants who report to the PM, who is the head of the PAP.

Over the decades, Singapore has learnt to entrust decisions on public transport fares, universal health insurance and screening of controversial films to citizen-led panels consisting of responsible, respected individuals.

It is time to set up such a panel of non-partisan, respected citizens to oversee the conduct of elections. An independent commission can decide on the timing of elections, oversee constituency boundary changes, and adjudicate on abuse claims.

As many people have noted, the nationwide swing back to the PAP suggests that the party need not have made those boundary changes anyway, and would still have won handsomely.

A party that keeps in step with voters, and is confident of its appeal, does not need to rely on any advantages to beat its competitors.

Unlike with the pioneer generation, the PAP does not enjoy as strong a bond with today's voters. The Edelman Trust Barometer shows trust in government here falling from 82 to 75 and 70 per cent from 2013, 2014 and then 2015. That level of trust in government is high by global standards, but the figures show a downward trend.

Fixing the political system to remove bias can help raise trust in government and faith in the democratic process.

As for the opposition, my hope is that it learns the lessons from GE 2015 as well as the PAP has learnt the lessons from GE 2011.

The opposition has to contend with a swing of 9.8 percentage points against it. The Workers' Party (WP) fared best, with a vote share in the wards it contested falling 6.8 points to 39.8 per cent.

Some opposition leaders and supporters have responded to the vote swing with a mix of anger and denial. One opposition leader petulantly likened Singapore to North Korea and China, saying Singaporeans got the government they deserved. (And he presumably got the vote he deserved – 20 per cent).

Even WP leaders were in denial about the town council issue, saying they did not think this swayed voters, or the swing against them would have been higher.

The argument can go the other way: Without performance issues on town council management, the opposition should have done much better, riding on a crest of rising support.

Many opposition supporters took to social media to vent their frustration. Some thought new citizens were to "blame" for the vote swing; many others insulted voters by saying they were cowed or had sold their souls for material benefits (in fact, there were no material inducements to vote PAP this time, unlike in some past elections).

Those feelings are part of the grieving process. But anger, denial and depression all must evolve to acceptance, before opposition parties and supporters can regroup to take a hard look at themselves.

Then they would know what they have to do. The smaller parties have to get their act together, go beyond personality-driven leadership and try to work together.

For the WP, the way to win voters is not by being brazen about its byzantine town council finances, but by being more upfront about its mistakes and correcting them. To grow to its next phase, the WP also has to become as serious in its policy proposals as it is about its political posturing. I hope new Non-Constituency MPs Dennis Tan and Leon Perera, who made good rally speeches, will lift the quality of WP's engagement with the PAP in Parliament.

If the opposition can raise its game, and the PAP can introduce changes to the rules to make the election landscape a fairer one, Singapore will have a politically more mature environment in GE 2020.

MYTHS IN THE GO-SLOW DEBATE

Taking economy out of the fast lane may not be all it seems

17 June 2012

Singapore is embarked on a national conversation about the model and pace of growth. But sometimes, the debate seems to be at cross purposes.

Take the issue flagged by Prime Minister Lee Hsien Loong on whether Singapore should go for strong growth when it can, or opt for a slower pace. He recently told members of the Economic Society of Singapore: "I know that some Singaporeans welcome the prospect of slower growth. Some want us to slow down even below our economy's potential.

"They argue that we already have enough material success, and should give less weight to economic factors, and more to social considerations. And that we should spend more on ourselves, and put aside less for the future."

There are two different questions here.

The first is: What pace of growth do we want for Singapore? The second is distributive: What level of social spending can Singapore afford?

The answer to the first is surely obvious: As much growth as we can get, while we can, in a way that does not make life difficult for the more vulnerable.

Past framing of the issue as one between "growth at all costs" and "slow growth" is an injustice to both camps. In fact, the debate is riddled with three mutually distorting myths.

Slow growth, less stress

The first myth is that slower growth equals lower stress.

Slower pace of life, fewer foreigners to compete for jobs with locals, cheaper housing with lower demand – what's not to like, then, about slow growth?

But slower growth also means the economy will shrink, some businesses go bust, workers lose jobs. It is the vulnerable workers who will bear the brunt of a shrinking economy: the elderly worker, the middle-aged technician or saleswoman who has worked 20 years in the same small company that folded and may not get another good position. When you lose your job in your 40s or 50s, chances are high that you end up permanently under-employed. You may still get a job, but at lower pay, with reduced benefits and on contract, with reduced hours.

Without a national survey, I cannot say how many Singaporeans seriously want the country to opt for a slow growth path. Those who already have means may find a leisurely pace of life intellectually and emotionally appealing. But the average Singaporean heartlander is still at an aspirational phase: he wants a good job, pay rises, a nice home and prospects for his children.

I am willing to venture most Singaporeans, if asked, would be quite happy with going for growth while the country is able. So long, that is, as they share in the benefits of growth.

Fast growth is unequal, so slow is good

This leads me to the second myth in this debate: the idea that fast growth breeds inequality, and therefore slower growth is better.

It is true fast growth exacerbates inequality. When the economy booms, those earning $100,000 a year may find their income tripling as performance bonuses stack up. Those earning $1,000 a month may get a $50 pay rise. The gap between the top and bottom incomes yawns wider.

But the solution is not to stave off growth. Size and distribution are different concerns. You go for a larger pie first, and then you figure out how to slice it more fairly.

Going slow is a choice

The third myth is the notion that Singapore can choose to go slow or grow fast. In fact, the choice will be made for us. As PM Lee noted, slow growth is unavoidable. You do not need an economics degree to understand that Singapore's mature economy is at a very high base, which means future growth will be slower. Its limited land and labour also constrain growth.

This is an accepted premise by all sides in this discussion. It is therefore important to understand what critics of "growth at all costs" are lamenting. They are not saying Singapore should slacken. In essence, they are saying fast growth should be conditional on benefits being spread equitably, and on maintaining quality of life. So there is no point in going for fast growth of say 8 per cent if:

- The benefits go only to those at the top, say, if incomes grow 8 per cent or more for those at the top, while the majority see their wages stagnate or even drop.
- Wage rises are wiped out by rising prices. If the cost of things like healthcare, transport and food goes up by more than 8 per cent, workers end up worse off than before.
- Growth worsens quality of life – for example, if you need to bring in so many foreigners to grow 8 per cent that the city gets overcrowded, and housing costs go up beyond your affordability.

In other words, it is the impact of high growth, unmitigated by social policies, that is being faulted. This is not the same as saying slow growth is preferred over fast growth. Rather, it is about saying: Go for growth that is balanced and sustainable, with benefits shared with the majority. If the alternative to 8 per cent growth is growth of 4 per cent, with real wage increases across the board and enough foreigners to fill jobs yet keep Singapore's pleasant living environment, then maybe Singapore should go for 4 per cent, this camp will say.

But in the end, these are hypothetical numbers. Economic growth is a function of inputs: with zero or minus population growth and low productivity, even slow growth will be a challenge. In this set-up, the debate over fast or slow is academic. As a price-taker in a globalised, cut-throat, capitalist world, tiny Singapore would be wise to take its growth when it can, and share the fruits of growth equitably.

Since a slower pace of growth is inevitable, I find it more meaningful to talk about how to prepare better for a world when jobs are harder to come by and incomes stagnate or even fall.

My own view is that our social safety nets have too many holes. The emphasis on self and family as the first line of defence against the usual life risks of unemployment, disability or disease worked well when real incomes grew steadily; the old age support ratio was high, with many young working folks per elderly person; and each successive generation was better educated, drew higher pay and could support their ageing parents.

Each of those three assumptions has broken down. Real incomes at the bottom and middle have see-sawed in the last two decades; the old age support ratio will plunge from six working adults per elderly today to two in 2030; and today's young born in the 1990s will start work and form families amid soaring asset prices, no longer assured of having a better life than their parents born in the 1960s who started on a much lower base.

There is an urgent need to rethink assumptions underlying Singapore's social policy approach, and do the hard policy work of coming up with alternatives, and the even harder political work of convincing people to buy into new kinds of social security programmes that share risks in a different way.

WEAVING A NEW SOCIAL SAFETY NET FOR S'POREANS

Forging new consensus among the people is most critical in this area

20 May 2011

Barely two weeks after the May 7 polls, it is becoming clear that the People's Action Party's (PAP's) promise of reform was not just election rhetoric. It is still very early days. But so far the PAP Government's actions suggest it wants to change not just its communication and style as some had assumed, but also its policies.

This was seen most clearly in the revamped Cabinet announced on Wednesday, which saw the exit of its two oldest members, Mr Lee Kuan Yew and Mr Goh Chok Tong, and the retirement of ministers covering issues voters had been unhappy about: the escape of terrorist suspect Mas Selamat Kastari, housing prices and overcrowded public transport. Ministers were also switched around so that 11 out of 14 ministries will get a change of leader.

Prime Minister Lee Hsien Loong is taking a considerable gamble with these changes. But if any of the new appointments or promotions don't work out, he always has the option to flow them out.

With voters showing no restraint in voting out PAP ministers, and a Prime Minister who does not shun from retiring incumbents in favour of new blood, a Cabinet appointment is now more like a fixed-term appointment for five years, than a decades-long tenure appointment. Voters fresh from having had their say at the polls, and with the memory of policy grouses ignored for years, may cheer this phenomenon. But it can have dire consequences.

The converse of policy ossification is policy flip-flops – when policies lurch from one end of the spectrum to the other in response to voters' signals, and to new ministers' preferences.

PM Lee wants his new team to review their portfolios with fresh eyes. If they do so, we may be talking not just about the transformation of the PAP, but also the transformation of Singapore. Will core policies undergo a change? Beyond changes already promised – a rise in income cap for Housing Board flats and a slowdown in influx of foreigners – will a Housing Board flat become more a home than an asset? Will the pool of foreigners dwindle, forcing small and medium-sized enterprises to close shop – and their local workers to lose their jobs – because they can't get workers? Will government subsidies to public housing, public transport and public healthcare increase?

These will require Singaporeans' consent. And it is by no means certain that the majority will support a change in, say, housing policy that leads to a fall in property prices.

This is why PM Lee has stressed the need to engage Singaporeans in making policies, and why there is so much talk about the need for a new consensus among Singaporeans.

This is most critical in the area of social policy.

Singapore adopts a fairly minimalist approach to welfare, restricting direct assistance to those too sick or old to work. For the rest, the approach is that the best welfare is a job, so those who cannot find one must be given training until they do. This view is at risk of becoming orthodoxy adhered to unthinkingly. Opposition candidate Hazel Poa raised a valid point, when she asked for statistical evidence – not just anecdotal stories – that the millions spent on training yielded jobs and higher wages for workers.

From a systemic point of view, one can see that apart from Public

Assistance for those who cannot work, Singapore's social safety net delivers many benefits through work: the Central Provident Fund, Workfare, training subsidies. But what of those who cannot get work or have lost their jobs? A system of benefits predicated on work obviously fails to meet the needs of those without work.

There is some unease among Singaporeans over the level of meagre state assistance to those who have fallen on hard times either temporarily or permanently: who are too old, too ill, or simply unable to support themselves and their families sustainably.

A leader from the social service sector Willie Cheng theorised in a recent article that it is not just the low-income, but also the middle- and higher-income, who are concerned about help for the poor. The well-to-do spoke up "through the ballot box" for the lower-income, he argued.

During the election campaign, half of about 90 voters interviewed by The Straits Times cited rising cost of living as one of their top two concerns. Some made it clear they were not in need themselves, but wanted the Government to do more for those who were.

The view that more can be done to help the vulnerable is not just based on altruism. A more generous social welfare system alleviates general anxiety, since the comfortably middle class today know they may be forced by ill health, prolonged job loss or other family circumstances into penury tomorrow, and may be in need of a helping hand.

This conviction that a rich nation like Singapore can afford to do more for the needy will gain traction as the income gap widens in the face of GDP growth.

Already, the signs of distress are visible around Singapore. During the hustings, I had lunch one day at Ang Mo Kio Central. An elderly woman with her right leg amputated below the knee propelled herself in a wheelchair, selling three tissue packs for $1. She told me she had met the Prime Minister at the MRT station a few days ago on his campaign rounds. She sought his help – not for a handout, but to write to the authorities to waive her many summonses (presumably for illegal hawking). She had five children but none supported her, so she sold tissue packs. She recalled how one kind lady gave her a hongbao of $200 during Chinese New Year – she wanted to thank the lady, but she had disappeared into the crowd.

Feisty old people like her may have family and internal resources, but could also do with some help from the state.

The new Acting Minister for Community Development, Youth and Sports Chan Chun Sing and Finance Minister Tharman Shanmugaratnam – who has been tasked to coordinate social policy – will have a challenging task ahead. They have to satisfy not only the low-income that government policies can help them, but also satisfy the middle-income that the social safety net is strong enough should they need it one day. And do all this without alienating the high-income who are the taxpayers. In short, forge a new social consensus on just how the poor among us should be helped.

A YEAR OF RUDE AWAKENINGS

29 December 2013

If there is one word to sum up Singapore's experience this year, it would be Vulnerability.

2013 is the year the People's Action Party lost whatever it might have retained of the lustre of invincibility.

In January, it had already lost a seat in the Punggol East by-election and was trying to beat a dignified retreat from the backlash unleashed by the Population White Paper's conclusion about preparing for a population of 6.9 million.

By the end of the year, it wasn't just the PAP but the entire Singapore system of governance that had shown its vulnerability.

High-profile trials for corruption underscored the way an organisation can entrench an anti-graft culture, yet have its own leaders behave with immunity against it, trading favours for sex and material gains. Squeaky clean Singapore suddenly became tawdry.

A fire broke out in SingTel's infrastructure in October, disrupting broadband services for days. The websites of the offices of the President and Prime Minister were hacked last month, exploiting a loophole called "cross-site scripting". IT experts said such hacking was "elementary". In other words, Singapore's IT fortress was found to have done the equivalent of forgetting to lock its gate even as it installed high-tech anti-burglary alarms all over its premises.

This month, hundreds of migrant workers rioted in Race Course Road, overturning and burning police cars. Orderly Singapore suddenly became dangerous.

Meanwhile, train delays and breakdowns have become such a common occurrence, they barely merit a spot as top news item of the day, or even a retweet. Some Singaporeans are asking: What is happening? Is this the beginning of the decline of the Singapore state as we know it?

It's easy to be an armchair critic and venture theories and opinions. One might say the recent episodes of failure are the result of decades of success. Having become accustomed to success, our institutions, systems and people are not used to picking up on signals of dysfunction and pre-empting problems, and are slow to react when things do go wrong.

Or we could put up a theory that we have become so reliant on systems and sophisticated technology, we have lost ground feel: the art of responding to what is here and now, of tackling today's problems to nip tomorrow's in the bud.

In the SingTel fire, a blowtorch used for maintenance that overheated materials was fingered as the cause. On the Little India riot, residents had complained for years about rowdy, drunken behaviour by migrant workers.

That brought to my mind the July 2012 Committee of Inquiry report on the December 2011 MRT breakdown, which pointed to "a gaping disconnect between what was formally on record and what was happening on the ground" when it came to MRT maintenance.

At the risk of tarring the public sector with the same brush, I do wonder if Singapore is facing the problems of success. A generation of people who grew up in complacent plenty are now in leadership positions. Across the public service, and in the private sector too, men and women in their 30s and 40s are heading organisations. They are smart and may even have First World exposure, having been schooled and trained with the best in New York, London and Fontainebleau. But are they schooled in the problems of the Third World? And more crucially, are they skilled in the ways of the street?

Increasingly, Singapore will have to deal not only with First World problems of success – managing income inequality, widening social safety nets, maintaining competitiveness – but also with Third World problems – overcrowding, preventing shanty slums (think slovenly dormitories), and maintaining basic law and order.

This is inevitable if Singapore is to continue its reliance on a large pool of migrant workers. Both First and Third Worlds are so densely packed into Singapore's tiny 716.1 sq km land area that they sometimes collide. Officials need skills to handle First World issues, Third World issues, and the interplay of both.

This year of Vulnerability is full of teachable moments.

For the innocent full-time national serviceman, the riot must have been a baptism of fire. Did all those hours of seemingly pointless training come to his aid when he faced down hundreds of hostile workers? For those watching on the sidelines, reading the voluminous online commentary, this is also a crucial year. Did we speak up and take a stand for what we think is right? Draw a line in the sand and say: that's enough? Or shrug off yet another insult, jibe, toxic comment?

For the many thousands of IT administrators, MRT maintenance staff, SingTel staff, and anyone remotely concerned with maintaining the computer, electrical, water, cable, or medical systems that make Singapore gel so wonderfully together, this year must be one of rude awakening. The things that shouldn't happen, can and did happen. Law enforcement vehicles can be burned, as can IT networks. Prestigious websites can be defaced.

Fortress Singapore is no more.

For a generation used to yawning when Singapore wins yet another new accolade – best workforce, most competitive economy, best performer in international examinations – the notion of Singapore losing its sheen of super-achieving invincibility can be traumatic.

And yet it is also a necessary part of growing up, as a people and as a nation. We are not the citizens to whom things are done by a government. We the people are Singapore.

If Singapore is no more fortress, what must take its place?

For me, there is only one answer. As citizens, we have to see that Fortress Singapore is no citadel of stone and steel built and protected by "them", but a society of us, made of flesh and blood that can tear and bleed.

WHICH OF TODAY'S ORTHODOXIES WILL BE TOSSED OUT TOMORROW?

Notion of risk-pooling healthcare funds was once deemed heretical

7 June 2015

It is now an article of faith that domestic wages were depressed for years in Singapore because of the too-easy access to a rapid influx of low-wage foreign workers.

So workers in low-wage sectors like cleaning and security have seen wages rise, as the Government tightened the tap on growth in foreign worker numbers after 2011.

On the front page of The Straits Times on Friday, in an article on productivity growth lagging behind wage growth, a bank economist was quoted as saying that wages have been playing catch-up only recently, after having been "generally depressed by an influx of foreign workers" for years.

Comments along these lines go unchallenged, and are hardly remarked upon. It was not always so. I recall parliamentary debates when MPs who suggested this were rebutted.

One Parliament news report from March 5, 2010 described Finance Minister Tharman Shanmugaratnam rebutting opposition MP Low Thia Khiang's claim that the Government had depressed wages of lower-income citizens by letting in more foreign workers.

Said Mr Tharman: "By allowing the economy to grow rapidly in the second half of the (last) decade, we were able to bring unemployment down and grow the incomes of Singaporeans."

To be sure, growing the foreign worker population helped drive the economy which raised wages across the board. But did it also extract a high cost on low-wage earners?

More pertinent, did that easy access to cheap foreign workers become a crutch for employers, so that they didn't invest enough in technology or more productive ways to do business?

It is now orthodoxy to say that the rapid influx of foreign workers from the mid-2000s depressed local wages at the bottom.

That got me thinking about other radical theories challenged by the establishment one day, which become orthodoxies years later.

One of these rebel-turned-establishment ideas is that of risk-pooling in health insurance. For years, the Government held fast to its principle that each individual and family should be responsible for their own medical bills. So the Central Provident Fund and its medical savings component, Medisave, were designed as individual accounts.

Whatever you put in remains yours, and isn't pooled. Never mind if you have $35,000 untouched in your Medisave, and someone else checks himself out of hospital because his Medisave has run out and he can't afford treatment.

After much soul-searching and hard arguments, the arm in government that argued for solidarity and risk-pooling won. Thus was born MediShield, which lets people pay premiums into a common pool and draw from it for medical expenses.

Today, there is also the CPF Life annuity scheme. It pools money from people's retirement accounts and spreads it out in an annuity payable for life. Even if you use up "your" portion of the money by, say, age 90, you can draw on the pool, funded by other people's savings.

It would all make some of our pioneer ministers turn in their graves. But today, such risk-pooling is universally applauded for giving individuals peace of mind.

In the economic and even social arena, once-radical ideas may become accepted. But what of ideas in the political arena? What ideas being discussed today might be before their time, but may one day become accepted?

Or to put it another way: What ideas that are so well defended today might crumble tomorrow and be discarded?

One such idea is that there is one right view of Singapore's history and that it is the duty and right of the establishment to defend it and use every resource at its disposal to propagate it.

The thing is, facts are indisputable. That Singapore is an island that lies one degree north of the Equator is a fact.

Existential realities, too, are of paramount importance and are hard to gainsay. Singapore is a tiny sovereign city-state in a volatile region, right smack in the middle of a maritime and air theatre in which big power play will unfold in the coming decades.

Military skirmishes escalating into conflict are a certainty; full- fledged war not totally unlikely. If we want to remain sovereign, there are certain things we have to accept and defend, certain behaviours demanded of us. These are cold, hard realities.

But what of historical events that brought us here – what is the role of the different players in those events? What motivated them? Some of that is contestable, and is being contested.

The best counter to such contestation of historical narratives is facts, not suppression.

If one scholar comes up with an interpretation based on one document, then let another scholar demand access to even more archives and records to come out with a different view.

While this contestation is going on, state authorities should resist the temptation to use their power to enforce one version of history over another. To be sure, the Education Ministry has to agree to a national education and history curriculum. It, therefore, has to "take a stand" and propagate the establishment view of history. Our school textbooks and our schools will tell that story to our students.

But other state bodies should act according to their mandate. For example, the National Library Board (NLB) should not start removing from its shelves books that articulate an alternative view of Singapore's political history. It should remain true to its mission of housing a wide variety of books for the population's edification and enjoyment.

Nor should the National Arts Council (NAC) start to use taxpayer funds to sponsor and support only works of art consistent with the national mainstream narrative of history. It should instead use artistic merit as its primary criterion.

Similarly, the Media Development Authority (MDA) should stick to its mandate of promoting media development and not filter out films with a point of view that runs contrary to that of the current government.

This is not to say these bodies should permit works that are seditious or run contrary to the national security interest. So some sanction remains necessary.

But these bodies should be ideologically neutral. They should permit works of art, films and books that espouse a diversity of views, some of which will necessarily run counter to prevailing mainstream views. It is not their role to censor such views – neither is it their role to actively endorse and promote them. But as bodies that act as facilitators and custodians of the cultural creations in our society, they should at least permit a free play of such ideas.

If these suggestions sound out of the box today, just reflect on the fact that the notion of risk-pooling healthcare funds was once deemed heretical. One day, the idea that agencies like NAC, MDA and NLB should do their jobs to promote art, and films, and reading, and not be used to defend and enforce the establishment's version of history, will become mainstream.

A LUXURY WE CAN NO LONGER AFFORD TO MISS

The time is ripe for the launch of a 15-week series of prose and poetry in The Straits Times Op-Ed pages

23 April 2016

My first exposure to English poetry came via my elder sister's secondary school poetry textbook.

It had a distinctive red cover, against which the black text stood out clearly: Rhyme and Reason. An Anthology. Raymond O'Malley and Denys Thompson.

In the long afternoons and weekends after primary school, I would open the book and read the poems. I'm sure I struggled with many. But in those days when a working-class family's home was sans television, sans Internet, sans mobile phone, I dipped into the volume of poems many, many times. I read them silently, declaimed some, mused over them, and somehow, without quite knowing it, fell in love.

Even today, I remember the cadence of Ozymandias, that sonnet by Percy Bysshe Shelley on the destruction of great political power by the passage of time.

I liked the rhetorical flourishes of Casabianca by Felicia Hemans:

The boy stood on the burning deck,
Whence all but he had fled;
The flame that lit the battle's wreck,
Shone round him o'er the dead.

Thus began my love affair with poetry and literature, and my growing appreciation of the English language, which I learnt in school at age seven, and had come to enjoy by the time I was 10 or 11, and reading those poems.

I went on to major in English literature in Cambridge University, England, spending three indulgent, angst-filled years reading through the canon of English literature.

I became a journalist, writing on social and political issues. In the background, like the heartbeat of a first love, my love for literature, for poetry, continued to pulse.

When I was put in charge of the Op-Ed or Opinion pages of The Straits Times more than four years ago, I thought of starting a literary page in the newspaper. But as a good Singaporean who understands the truth of Lee Kuan Yew's words in 1969, that poetry is a luxury we cannot afford, I set it aside.

Instead, with my editors' prompting, The Straits Times launched its By Invitation series, featuring opinion leaders in Singapore and the region. Over the years, we carved out a niche for the paper's Opinion pages as a place where readers get access to viewpoints from both East and West, on matters from terrorism to technology, on issues from healthcare to dying with dignity, on power tussles in the South China Sea to the Arctic.

Last year, to mark Singapore's 50th anniversary and to look towards the future, we worked with leading thinkers including Peter Schwartz (of *The Art Of The Long View* fame) and Saskia Sassen (*The Global City* guru) to launch a series of 20 essays on SG100.

Then 2016 came.

With the onset of 51 (the nation's age, not mine) and middle age – that period when people are said to revive adolescent dreams as age presses on them – I thought the time was ripe to float the idea of a literary page in The Straits Times.

The National Arts Council's (NAC) deputy CEO Paul Tan, a former colleague who went on to direct four successful editions of the Singapore Writers Festival, linked me up with May Tan, who looks after the development of literary arts at NAC. We brainstormed ideas and writers. May suggested going beyond prose, to include poetry. I was thrilled. But poetry in the Op-Ed pages?

I found out that it wasn't really such a radical idea. British newspapers have run poetry for centuries. In fact, Alfred Tennyson's The Charge Of The Light Brigade first appeared in The Examiner on Dec 9, 1854. Victorian newspapers published poems regularly. During World War I, patriotic poems were published almost on a daily basis.

Former Bloomberg News editor Michael Silverstein argued for precisely this in an article titled "A call for more political poetry on America's Op-Ed pages" on Feb 26, 2004. He wrote: "Poetry was a standard feature in American newspapers. Some papers even had in-house poets. The most famous was probably Edgar Guest, who wrote a daily poem for the Detroit Free Press well into the 1950s, and was also widely syndicated. Today, many smaller newspapers and even some national ones (such as The New York Times) still have sections that occasionally run verse.

"Poetry on Op-Ed pages, however, poetry that regularly speaks about political, economic and social issues of immediate interest to a wide audience, is nowhere to be found. And this is a serious loss to the public. Robert Frost described poetry as 'the best possible way of saying anything'. No one could argue against the need for 'the best possible way of saying anything' on Op-Ed pages, where public policies that affect us all are debated and shaped."

For poetry to appear in Op-Ed pages, Silverstein argues that poets need to break out of their self-referential habits of writing for a small circle of learned professionals. On the newspaper side, what's needed are editors "who recognise poetry as a real-world way to look at the issues covered in their pages".

His words resonated with me.

And so, today, we present the start of the Rhyme and Reason page – a literary series that will run for 15 weeks. Today is, aptly, Shakespeare Day – the 400th anniversary of the death of The Bard. William Shakespeare parsed politics in his poetry; waxed lyrical in his prose; and encapsulated all his prose and poetry and passion within the form of drama. He was an inveterate cross-genre writer.

What follows every Saturday till July 30 will be one literary page a week in The Straits Times Opinion pages. There will be one prose essay and one poem each week. They are written by writers – poets, playwrights, novelists, essayists – who could be Singaporeans, or were born in Singapore, or have made Singapore home.

Their choice of subject is eclectic, but grounded in issues of the world. There will be stories of cabaret women and a general's daughter; meditative essays on the sound of nature and on the nature of memory; philosophical pieces on urban design and rural kampungs. Poets grapple with carparks and trees; gawk at artworks and flower domes; muse on shadow play and terror; and reflect on the Smart Nation and citizenship.

I hope readers will enjoy this addition to The Straits Times diet of commentary, and that these writers will find in The Straits Times, and its ancillary digital platforms, new ways to reach more readers.

This week's literary feast includes an essay by Meira Chand, the author of *A Different Sky*, one of the best Singapore novels written so far. She is of Indian-Swiss parentage, went on to marry an Indian man and moved with him to Japan, and found home and relevance in – where else but – Singapore, this hotch-potch island nation of many races, many religions, and many more cuisines.

We also offer here three previously unpublished poems by Edwin Thumboo, who remains active and prolific into his 80s, and generously shared his oeuvre with readers of The Straits Times. Like many other writers I approached, Edwin was enthusiastic in his support of a literary series.

I think their enthusiasm springs from a sense that the time is right for Singapore to indulge in this luxury. We are a nation not only of merchants, bureaucrats and engineers. We are also a nation of dreamers, artists, poets. We need nourishing not just of the body and mind, but of the soul.

Good prose and poetry stir the heart and quicken the soul while teasing the mind. When they dwell on national or current affairs issues, such writings, at pivotal times, can speak for an epoch, to an entire generation, and indeed can speak for an entire nation. Scottish poet laureate Carol Ann Duffy wrote a poem for The Guardian newspaper, a day after the September 2014 Scottish referendum on independence. Drawing on the symbols of an English rose and a Scottish thistle, she penned:

A thistle can draw blood,
so can a rose,
growing together
where the river flows, shared currency,
across a border it can never know.

If Singapore has a poet laureate, it would be Edwin Thumboo, the man who gave Singapore the by-now iconic poem Ulysses By The Merlion, in which the poet imagines Ulysses, the Homeric hero, stopping by Singapore and puzzling over the strange "half-beast, half-fish" Merlion creature, crafted by people who are beyond his ken:

They make, they serve,
They buy, they sell.
Despite unequal ways,
Together they mutate,
Explore the edges of harmony,

Search for a centre...
Perhaps having dealt in all things,
Surfeited on them,
Their spirits yearn for images,
Adding to the Dragon, Phoenix,
Garuda, Naga, those Heroes of the Sun,
This lion of the sea,
This image of themselves.

Having surfeited on things, we are at a juncture in our history when literary writings and poetry are no longer luxuries we cannot afford. Instead, I would submit, they have become essential to a more rounded, richer understanding of ourselves.

THE PROMISE AND PERILS
OF DIRECT ELECTIONS

**To lower risk of rogue leaders being elected, educate and expose
voters to election process to help them vote wisely**

28 February 2016

My first introduction to the promise and perils of democracy came in
secondary school. That was when we students came together to elect our
head prefect .

The head prefect worked with the principal and teachers to enforce
discipline and to organise activities for the school. Yet, in seeking our
vote, she would have to be a representative of the students and champion
our welfare. She would have to be both advocate and regulator.

I remember the quietly competitive campaigning that went under
way, as each candidate and her supporters put up campaign posters and
organised "rallies".

Even within the confines of a school election for head prefect, we
somehow knew there was an "establishment" candidate, a girl from the
top Science class said to be favoured by the principal and teachers. Then
there was a "grassroots" candidate, a girl from a humble background
with a likeable demeanour.

As I recall it, it was bread-and-butter issues like recess time and
canteen food – not education policy – that dominated campaign talk.

The grassroots candidate won. She proved to be a steady head prefect
and school life carried on as usual, without dramatic changes.

I have often reflected since on how progressive it was of the principal and teachers to have a head prefect elected by the student body. To be sure, the risk of having a feckless or reckless head prefect is small, compared to the risk of having one such national leader. But it would have been irksome, to say the least, for the teaching body to have to deal with a troublesome head prefect for a year.

Yet, the adults at Raffles Girls' School in the 1980s, when I was a student, saw fit to entrust a bunch of over 1,000 teenagers with the vote to choose their student leader.

I have been thinking about the RGS head prefect election since news broke about impending changes to the Elected Presidency in Singapore. The Elected President in our system acts as a custodian to safeguard Singapore's stability, as he has veto powers over spending of past financial reserves and key public-sector appointments. The idea is that he should act as a check on the elected government of the day and prevent the latter from squandering hard-earned past reserves.

To weed out frivolous candidates, criteria were set to make sure only people with vast management or financial experience will qualify. The finely balanced mechanism is meant to act as a "second key" to protect Singapore's inheritance.

But the last presidential campaign troubled many Singaporeans, including myself. We saw with deep concern how even candidates from the requisite backgrounds campaigned as though the Elected President was the head of an alternative government which could institute alternative policies.

Such candidates behaved as though they did not understand the constitutional limits to their role – or if they did, were unwilling to be constrained by them. The result of such wrong-headed thinking was a confused campaign that confused voters.

To avoid a repeat of such confusion, the institution of the Elected Presidency clearly needs fixing, and urgently, before the next election is due by August next year. It was no surprise then, that this was among the top items of the Government after winning a handsome mandate in the September 2015 General Election.

A few people, including my colleague Warren Fernandez and eminent diplomat Kishore Mahbubani, have argued in The Straits Times that it is worth considering going back to the practice of having Parliament choose someone to become the President.

Warren argued last week: "Sooner or later, a president with his own electoral mandate will inevitably emerge as an alternative source of power, at odds with an elected government. No amount of tinkering with the selection criteria or process will address this."

Kishore wrote: "While we worried about a rogue government in the past, we did not consider the possibility that a rogue president could be elected. It is true that democratic electorates can display wisdom. They demonstrated this when they gave the People's Action Party government a solid mandate in the 2015 elections. Sadly, it is also true that democratic electorates can display a lack of wisdom."

I agree with both that the current set-up for the Elected Presidency turns it into a huge political risk, a point many observers noted after the August 2011 Presidential Election. The Presidency has become Singapore's Achilles heel in politics.

This is due, in part, to the nature of elections and politics. The perils of direct democracy are all too evident this season, as the contest for presidential nominees gets under way in America. The world watches in horrified disbelief, as the extreme antics of Republican candidate Donald Trump help him trounce rivals; and gasps at the way Democratic candidate Bernie Sanders promises free healthcare and free college tuition, as they try to clinch their respective parties' nomination.

In a frank commentary in Huffington Post, Professor Robert Reich, who was Secretary of Labour in the Clinton administration, warned about "The Perils of Circus Politics". In the article, he wrote: "Paradoxically, at a time when the stakes are especially high for who becomes the next president, we have a free-for-all politics in which anyone can become a candidate, put together as much funding as they need, claim anything about themselves no matter how truthful, advance any proposal no matter how absurd, and get away with bigotry without being held accountable. Why? Americans have stopped trusting the mediating institutions that used to filter and scrutinise potential leaders on behalf of the rest of us."

He identifies these mediating institutions as political parties (now disdained), the mainstream media (seen as biased), and opinion leaders (none of which can sway a broad swathe of public opinion).

Singapore is not the United States and the solution to our flawed presidential system must be our own. I think the solution must be two-pronged. The first prong of measures – already being undertaken by the Constitutional Commission on the presidency – is to raise the bar to ensure quality candidates, and to embed the powers of the president more tightly within the embrace of the Council of Presidential Advisers.

The second prong must be targeted at voters: to inculcate in Singaporeans an understanding of what the vote means, so they will not support demagoguery or bigotry.

A campaign to explain the presidency's limited role is essential so they can see through candidates who try to win them over on false premises. Beyond that, we can introduce Singaporeans to elections at a young age.

Educate students on politics in school. Hold elections for class monitors and head prefects, and give them power to decide on things that students care about, like canteen food, school uniform, hair lengths and outings. Have elections for mayors, town councillors and Residents' Committee members.

Then, we see elections up close and live with the consequence of our vote in the school, neighbourhood or town. When it is time to choose national leaders, we would hopefully have lived through and learnt from the folly of supporting incompetent or populist leaders, and learnt to cast our vote more wisely.

The way to deal with the dangers of democracy is not to back away from it by withdrawing suffrage, but to get people to see and experience both its potential and its limits – and as early on in life as possible.

I admit my view is based on an optimistic view of human nature and of politics. There will be risks, and certainly much time and effort will be spent on school and local elections.

But the alternative – reducing the franchise, or removing the vote, because of the risk of a rogue candidate being elected – leads us down a far worse path.

WHEN I'M 64... WHAT KIND OF SINGAPORE CAN I GROW OLD IN?

Changes to the nursing-home model and retirement financing will be too late for me, but I hope they come in time for younger Singaporeans

7 August 2016

As I grow into my late 40s, I find myself ruminating on what kind of Singapore this will be like to live in when I'm old. Will I have enough to live on? What kind of home can I live in? Will there be support in daily living needs as I grow frail?

As I have no children to count on, will I have to grow old in one of those nursing homes with long rows of beds filled with sad-looking old folks? Or can I age in my own home, or my own room, among friendly people?

Last week, two issues in the news sparked both despair and hope in this area. First, hope.

After dismissing as unsustainable a care model that would let elderly people live in home-like settings in single- and twin-bedded rooms, clustered around a dining and kitchen area, the Ministry of Health (MOH) has relented somewhat.

The Lien Foundation had proposed this kind of care home last year for an existing facility, but aborted the subject when MOH refused to provide it with the usual subsidies for eldercare patients, saying it would be financially unsustainable to provide subsidies for patients living in rooms that are "designed to proxy private or A-class ward configurations such as single- or double-bedded rooms only".

Most nursing homes today have dormitory-style beds in institutionalised settings.

The Lien Foundation and the Khoo Chwee Neo Foundation got research consulting agency Oliver Wyman to research on the costs. Its consultant, Dr Jeremy Lim, wrote: "Transitioning the 5,000 nursing-home beds in the pipeline to a Jade Circle-type model would cost Singapore an additional $8 to $13 per nursing home resident per day or less than $20 million a year in total."

MOH has since said it will study the report and work with Lien Foundation. It also stressed that it "appreciates the aspiration for our seniors to age in more homely environments that provide dignified and enabling care" and would "work with providers to explore new models of care that give residents greater independence and autonomy".

I am rooting for the Lien Foundation and its partners to convince MOH to widen its fiscal horizons, and include home-like nursing homes within its funding formula.

Then, when I'm 64, perhaps I can start my "young old" days in a Housing Board flat near coffee shops and amenities. As I age and need more care, I hope to have access to home-care assistants, or nursing help, or doctor's visits, or meals in a communal dining area so I don't have to cook for myself.

As I get more frail, and advance into my "old old" age, I hope to move into a nursing home in the same block or nearby, living out my last days in a single- or twin-bedded room, decorated the way I like it, with my favourite objects around, and elderly friends nearby.

But while the Lien Foundation's advocacy gives me hope for change, I'm not holding my breath.

What I find frustrating whenever we discuss ageing issues is that there has been so much talk over the last 20 years, and not enough action.

In the 1990s, a slew of reports suggested changes to housing options, and to financing. There was much talk of sheltered housing – that lets people age in home-like surroundings, with supports for medical and living needs nearby.

In 1997, The Straits Times did a survey that I reported on. It found that four in 10 worry about housing for their old age. One-third of those with children do not want to live with them when old. Thirty-eight per cent said they could live in a retirement block within an HDB estate; 27 per cent would consider commercial retirement homes; and 14 per cent would consider a nursing home.

Even back then, 19 years ago, the nursing-home option was the choice of a mere 14 per cent. Yet, for most frail elderly that can't hire a full-time caregiver at home, that remains the only viable option today.

Singapore, in other words, hasn't moved much when it comes to caring for its frail elderly.

The Oliver Wyman research report on nursing-home economics noted that countries like Japan, that began with dormitory-style institutionalised nursing homes, have moved on to provide residents with more homely settings today. In Singapore, progress has been painfully slow.

I hope nursing-home models will change by the time I need one. I turn 62 in 2030, and will be one of the one million people who will be above 60 in 2030. One in three of us then is projected to need some form of eldercare service by then. The window of 14 years between now and 2030 gives me some hope for change to happen in time for when I age.

When it comes to retirement financing, however, 14 years is too short a horizon for those in my age group to benefit from whatever changes may be effected to the status quo.

Last week, a panel advising the Government on Central Provident Fund changes proposed the setting up of a series of passively managed life-cycle funds that CPF members can invest in.

This offers an alternative to their current two choices: the zero-risk, guaranteed return of keeping their monies with CPF; and the wild wild west of using their CPF funds to invest in over 200 approved unit trust and other funds under the CPF Investment Scheme (CPFIS).

Finance professor Benedict Koh (on the CPF advisory panel) wrote in The Straits Times in 2014 that 47 per cent of CPF members who had withdrawn their Ordinary Account (OA) savings to invest in the CPFIS had incurred losses on their investments between 2004 and 2013; 35 per cent realised net profits equal to or less than the default 2.5 per cent per annum OA interest rate; and just 18 per cent generated net profits in excess of the OA interest rate.

In other words, eight in 10 would have been better off, or just as well off, if they had just left their money in the CPF. What this shows is that most of us don't make very good investment choices with our CPF funds.

This, however, shouldn't lead us to think we're better off just letting the CPF Board handle the money and being content with 2.5 per cent a year.

If one of those passively managed exchange-traded funds was available and we had just left the money there, how would we have fared?

Imagine a fund that tracked the benchmark MSCI World Index. In the last 10 years, this index grew at an annual 5 per cent a year. That's twice the OA interest rate. How much difference would that make?

If you left $10,000 in your CPF, 10 years later, you would get $12,837. If you had put it with the index fund that generated 5 per cent, you would get $16,487.

The difference of a few thousand dollars may not sound like much. But over 30 years, it can make or break your retirement piggy bank.

Over 30 years, $10,000 at 5 per cent interest compounded monthly swells to $44,677. At the CPF rate of 2.5 per cent, you get just $21,153. The difference is twofold. This is the power of compound interest over time.

This is why I despaired when I read that the panel was proposing the setting up of these funds.

Proposals to set up private pension funds or privately managed pension funds or private pension plans have been around since the mid-1990s. The exact nomenclature changes depending on the mood of the times and the specific suggestion, but the idea is of low-cost funds that are cheaper to run than retail unit trusts, and that offer investors a few, carefully selected, choices that match their life cycle and risk profiles.

Each time, some committee or other would recommend it, there would be lots of talk, it would be studied – then, nothing.

And after over 20 years of talk, we get another proposal. It will take a few years to study this, and another few more to operationalise this. If it even gets beyond the "study" stage.

I know retirement financing is serious business, affecting people's lives. It takes leaders with confidence and conviction to propose changes. No politician will want to get flak when the market turns, and returns dip. Citizens too will also have to understand the risks and returns, and not blame the Government if they make poor decisions. So time for considered study is important.

But each delay in action means another cohort of Singaporean workers is growing old with safe but low returns on their CPF funds.

Each cycle of talk-explore-no-action means another generation of average workers will lead harder lives in old age.

Will this time prove different? For the sake of younger Singaporeans, I sincerely hope so.

For myself, and those of my age group, it is too late. I have seven years before I hit 55, when my Retirement Account in CPF is due to start. That is barely time to operationalise the proposal, let alone to enjoy the compounded interest that may come with higher-yield funds.

My mind goes back to the lyrics of the Beatles song When I'm 64: "Will you still need me, will you still feed me, when I'm 64?"

What I'd really like to say, though, is this: "Will you heed me, will you change for me, before I'm 64?" I won't hold my breath for myself.

But I hope today's generation of decision-makers will take action on retirement financing, so that younger Singaporeans just building up their CPF nest eggs today will benefit from their decisive action this decade.

WHO WILL BE THE NEXT PM AFTER 2020? I HOPE BY THEN, IT WON'T MATTER SO MUCH

3 October 2015

The past week has been rife with speculation as people waited to see who would be appointed to the new Cabinet, and to what portfolios.

When Prime Minister Lee Hsien Loong announced the new Cabinet line-up on Monday (Sept 28), the news spread quickly through social media. Swift on its heels came analyses aplenty.

I followed the reports from a haze – literally, as the Pollutant Standards Index rose. I coughed – not only from the haze – when I read the startling analysis that said PM Lee was sidelining his two deputy PMs by stripping them of their portfolios (he elevated them to coordinating roles and handed over their Home Affairs and Finance portfolios to younger ministers).

I took part in many pleasant, speculative sessions with friends and work associates, discussing this minister, that minister; who said what, when; as we marinated ourselves in that mix of information, insight, and gossip that makes for political conversation over dinner.

One friend said the key issue was who would be the next PM after Mr Lee. Would it be Mr Heng Swee Keat, who is the most experienced of the newer lot of ministers?

Or one from the 2011 batch like Mr Chan Chun Sing, with his razor-sharp brain and his instincts for the common man?

Or maybe one of the new candidates of ministerial calibre from the 2015 batch might prove himself to have the X-factor.

Mr Ong Ye Kung, who impressed many in the election campaign with his visionary, passionate rally speeches? Or former chief of defence force Ng Chee Meng, with his equable demeanour belying the considerable organisational skills and stamina of the man who oversaw the massive state funeral arrangements and logistics in the mourning period after Mr Lee Kuan Yew died?

A left-field theory has it that Mr Tharman Shanmugaratnam will be the next PM after Mr Lee, holding the fort till one of the fourth-generation candidates musters sufficient political support.

But perhaps who becomes the next PM is less important than the question of whether the new group leaders can all "shake down as a team", in the vivid words of PM Lee, who has said he hopes to have a new team in place to hand over the reins of leadership after the next election, which is due by 2020.

PM Lee said of the new Cabinet: "They have to be tested, learn the ropes, prove themselves, and shake down as a team. Increasingly they will carry the Government's programme – initiating, explaining and executing policies, and persuading people to support these policies, which will increasingly be their policies."

I've been asked by various people who I think the next PM will be, and who I think would make a good future PM for Singapore.

Who will be the next PM?

It all depends. No one can predict politics, or the mood of the people, or group dynamics. Your guess is as good as mine.

Who would make a good PM?

That depends so much on the kind of Singapore we become.

In this respect, it is my hope that we will become the kind of society that depends less and less on one man, and more and more on a group, and on institutions, and on its citizens.

PM Lee Kuan Yew was a tough leader not averse to "knocking heads" – in his own words – which was probably necessary for the founding era. His successor PM Goh Chok Tong was more genial, although he played hardball in electoral politics. PM Lee Hsien Loong is collegial, and appears to give his ministers quite free rein.

The next PM should be someone with vision to lead; who has the emotional energy and charisma to communicate and reach out incessantly to people; and, I would argue, with a nurturing, positive personality capable of getting the best from his colleagues in government. For, increasingly, it will not just be the PM who leads Singapore, but a team.

I hope, too, that our institutions evolve: that the executive, the legislature, judiciary, academia, media, are all strengthened to play a more robust role in Singapore's evolution.

Then, the question of who will be the next PM of Singapore will still matter, but will not be the arbiter of the nation's future – because there are many other people, and systems, keeping the country going.

PICKING SINGAPORE'S NEXT PM: THE 4G16 HAS SHOWN ITS HAND AND IT IS GOOD

"We've got this" – that sums up the approach in the statement from the 4G political leaders. It speaks of their decisiveness and collegial approach to leadership

6 January 2018

I must confess to feeling rather nonchalant about all the discussion about the future 4G or fourth-generation leadership in Singapore.

When friends or work associates want to discuss who's going to be the next prime minister in Singapore, I'm sometimes inclined to put on my contrarian hat and say who cares, or throw a spanner in the works by saying it might be someone from an opposition party.

I mean, current PM Lee Hsien Loong has been talking about the importance of political succession since at least 2005. Every election since Mr Lee took over as PM in 2004 has been fought in part on the urgency of political renewal: Vote for this slate of young promising candidates, so the country will have good leaders to choose from.

Fast forward to 2018. We all know Mr Lee, now 65, has said he intends to hand over the reins of government to a successor by the time he is 70, in 2022. Meanwhile, his two Deputy PMs, Tharman Shanmugaratnam and Teo Chee Hean, are aged 60 and 63.

If there is to be political renewal, a younger set of leaders has to step up. In the PAP style of political succession, not much is said explicitly but much is assumed. Every sentient political creature in Singapore knows that the front-runners for PM are Heng Swee Keat, 56 (temporarily disqualified after his stroke in 2016, but back in the game after his remarkable recovery); Chan Chun Sing, 48; and Ong Ye Kung, also 48.

Expectations are for a Cabinet reshuffle after the Budget debate in March, when one or more of them might be promoted to DPM ranks.

As Mr Heng is first among equals, he may become first DPM. Mr Chan might be next in line, as he is considered more experienced than Mr Ong, having entered Parliament one term earlier. Mr Ong was fielded as a candidate in the losing PAP team for Aljunied Group Representation Constituency (GRC) in 2011 and made a comeback in 2015, under the safe Sembawang GRC seat helmed by Khaw Boon Wan.

The two current DPMs may then stay on in advisory capacities, while retaining their coordinating minister functions, so the reasoning goes among the politically attuned.

It is all pretty standard PAP thinking. Reasonable, steady, and a bit predictable.

Until the young ministers broke with tradition by issuing a statement on Thursday, Jan 4. When someone brought my attention to it, I thought it was fake news.

A group of 16 young ministers ganging up to essentially tell their senior colleagues to just leave us alone, we will decide who among us will be the leader, in good time?

But it wasn't fake, it was true.

The statement said: "Political stability has been the hallmark of Singapore and smooth leadership succession has instilled confidence among Singaporeans and our friends around the world.

"The younger ministers are keenly aware that leadership succession is a pressing issue and that Prime Minister Lee Hsien Loong intends to step down after the next general election. We are conscious of our responsibility, are working closely together as a team, and will settle on a leader from among us in good time."

It was signed by 16 PAP MPs, who included the three front-runners for PM as well as ministers like Lawrence Wong and Ng Chee Meng and ministers of state. Aged 42 to 56, they included four women; four non-Chinese; and Tan Chuan-Jin, who had faced the embarrassment of being considered demoted after he left Cabinet and was appointed Speaker of Parliament.

When I read the statement and glanced at the list of names, I felt cheered.

There's a simple reason.

By issuing that statement, the 16 members, who will likely form the core of the next generation of political leaders, are telling their political elders and Singaporeans: We know what's at stake; we take succession seriously; and we will do things our way, in our time.

Or in three words – the three words counsellors say signify a rock-solid marriage, that partners love to hear even more than "I love you": I've got this.

I liked the way they were essentially telling people like Mr Goh Chok Tong to lay off their case. Former PM Goh had had a clear designated successor from the first day he took up office in November 1990, and might have felt the 4G leaders were dragging their feet picking a leader. He had, on Wednesday, asked them to choose a leader among themselves in six to nine months' time – so that PM Lee can formally designate a successor before the year's end.

I liked that the statement was issued not by one, or two, or three, of some inner group of future leaders, but by 16 of them. The group is quite diverse, and inclusive, and egalitarian. Names were arranged not in order of seniority, but in strict alphabetical order.

I liked that the statement was issued quite suddenly, without public testing of the ground. It did not come across as orchestrated or premeditated, unlike a lot of PAP-engineered events or pronouncements.

It was, however, responsive to an emerging situation – a sense of greater pressure to name a leader among them. I was glad the 4G16 did not look the other way and pretend there was no issue brewing, as though the controversy could simply be shrugged off or ignored out of existence.

If Singapore is to have a chance in the brave new world of disruption, we will need a political leadership that acts more like this – quick to respond without being defensive, tackling a difficult decision head-on, collegial in nature, while being cool-headed and not panicking into a rushed decision.

I have long thought the focus on who the next PM will be is over-intense. It is human nature to want to rally around a central figure. But no one person will define the fate of Singapore. An increasingly complex society like Singapore requires a group of leaders who are capable, honest and can pull together as a team. As I have argued in the past, Singapore's ability to sustain its success will depend on whether it can foster networks of leaders across sectors, who can come together for the common good. It will be less dependent on its ability to replicate the old PAP-style of dominant leadership coalescing around one central figure (or one political party).

To me, it matters less which individual will become PM, and more how the rest of the team will rally around him or her. The PM can be the captain, but he will need strikers, defenders, goalkeepers, and midfielders – not to say a supportive audience – to nurture a winning team that can bring in the goals.

WHY CABINET TO SPEAKER-PLUS CAN BE AN UPGRADE

Cabinet should not be a one-way street. More fluid leadership networks are needed in the new economy

11 September 2017

There's the old economy, business-as-usual way of looking at the move of Mr Tan Chuan-Jin from the Cabinet to that of Speaker of Parliament.

And then there's the disruption-friendly, start-up way.

First, the old, hierarchical way of analysis. This says that Mr Tan has been given a demotion.

From being a full Cabinet minister in the Ministry of Social and Family Development, with hundreds of staff, important policies to make and reportedly an annual seven-figure salary, he is being put up for the role of Speaker, with sway over a tiny staff and a salary reportedly in the mid-six figures.

His main decisions won't be on governing Singapore, but within a narrow ambit of overseeing the Parliament staff, and presiding over debates in the House. He will also lead Singapore's delegation in international parliamentary gatherings.

By the matrix of power and money – the two most common indicators of success in life – there is no doubt that moving from minister to Speaker is a step down.

Prime Minister Lee Hsien Loong had said that he would nominate Mr Tan for the role of Speaker, which is vacant after Madam Halimah Yacob resigned to contest the presidential election.

Online and off, chatter exploded over this unexpected move, as past

Speakers were usually backbench MPs, not ministers, unless they were near retirement. Mr Tan is 48. Many see this as a demotion.

But there's another way of looking at the move, from the lens of a society in the throes of disruption.

As digital transformations turn old industries upside down and threaten most of our jobs, surely our politics too must change, and our assumptions alongside.

Reframing politics

So here's my take on how this move can be viewed as an opportunity for Mr Tan, for the Government, and for all of us to reframe our views of politics in Singapore.

Cabinet is not a one-way street

First, Cabinet should be seen as a flow-through position, not a one-way street.

It's going to get tougher to persuade very capable, very successful career people to enter politics, and to take up a Cabinet post. The stakes are even higher if citizens see becoming a Cabinet minister as the acme of professional success. If we see things that way, then anyone who leaves Cabinet is (looked at askance) as a failure.

This should no longer be the case. Instead, Cabinet should be viewed in flow-through terms. People get picked to become a minister. They try it for a term, or two. Some take to it. Those who don't, leave – with little or no stigma. They go on to fulfilling careers elsewhere.

In the last few years, a few former ministers have taken this path.

Mr George Yeo moved from Foreign Minister to the private sector, joining a logistics company based in Hong Kong. Mr Raymond Lim left as Transport Minister, back to asset management. Mr Lui Tuck Yew, who resigned as Transport Minister, was just appointed Ambassador to Japan.

There is life after Cabinet, abundant life.

It's time Singaporeans stopped seeing an exit from Cabinet in cataclysmic terms. There are only about 15 ministries. Even with senior and second ministers, only about 20-something people are needed in Cabinet.

The pace of change these days is supersonic. Two years ago, any minister who didn't understand Facebook or Twitter would be out of touch. Today, if you don't Snapchat, Insta or Uber, you won't really understand the forces of change transforming our society. Alexa and Echo are creating waves overseas and will be on our shores soon. Before we know it, artificial intelligence-empowered robots will be ubiquitous in homes, and we'll realise Pepper was nothing.

I can't even imagine what the world will be like in 10 years.

In this disrupted world of rapid change, Singapore needs a more fluid system of political leadership. It's better for people to go into and out of Cabinet, than to be stuck with Cabinet ministers appointed in their 40s who then stay there for the next two to three decades.

In Singapore, we often talk these days of entrepreneurship, of not being afraid to fail, of moving away from a narrow definition of success.

In the same way, we need to broaden our conception of what makes for political success.

Making it to Cabinet is the equivalent of scoring straight As, and getting into an Ivy League university. But it's not the only kind of success we should recognise as a society.

When Singapore's political history is written, would a normal Cabinet minister get even one mention, or would opposition leaders J.B. Jeyaretnam and Chiam See Tong, for their long, brave sojourns as solo opposition MPs in Parliament for years?

Or Mr Low Thia Khiang, for leading an opposition team to a breakthrough win in a Group Representation Constituency?

Or, perhaps one day, former Nominated MP Siew Kum Hong will be feted for his far-sighted attempt to repeal Section 377A that criminalises homosexual acts. Success comes in a myriad of forms.

Also, change is constant in politics, as in life. The truism holds fast here: When one door closes, another opens.

From authority to influence

For Mr Tan, the door of the House is now wide open. As Speaker, his role is procedural and highly circumscribed. It is devoid of executive power. In the House, he has authority. Outside it, he lacks authority, but can have lots of influence.

Authority works in a command and control structure. You're the minister, you give an order, those down the line follow.

The real world is messier. You want something done, you use your influence, your people skills. This is where Mr Tan can make a difference.

Already, protocol-wise, moving from minister to Speaker is an upgrade, as he ranks just after the president, prime minister and deputy prime ministers, and the Chief Justice.

He can also do more to extend the influence of the role.

As Speaker, Mr Tan has authority over who gets to speak in Parliament, for how long, and when. That influence can be parlayed into a force for good.

Having watched parliamentary proceedings quite closely for over 20 years, I've seen how a Speaker can set the tone for the House.

Former Speaker Tan Soo Khoon was firm but studiedly fair, even going out of his way to give minority voices a chance to be heard.

Mr Tan Chuan-Jin is reportedly "sincere" and someone who "really cares" – words often used by those who have dealt with him. If he has a true heart for the marginalised and a true conviction to be inclusive, there is a lot he can do as Speaker to shepherd the tone of debate in the House along those lines.

Being impartial and giving equal weight to front and backbench speeches, and ensuring that the opposition gets heard, will also set the tone for respectful, fair, political debate, no matter how heated.

His influence will go far beyond Parliament. Parliamentary debates are widely watched by citizens, especially when edited into bite-sized video clips shared on social media.

Video clips of the Speaker making time for the social or political underdog in Parliament will create waves of positivity across the nation.

Mr Tan himself will continue to have influence, via his networks, friendships and access. For he won't just be Speaker of Parliament. He continues to head SG Cares, a national movement that encourages Singaporeans to volunteer. He will be appointed adviser to the National Council of Social Service.

PM Lee said Mr Tan has taken "a deep interest in social issues, and in helping the needy and disadvantaged". He should continue to be an active advocate in these areas, using his influence, his networks and his passion to help advance their causes. He can be Speaker-Plus-Social Advocate.

Moving Mr Tan from Cabinet minister to Speaker, in my view, does not put him out of the core of the fourth generation of new leaders. On the contrary, it presents an opportunity for us all to redefine the kind of political leadership we need to take Singapore forward into one where we stop seeing the Cabinet as the political acme and core of public life.

The Cabinet will always be powerful by virtue of its authority over executive decisions. But other centres of political power and influence must develop. For example, an influential Speaker who can act as a check on the frontbench by making time for parliamentary debates on difficult issues, ensuring that ministers answer MPs' probing questions on difficult issues, and chiding them when they are evasive.

Outside the House, having an influential former minister engaging with the ministries he used to head, but this time on behalf of activists and non-profits, can invigorate policies. This requires ministers and civil servants to embrace his contributions, not stonewall them.

Personally, I think continuing to have a rigid understanding of power politics overly centred on a few Cabinet ministers will constrain us from progress, for citizens will then always look to a top-down state to do things.

Instead, a society deep in disruption, in a fast-moving world, needs a more fluid understanding of true political leadership, full of people who can move in and out of power positions, into networks where they may not have authority but heaps of influence. Where things are done not by fiat, but through persuasion and influence, bound together by conviction and passion.

Increasingly, we need people who can work collaboratively across boundaries – of organisations, of political parties, of sectors.

Thinking in ministry silos and putting Cabinet positions on a pedestal over other leadership positions is just so last millennium.

POST-LKY ERA, WE ARE IN THE AGE OF CONTESTATION

Members of the establishment are coming out with alternative
ideas, sparking debate. It's time for rules of
engagement on such debate

8 July 2017

We have been in the post-Lee Kuan Yew era for just over two years, and it is already clear Singapore is deep into a different era. We are in the Age of Contestation.

Examples include the three-week-long public spat between Mr Lee's three children, as the two younger siblings Hsien Yang and Wei Ling took to Facebook to allege that their elder brother, Prime Minister Lee Hsien Loong, misused his position to thwart their father's wish to have the family home demolished on his death. The Lee siblings have since agreed to settle their dispute privately.

Private family feuds with political overtones used to be the stuff of television drama and a feature of other countries' political systems.

That it is now playing out in Singapore shows just how much the political landscape has shifted in the short 27 months since founding prime minister Lee Kuan Yew died in March 2015, aged 91. In his time as PM and after, Mr Lee's iron will and people's reverence for him personally, kept in check more than family disputes.

With his passing, more members of the establishment are openly quarrelling among themselves.

Foreign policy options have been the arena for another battle of words. Former diplomat Kishore Mahbubani, in a candid, controversial article published in The Straits Times, said Singapore should learn from Qatar's plight and behave more like a small country.

In his time, Mr Lee Kuan Yew had spoken freely on great power matters, but that was because "he had earned the right to do so because the great powers treated him with great respect as a global statesman", Mr Mahbubani said, adding: "We are now in the post-Lee Kuan Yew era. Sadly, we will probably never again have another globally respected statesman like Mr Lee. As a result, we should change our behaviour significantly. What's the first thing we should do? Exercise discretion. We should be very restrained in commenting on matters involving great powers."

Mr Mahbubani also wrote: "Consistency and principle are important, but cannot be the only traits that define our diplomacy. And there is a season for everything. The best time to speak up for our principles is not necessarily in the heat of a row between bigger powers."

That article drew a fusillade of repartee. Law and Home Affairs Minister K. Shanmugam retorted: "Mr Lee never advocated cravenness, or thinking small. Did we get to where we are now, by thinking 'small'? No."

Another seasoned diplomat Bilahari Kausikan launched a spirited rebuttal: "His first lesson – that small states must always behave like small states – is muddled, mendacious and indeed dangerous." He added: "I am profoundly disappointed that Kishore should advocate subordination as a norm of Singapore foreign policy. It made me ashamed. Kishore will no doubt claim that he is only advocating 'realism'. But realism does not mean laying low and hoping for the leave and favour of larger countries. Almost every country and all our neighbours are larger than we are. Are we to live hat always in hand and constantly tugging our forelocks? What kind of people does Kishore think we are or ought to be?"

Mr Kausikan's rebuttal was posted on his Facebook page.

Another diplomat Ong Keng Yong also responded with an article arguing that Singapore should not be cowed by others due to its size, and agreed with Mr Mahbubani that it had to uphold regional institutions.

A few other writers came out to defend Mr Mahbubani. One is Mr Marcus Loh who wrote that the article was consistent with Mr Mahbubani's role as a "naysayer": "Kishore too has never been shy of taking a contrarian viewpoint to trigger debates to arrive at out-of-the-box scenarios, or to stand up for one's principles."

Noting that Mr Mahbubani "railed against Western arrogance while standing up for" Asian values, Mr Loh added: "Kishore's track record of standing up for Singapore runs contrary to the impression that the Dean had implied that Singapore should take on a subordinate position when dealing with larger powers."

Mr Lee Kuan Yew's death marks the ascendance of a new Age of Contestation. If we are to look at modern Singapore history in broad arcs, one could say that the 1950s and 1960s was the age of confrontation, when political parties fought for the hearts and minds of the populace. Political battles were intense and fraught, with anti-colonialists, communists and communalists jostling for power.

With the victory of the People's Action Party came the period of consolidation in the 1970s and 1980s when the country buckled down to build up the economy, build schools, provide mass housing, and build an army from scratch. So successful were most of those attempts that by the 1990s and 2000s, we were entering the age of consensus-building. Singapore was engaged in a widespread move to forge national values, develop a stronger national identity, give people a greater sense of ownership in society, and widen participation and build consensus.

The period from 2011 can be described as the Age of Contestation. 2011 was of course the year when the landmark General Election saw the ruling party's vote share fall to a historic low (albeit still 60.1 per cent). More political parties with credible candidates entered the political arena, and the rise of social media allowed a growing slew of public intellectuals and armchair critics to challenge the dominant intellectual narrative in Singapore and gain followers.

Mr Lee's death in 2015 gave momentum to the spread of contestation. With the exit of the "referee" of public discourse, so to speak, other members of the establishment felt freer to offer alternatives to the Singapore way.

In the last few years, even before Mr Lee's departure from the scene, we have seen former permanent secretaries like Ngiam Tong Dow criticise government policies; former PAP MP Tan Cheng Bock challenge and nearly triumph over a government-endorsed candidate for the elected presidency; and a host of former senior civil servants like Yeoh Lam Keong and Donald Low challenge government policy on sociopolitical issues in their Facebook posts, many of which are widely shared.

I think this week's debate on foreign policy options is a precursor of more heated discussions to come on Singapore's fundamentals. Here, the doyens of the foreign policy establishment are countering each other's positions, openly and robustly.

As a citizen and a journalist, I think this is a welcome development. Foreign policy is vital to Singapore and we are living in changing times. Should our foreign policy stance shift? As Professor Chan Heng Chee commented in a speech at a launch of a book by Mr Kausikan before the spat broke out, Singapore has to balance pragmatism with principle, and has to rethink its options in a post-US world order. The way forward for Singapore to maximise its geopolitical space may be different from that of the past, when the Little Red Dot could nestle under the American security shield and hitch a ride on the US-centric bandwagon in the region.

Just what can change, and how, layman commentators like me can't say. So it is useful when the experts have public exchanges, as they are then educating the population on the realities of our shifting geopolitical landscape and exploring some alternatives. That can only be positive for a maturing polity.

But I think we can improve the manner in which that public debate is conducted in this Age of Contestation. Elite diplomats, retired or not, also have a duty of care to be civil in their exchange. Some rules of engagement to consider:

1. ATTACK THE ARGUMENT, NOT THE PERSON
Ad hominem attacks on a person's character, or discrediting someone's views by virtue of who he or she is, must be called out.

2. DON'T PUT UP A STRAW MAN TO KNOCK DOWN
Describe your opponent's arguments fairly before you criticise them. For example, I don't think it was fair to characterise Mr Mahbubani's article as one that called for subordination to be the norm in foreign policy. Mr Mahbubani advocated discretion and choosing one's time to speak – those are traits of prudence, not submission.

3. ENGAGE STRONGLY BY ALL MEANS, BUT WITH RESPECT AND CIVILITY
The tone of some exchanges and rebuttals, including from people in leadership positions, has sometimes made me cringe. It is incumbent on those in positions of power and authority to avoid bullying tones when they respond to criticism.

4. FACEBOOK IS NOT ALWAYS THE BEST AVENUE FOR AN EXCHANGE OF SERIOUS VIEWS
Taking time to pen a serious rebuttal for a newspaper Opinion page is probably, sometimes, a better option than shooting off a Facebook post. (Disclosure: self-interested argument here, since I edit The Straits Times Opinion pages and am constantly on the lookout for well-reasoned arguments on issues of public interest.)

5. NATIONAL INTEREST FIRST, EGO SECOND. OR THIRD

Writers have egos. People who rose to high positions in the establishment tend to be even more sensitive about their ego and public image. But when engaging in a debate on Singapore's future, it is my fervent hope that establishment figures, and all the rest of us, think of how the exchange is advancing the national interest. It is always satisfying to your ego to try to demolish your opponent; but I hope we can all desist if that means bringing down the national interest.

I am sure that many other issues will be challenged in the months ahead. It is incumbent on all of us, and especially those who are leaders of the establishment, to engage with each other with civility. When government leaders or members of the leading family slug it out, there is no more referee, teacher or parent figure we can turn to to mediate; they themselves must learn self-restraint.

The Age of Contestation is upon us in Singapore. I hope it does not degenerate into an Age of Conflict. Contestation can sharpen debate, make us consider alternatives, and result in a better Singapore. But only if we all learn to engage like adults with each other, civilly and with respect.

HAS TRUST IN THE GOVERNMENT BEEN ERODED? IT'S TIME TO TALK FRANKLY

Leaders talk of maintaining trust, but some say trust has already been eroded

1 February 2018

Trust – that perennial issue – has been in the news again in recent weeks.

Last November, Prime Minister Lee Hsien Loong stressed the need for the ruling People's Action Party (PAP) to maintain the trust of citizens. Speaking at the PAP party convention, he said: "The PAP earned the people's trust the hard way, and we must never take it for granted or fritter it away."

More recently, Minister Chan Chun Sing returned to the theme, in a speech on Jan 11 when he stressed the need for exceptional leadership that is able to build trust with Singaporeans, and in an interview with my colleague, Straits Times editor Warren Fernandez, last week.

Like PM Lee, Mr Chan warned against a trust deficit developing in Singapore. Mr Chan diagnosed that trust erodes if citizens feel their lives have not improved; and if they feel their government – or the media in this era of "fake news" – was not honest in their statements or efforts on how to improve citizens' lives.

He summed it up aptly: "The first question is a question of competence, the second is a matter of integrity."

He also stressed that leaders should be forthright and honest about the challenges and options facing the country.

That view of trust and its importance is something many Singaporeans will agree with. As Mr Chan has noted, founding prime minister Lee

Kuan Yew once described the trust between government and people as the greatest asset.

But I also wonder if Singapore's leaders have listened hard enough to another group of Singaporeans – the one with deep-seated gripes about the Government – or simply waved their concerns aside.

For this group, maintaining trust in government is not the issue, because it has already been eroded. They may be a minority, but they are vocal, and with social media and technology, their views spread quickly and are amplified.

As someone from the media with some access to the political elite, who remains friends and in touch with ordinary folk remote from the centres of political power, I sometimes feel like I live in two worlds.

I defend the Singapore system to those who have lost confidence in it. I am proud of my country. I am also a product of the same system that produced the political elite – some schoolmates are in the top rungs of the public and political service. I too believe in the importance of exceptional, competent, honest government. I give our leaders the benefit of the doubt; I believe most mean well and are doing their best.

And I try to articulate the anger and despair of those who feel betrayed to the elite. For example, what might explain this erosion of trust among that group of Singaporeans so vocal about the issue?

I think one factor is that today's citizens may be expecting too much of their leaders, thinking back to the pioneering generation. In turn, leaders who hark back to the pioneering generation of ministers inadvertently invite such comparisons.

The pioneer generation lived through a world war, the Japanese Occupation, the fight for independence and economic upheaval. The bonds forged were deep. People looked up to leaders who were in general better educated than the masses, yet sacrificed professional careers and wealth to lead the country through independence and economic transformation.

Today's leaders oversee a mature economy with slowing growth. Many citizens are as well-educated, if not more, than their political leaders. Many have more global or business exposure than today's ministers, most of whom worked in the public sector before entering politics.

The intellectual and achievement gap between the ruler and the ruled has narrowed. Meanwhile, news and images of frequent train delays, lift malfunctions, decaying trees and bursting water pipes, widely shared on social media, all add to a sense that government agencies are falling short even on maintenance matters. If performance forms the bedrock of a trusting people-government relationship, alas, in some people's minds, even that is faulty.

Worse, when things go wrong, so the whispers go, blame is pushed down to the lower rungs.

Both Keppel Corp and SMRT have been in the news for what appear to be systemic issues. A Keppel subsidiary was fined by the US authorities for giving bribes in Brazil. The corruption trail lasted 14 years, from 2001 to 2014.

In SMRT, pumps were not maintained; worse, maintenance reports were falsified for over a year. These were discovered only after MRT tunnels were flooded last October when a pump failed to work.

In both organisations, those involved in the wrongdoing or their superiors faced disciplinary action, were dismissed, or are being charged or investigated. These are perfectly reasonable courses of action to take. But it says something of the corrosive climate of distrust that in some quarters, the grumble on the ground is that the penalties stop short of those at the top.

If such invidious views gain credence and become widespread, Singapore will be in serious trouble. The trust deficit can bankrupt the reservoir of goodwill between people and government.

The chorus of critics seems to be getting louder, and even erstwhile members of the political elite appear to be chiming in.

One sobering recent analysis came from former PAP MP Goh Choon Kang. In a commentary in Chinese daily Lianhe Zaobao, translated and reprinted in The Straits Times on Dec 13, he wrote about the loss of trust between the elite and the masses. He was referring mainly to Western societies, not Singapore.

But he did warn against Singapore going the way of those Western democracies, where the elite had turned their back on the masses: "They lose touch with the masses even though they are in leading positions. They feel that their achievements today are based solely on their own capabilities and talent within the meritocracy implemented by society. They bask in their own successes, sing their own praises and no longer have the slightest empathy for the people, with the political parties fighting for power but unable to understand and sympathise with the public feeling.

"The system becomes such that it is your own problem if you cannot keep up with the times or are left behind. As a result, many pressing issues do not get proper attention. For example, jobs being outsourced or becoming short-term hired labour because of globalisation, job losses, workers facing job instability, wage stagnation, uneven distribution and a widening gap between the rich and the poor...

"Like mainstream political parties in other countries, the PAP may encounter issues of being too comfortable, of arrogance, slackness and losing touch with the grassroots because of its long-term rule, if it does not have sufficient awareness of potential problems or is unable to correct some possible problems in time."

Mr Goh's warning should be heeded.

Trust is a valuable commodity. It takes two to trust. A government that asks its people to trust it more, must be deserving of that trust. Trust is not a natural legacy a new generation inherits from its elders. As Mr Chan said, it has to be earned and maintained by each generation.

If some segments feel that trust has been eroded, the Government has to first acknowledge that, before it can seek to restore and enhance it.

I think the political elite has to start addressing the reality: Trust has been chipped away in some quarters, although hopefully it is not pervasive or deep-seated, and can be repaired.

There are some encouraging signs that people-government relations can be put on a stronger footing.

First, the apathetic citizen is no more. Many Singaporeans who grew up on a diet of online news and discussion are politically engaged and interested. More are forming interest groups organically to reach out to others or help the less privileged. Many are involved in activist groups. Discussion on alternative routes for Singapore – in the social, political or economic realm – is robust and lively. All that is needed is for government leaders to open their doors and minds and engage with these active citizens. For a start, begin a serious, honest conversation about trust.

Second, this period of leadership transition, when the so-called fourth generation of leaders (4G) steps up, is a time of opportunity for a new generation of leaders to forge a new kind of bond with citizens.

The group of 4G leaders – who signed a statement saying they will decide on a leader among themselves in good time – is made up largely of those born after independence. They are more in tune with the mood of today's citizens.

They should step up more, articulate their vision of Singapore, and explain to Singaporeans just what they stand for. Apart from continuing with the usual narrative about the need for exceptional leaders, they could be telling a more nuanced story about the need for engaged citizens and how we can all work together for a better Singapore.

A government that trusts, empowers and consults citizens, making them feel respected and co-creators of the country's future, may be the best antidote to vocal critics and the cynics.

THE WORLD OF SPY FICTION BECOMES REALITY

News of Chinese operations to influence policy in Australia reminds us that espionage is real

11 June 2017

I grew up reading thrillers, especially espionage fiction in which brave men with troubled pasts (they usually had troubled pasts) went into target countries to carry out their duties – which might be to assassinate someone, recruit or rescue someone, plant or retrieve something, or just disrupt the smooth flow of a society.

John le Carre, Jack Higgins, Robert Ludlum, Len Deighton and Frederick Forsyth were constant companions. I even wrote my undergraduate thesis on le Carre's novels.

I thought being a spy would be an exciting profession. But I became a journalist – and realised I'd make a very bad spy because I'm too upfront. I find it hard to dissemble and hate to lie; and I like to share what I know with people, not use it to manipulate them.

But, of course, the world of espionage, intelligence and counter-intelligence is far more complex than fiction, and it strikes societies in many more guises.

These days, I sometimes feel that the fictional world of espionage has leapt from the pages of novels into real life.

There's news of Russian actors, possibly state-backed, meddling in the United States presidential election last year via cyber attacks, releasing sensitive information at opportune times, or outright creating false information to be disseminated to sway votes.

Those reports triggered fears across Europe this year that similar attempts might be made to influence the French, British and German elections.

Last week, a five-month-long investigation by Australia's leading media companies, Australian Broadcasting Corporation (ABC) and Fairfax Media, concluded that the Chinese Communist Party (CCP) was secretly infiltrating Australian domestic politics and society to influence policy and opinion.

Business leaders allied to Beijing are said to use donations to major political parties in Australia to gain access and influence, even tying donations to pro-China policies that may be against Australia's national interest.

My colleague in Australia, Jonathan Pearlman, reported that one of the individuals named in the report is a Chinese developer called Mr Huang Xiangmo. He wrote: "Mr Huang allegedly threatened to withdraw a A$400,000 donation to Labor last year over the party's call for Australia to conduct a freedom of navigation patrol near disputed parts of the South China Sea.

"A Labor MP and power broker, Mr Sam Dastyari, appeared with Mr Huang the next day and softened Labor's position – but the MP denied he knew about the donation. He resigned from Labor's frontbench soon after over the foreign donations scandal."

Last year, the Australian media landscape was rocked by reports that even stalwart dailies such as The Sydney Morning Herald (SMH), The Age and Australian Financial Review were accepting multi-page pull-out supplements prepared by the CCP's official English-language China Daily. These advertorials carry the Chinese government's point of view, straight into Australian homes.

SMH's correspondent Philip Wen, reporting on this trend last May, said: "Individually, the deals offer compelling commercial opportunities. But, viewed collectively, they underline the coordinated nature in which China's propaganda arms are seeking to influence how the Communist

Party is portrayed overseas – the potential pitfalls of which were highlighted when the Australian Broadcasting Corporation was caught self-censoring news reports on its Australia Plus website."

As you sip your coffee this morning in bucolic Singapore, you might wonder: What's this all got to do with us?

My answer is: Everything.

What is happening elsewhere can happen in Singapore too. Just as the country is a terrorist target, it is also a target for whatever espionage or "black operation" a foreign power might mount.

Singapore is tiny, but influential. It is also at the heart of the cross-flows of finance, shipping routes, information, trade, commerce and air links. It is a fulcrum in South-east Asia, theatre of what is probably the No. 2 geopolitical hot spot (after North Korea).

Singaporeans may just want to get on with their lives, but likely won't be allowed to as long as there are bigger players that want to influence them.

I think a hard-headed look at the changing world we live in today will reveal the truth that the world is not a benign place for a small, rich country.

We are in a an era marked by divisions. Even as Singapore works with others to build up cooperative institutions, it must live as though its future depends on itself alone.

This is why, while I chafe at some of the moves, I understand completely why the Singapore Government has made certain decisions in recent months that appear to take Singapore backwards.

For example, the move to delink government computers from the Internet looked excessive when The Straits Times first reported on it last year. Today, in the wake of a few pervasive cyber attacks, some possibly state-sponsored, it begins to look less extreme and may one day appear forward-thinking.

Then there was the decision to ban foreign sponsors of the Pink Dot event that supports LGBT (lesbian, gay, bisexual, transgender) issues. When news of that ban broke, many people, including myself, assumed that the move was meant to hobble the Pink Dot rally by starving it of funds. But local sponsors stepped up and the event will go on as scheduled, on July 1.

Then came more reports that actually, foreigners aren't even allowed to take part in Speakers' Corner events – which meant they can't even go to the Pink Dot event.

Again, like many others, I thought this was a move by the moral police to try to curb the spread of Pink Dot's pro-gay message. But more reading around the issue made it clear that the locals-only rules apply to all Speakers' Corner events, not just Pink Dot. These rules specify that only Singapore entities, and Singaporeans and permanent residents, are permitted to sponsor, protest or participate at such events. Foreigners can do so with a permit.

So if the move wasn't targeted at Pink Dot, what was the target?

Why keep foreigners out of Speakers' Corner?

It sounds retrograde, especially for such an open society like Singapore that is told to welcome foreign workers and appoints any number of international advisory panels to guide its research and economic policies.

The move, however, makes more sense when you consider it against the backdrop I painted earlier in this article: a world of espionage, where states use their soft, hard and financial power to influence events and shape policy to their own advantage; where others will work against your national interest, operating often unseen, via a word here, a cheque there, nudges everywhere.

Singapore has long been suspicious of foreign funding that goes to its domestic politics and media and has taken stern action against any such "black operations". In the 1970s, the Government closed down the Eastern Sun newspaper, an English daily, after disclosing that its proprietor had received loans made by Chinese communist agents in

Hong Kong. Another paper, the Singapore Herald, was also shut down over "black operations" charges of receiving questionably-sourced foreign funds. Foreign donations to political parties, candidates and associations are curtailed.

In Australia, a foreign donor conditions political donations on foreign policy. Last week's ABC-Fairfax report also said China was funding Chinese students in Australia who took part in pro-China protests and activities, and intimidating those who took part in pro-democracy activities.

It is not too far-fetched to imagine a dubious foreign organisation funding a Speakers' Corner event or protest to foment discord on an issue for its own ends.

It is, of course, possible that my view of the world, which is subjective, is out of sync with reality.

If so, then consider this a mental exercise that skirts close to fiction.

But, as a literature student, a good Singaporean brought up on a diet of the survivalist narrative, and a battle-scarred woman who has lived through poverty, cancer and failures, I also know that truth can often be stranger than fiction.

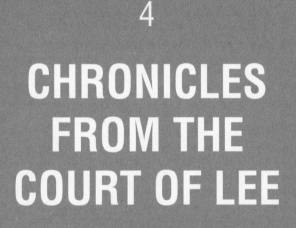

4

CHRONICLES FROM THE COURT OF LEE

Journalists, they say, dine with kings. In the Republic of Singapore, the closest one gets to a royal family is that of the Lee family. I did not dine with kings – but I did get to dine with Mr and Mrs Lee Kuan Yew at the Istana poolside, as part of a media team that worked with him on his memoirs. By some quirk of fate – or the decisions of various editors – I also had the chance to interview or observe the Lee family on various occasions in my career.

Lee Kuan Yew was Singapore's founding prime minister who stamped his personal and political style on a nation. Famously austere and frugal, he begat a city in his own image – sans spitting, sans neon signs, sans gambling, sans frivolity and chaos. At least, he tried, turning a rambunctious colonial-era Singapore into a disciplined, tidy city-state that topped economic charts but that was routinely criticised for being boring. He stepped down as Prime Minister in 1990, handing the reins to Mr Goh Chok Tong.

I joined The Straits Times in 1991, just after Mr Goh became PM. Some of my older colleagues confessed how hard it was for them to call Mr Goh PM, so used were they to calling only Mr Lee Kuan Yew by that title. PM Goh handed over the premiership in 2004 to Mr Lee Hsien Loong – the eldest son of Mr Lee Kuan Yew – who had been in politics since 1984. When Lee Jr became PM, he told some journalists he preferred to be addressed as plain Mr Lee, presumably out of discomfort at inheriting his father's title. I was then a fairly seasoned political journalist. I remember laughing and telling him everyone would soon call him PM Lee and he had better get used to it.

When Mr Lee Hsien Loong was still Deputy Prime Minister in 2003, I had a long, one-on-one interview with him. Here was a young man – who had grown up in the public eye, who had acquired a bit of a reputation for being a hardliner when it came to policy and who had survived a bout of cancer – who was about to become PM. Singaporeans deserved to know him better. My editors gave me that task, to try to get behind the public persona of Mr Lee Hsien Loong to the private man.

On the allotted day, there were three people in the room – his then-press secretary, a very amiable young man; Mr Lee; and myself. The press secretary later commented that his boss was unusually relaxed throughout the interview. I had sent over questions in advance; and true to his promise, no questions were off limits. I grilled him about being his father's son; whether he would keep his father in Cabinet when he became PM; whether he would be able to ask his own father to step down if he ever assessed the elder Lee was becoming a liability. I also asked him about his wife Ho Ching, who headed Temasek Holdings, and the awkwardness of him being Finance Minister at that time, overseeing a government-linked company headed by his own wife.

It wasn't all politics. I asked about his difficult moments. When he spoke about his first wife who had died after a difficult childbirth, he teared. In some private exchanges – I think before the interview started – we exchanged notes on two common experiences. I had been diagnosed with cancer over a year ago and had completed treatment and returned to work when I did the interview. We swopped notes on chemotherapy. I had just returned from a Master in Public Administration programme at Harvard, where he had been years before. I told him one of his professors still "boasted" about his star student at lectures.

I spent some time around 2003 and 2004 working on a series of features on Mr Lee. For one profile article, I sought out his friends, former classmates and former army mates. For two straight weeks, I ate, lived and breathed Lee Hsien Loong. My bosses also wanted personal family photos, and Mr Lee agreed to a photo shoot with his wife and "whichever children are available". So one Sunday morning, I went to Changi Point with the photographer. I remember the two younger boys Hongyi and Haoyi turning up, rather reluctantly, posing with their parents for photos and grumbling audibly – glancing in my direction – about how "fake" the session felt. I remember thinking they were rather likeable typical teenagers.

Several years later, I was part of a team of Straits Times journalists who spent months interviewing Mr Lee Kuan Yew for a series of books. The team was led by then-Straits Times editor Han Fook Kwang.

Unlike his son, the elder Mr Lee was an interviewee harder to build rapport with. I was always grateful not to have a one-on-one interview with him. As a team of journalists, there was strength in numbers. I was always relieved that Fook Kwang sat opposite him across a table, directly in the line of fire. My boss had a way of speaking to Mr Lee in a measured, even tone; facing him calmly as the elder man fired his testy responses, drew sharp intakes of breath or glared around the table. Over the years, as we trooped in and out of Istana doing these interviews, Mr Lee moved in my mind from being a distant figure to becoming a person, and then, as he grew frail, he became just an elderly man struggling with ill health. Somewhere along the line, as I wrote in my essay "He Changed My Life: My Father and Our Founding Father", I grew fond of the old man.

I've always tried to find common ground, and build rapport with people I interview. Rapport smoothens exchanges; it can also disarm, and the journalist in me understands that an interviewee who feels at ease is more likely to loosen his or her tongue. But when an interview is under way, I am on the trail – seeking information, looking out for inconsistencies or openings, clarifying, probing, questioning. People may parry or push back; I back off, circle, try again.

When interviewing powerful people, I try to remember that I am there as a member of the media. I am not just representing myself; I come imbued with the power of the readers of my newspaper – all one million or more of them. When I grill ministers on policies, it is not just I who ask, but Every Citizen affected. Unlike most citizens, I have access to the people who make policy decisions. Access is a privilege that comes with responsibility. A journalist's responsibility is to represent the interests of readers in an interview, in press conferences, in the articles he or she writes.

A journalist is first and foremost, a witness – a witness to history in the making as events unfold; a witness to the lives of the poor and the powerful as we see them; a witness, if we are given the access, even to the birth and death of life.

I think because I write both from the head and the heart, I have been called on too many times to cover funerals of prominent state figures, including former Chief Minister David Marshall in 1995; former President Wee Kim Wee in 2005; and former Deputy Prime Minister S. Rajaratnam and former minister Lim Kim San in 2006. I was also one of the few reporters given access to the private family funeral for both Mr Lee Kuan Yew, who died in 2015, and that of his wife Madam Kwa Geok Choo, who died earlier, in 2010.

It was a surreal feeling being witness to the family farewell for Mr Lee at the Mandai crematorium. The week of mourning had heightened emotions. After the lying-in-state and the remarkable outpouring of grief and respect for the late Mr Lee, it was time for the family's final farewell as his body was moved to Mandai for cremation.

A television crew and a handful of reporters were allowed to watch the event. As the funeral procession rolled up at the Mandai viewing hall, with family members and friends streaming in to fill the seats, I felt my presence like an intrusion. I had been told that the photographers and videographers could beam images out after the event was over but the reporters were not to write a report about it. I grumbled to myself that in that case, any rookie reporter could have been assigned that watching brief, not a middle-aged one feeling hungry and grouchy. But since I was already present, I managed to persuade officials to ease the rule, promising to write just a simple report on the funeral. I understood they feared histrionics or over-sentimentality. When I got back to my office, I wrote up a straightforward report of the event, quoted from some of the eulogies, and filed the story. It was posted on The Straits Times website and shared on our Facebook page shortly after.

I then began work on the report for the next day's print edition of The Straits Times and finished about an hour later. I decided to check on my online story and clicked to look at it. I discovered to my shock that it had already been shared over 100,000 times on Facebook. In that moment, the uncomfortable hour or so I had spent at the Mandai crematorium became worthwhile. Singaporeans grieving the loss of Mr Lee Kuan Yew were hungry for information, news and insights into all aspects of the mourning of this great man. And mine was the only report of that private family farewell that evening. That night, I felt afresh both the privilege and the burden of being a journalist and a witness.

Mr Lee's death has a definite *fin de siècle* feel to it – the sense of a distinct ending of an era. In the months after, many articles would hark back to the days when he was alive. Mr Lee would have done things differently; would have cleaned things up; would have put a stop to all this nonsense, many people felt, said, and wrote.

The clearest, sharpest, saddest reminder that Mr Lee was no more came when the Lee children had a public quarrel on Facebook and social media over what to do with the family home at Oxley Road. The younger siblings – Wei Ling and Hsien Yang – accused their elder brother PM Lee of going against their father's wishes to have the house demolished, saying he wanted to preserve it for his own political ends.

When the spat broke out, a few of my close friends and family members advised me not to weigh in on the issue. Public sentiments were riding high on the matter, and the family members were highly emotional. When powerful people fight within a family, wise bystanders stay neutral and on the sidelines, hoping things will cool down. So when my boss asked me to consider writing a commentary on it, I hesitated. But once again, I felt that responsibility – or is it just hubris? – of being a journalist with some access, and of being a witness to power. Like many Singaporeans, I felt that the public spat would have grieved their father. Unlike most Singaporeans, I had met and spent hours with Mr Lee. I was part of the interview panel that had asked him about his plans for the house.

So I told my boss I would try to write something on the Lee family feud over the house. I finished the article barely two hours later. It had all been simmering in me, waiting for an outlet. The article was a heartfelt plea to honour their father's memory and spare the nation's feelings by taking their feud private.

Singapore, Disrupted is the theme of this book. The death of Mr Lee and the unfortunate public family feud that erupted shortly after was certainly an event that threw the country into disruption mode. It was jarring and unsettling to see public, respected figures fight so bitterly over family issues. Accusations of dynastic ambitions and abuse of power were hurled. Among the chattering classes, much energy was spent dissecting the statements of the siblings and speculating on their intentions. It got so toxic that the third generation of Lees had to speak up. The sons of the two Mr Lees were forced to answer the charges of dynastic ambitions.

PM Lee's son Li Hongyi said: "For what it is worth, I really have no interest in politics." Mr Li Shengwu, the elder son of Mr Lee Hsien Yang, went further: "Not only do I intend never to go into politics, I believe that it would be bad for Singapore if any third-generation Lee went into politics. The country must be bigger than one family."

As a political journalist given rare access to two generations of Lees, I know it is time for me, too, to move on. Singapore's future will be written by a new generation of leaders – and recorded by a new generation of journalists. It is my hope that future journalist colleagues will take seriously their duty as witnesses and to chronicle, and critique or champion as they see fit, the doings of a new (political) court.

PRIVATE SIDE OF DPM LEE

19 October 2003

To understand Deputy Prime Minister Lee Hsien Loong's private side, look no further than his desk at work.

It's strewn with files and paper. Unlike his father, Senior Minister Lee Kuan Yew, who is pristinely tidy, the son is more forgiving of clutter. Several photos of his family sit in a corner by the telephone, testimony to the importance that family holds for him. Prominent among them is one of his first wife, Wang Ming Yang.

She died in 1982, aged 31, leaving behind their 19-month-old daughter Xiuqi and three-week-old son Yi Peng.

But recalling her even now, his eyes grow red and brim with unshed tears.

What were the darkest moments in his life?

"My first wife Ming Yang died, it was... you know, my whole world fell apart. But life went on. I coped with help from parents and also my mother-in-law who stayed with me and helped to bring up the children."

Does he still think about her, talk to his children about her?

"Yes, from time to time."

What does he tell them?

"It's a long time ago," says Mr Lee. His voice softens. He pauses and blinks back tears.

His mind no doubt went back to their 4½ years of marriage and the times they shared.

His eulogy at her funeral 21 years ago: "She was my wife, lover, companion and confidante. She loved me, cherished me, honoured me, comforted me... I tried to do the same for her. Now death has parted us. We shall all have to learn to live without her."

It's a brief moment in the 90-minute interview when DPM Lee was moved to tears, but it gives a glimpse of the private man behind the public figure.

Here is a man of deep emotion and strong attachments, who's not afraid to show his feelings. He's as game talking candidly about past tragedies and failures in his life as taking on sensitive questions about the Lee family's involvement in politics.

So from losing his first wife, he talks about his fight with cancer in 1992, when he was diagnosed with lymphoma. "It was quite frightening but a less dark moment. The family helped to carry me through again. These things happen to everybody."

Cancer has given him a sense of equanimity.

He says: "You accept your limits better. You accept that there are some things you can't predict or control that may happen to you. You accept it as it comes and carry on from there. And also you accept other people as they are."

It also reminded him to maintain a sustainable pace of work.

His day begins at about 7am, when he checks e-mails and reads The Straits Times and other papers online. Then he limbers up and stretches, breakfasts, and works out for about 45 minutes at home, before having a shower and heading off to work. If he has no morning functions, he is in the office at the Finance Ministry at around 11am.

At work, his swift response to e-mails is legendary in the civil service. He's known for being an early adopter of technology. For example, he tried wireless networking in his home but gave it up, and was one of the ministers who tested the Blackberry wireless e-mail system earlier this year.

He's home for dinner around 7pm if there are no evening engagements.

Then it's "homework" time: more e-mails, or reading up on papers for the following day, or drafting or editing papers or speeches. He works on major speeches in the evening, away from the bustle of day-to-day decision-making.

He says: "Physically I try not to go over the limits so I usually try and have a short break in the afternoon and rest and calm down for an hour, if I can."

It has been 11 years since the cancer, and he's put it behind him. But is his physical stamina up to being Prime Minister, as he is expected to become some time next year?

"The cancer hasn't affected my physical stamina. As you grow older, of course you notice that you don't bounce back quite as quickly as you used to but I am sure I will manage."

He usually does – manage, that is. Those who have known him over the years say he is technically brilliant: as an army officer, a policymaker or a student.

Mr Choo Thiam Siew, president of the Nanyang Academy of Fine Arts, was his classmate at Catholic High School for several years. He remembers that the young Hsien Loong was fluent in English, Chinese and Malay, excelled in Mathematics and Physics, and mastered the clarinet in two years to perform the Mozart clarinet concerto while fellow band members struggled with simple brass band tunes.

One public success was in 1983, when Mr Lee directed the rescue of 13 people trapped in cable cars after seven people fell to their deaths when a cable snapped. Mr Boey Tak Hap, who served with him in the army, notes that DPM Lee was then 31, with just eight years' experience in the armed forces.

So has he ever failed at anything he did?

DPM Lee recalls a band competition in school, when he was drum major. "We had worked out the drill and the routine and so on. We went there and the whole thing fell to bits. Somebody was in the wrong place and the whole formation ended up in a shambles all over the basketball court." The team did not win and as drum major, he felt responsible.

On policies, he reckons that some could have been done differently with the benefit of hindsight. For example, banking reforms could have been introduced earlier. Perhaps the use of Central Provident Fund savings for property was over-liberalised. "But as I was when I was at that point, I did what I thought was the right thing to do."

With a keen eye for details, he is known for refining policy proposals down to the nitty-gritty.

Mr Goh Yeow Tin, secretary of the People's Action Party branch in Teck Ghee, recalls showing Mr Lee a quote for a computer system for the branch that amounted to $18,000. Several weeks later, the branch officials submitted the final invoice for $16,000, as they had whittled down the sum. DPM Lee noticed the difference right away. Mr Goh says: "We didn't want to bother him with small details but he remembers!"

His grassroots leaders say he is approachable and they are clueless about why some people perceive him as tough and uncompromising. "He mixes freely with us, no airs," says Mr Loh Bak Song, a grassroots leader.

"A good listener," adds Mr T. Krishnan, another veteran grassroots leader. He says that DPM Lee invites grassroots volunteers to his home in the Tanglin area every Chinese New Year for a tea reception.

Friends say he has a warm, caring side.

Architect Joey Yeo, 48, who served in the same battalion as DPM Lee in 1981, recalls: "When my son was born in 1988, the Year of the Dragon, I remember sharing the good news with him.

"He was in his constituency office, which has a calligraphy of the Chinese word 'Dragon', which is what the name Loong means, as he's also born in the Year of the Dragon. He congratulated me and wanted to take down the scroll and give it to me! I didn't accept, I was too embarrassed. But it just shows what a warm, spontaneous person he is."

Mr Boey, who used to be Singapore Power CEO and Chief of Army, says: "Some time around 1985, he called me one day and asked if I wanted to join him at a 'crabbing party' in Sentosa.

"On the day, we assembled at Sentosa ferry terminal. I thought a launch would have been arranged to bring us across. But no. He queued at the ticket counter like everybody else, and bought tickets for all of us. There were three or four families. And there he was with Ho Ching.

"We all spent the day at the beach and then had a seafood dinner. We never did catch crabs, although I think we did have it for dinner.

"That was the first time we realised he and Ho Ching were courting! And that was his way of introducing her to us."

DPM Lee married Madam Ho Ching, an engineer who is now executive director of Temasek Holdings, in 1985. They have two boys, Hongyi, 16, and Haoyi, 14.

All those interviewed highlight one thing about him: He always makes time for those who need him.

Mr Yeo tells this story: Last year, his daughter was accepted by several universities. He e-mailed DPM Lee for advice as to which one she should go to, as DPM Lee had been to Cambridge and Harvard and his wife went to Stanford. He expected an e-mail reply or perhaps a phone call.

Instead, DPM Lee and his wife asked Mr and Mrs Yeo out to lunch at Halia restaurant in the Botanic Gardens and discussed the pros and cons of the universities over two hours. Mr Yeo's daughter is now in Harvard.

In his down time, DPM Lee likes listening to music – including composers Beethoven, Brahms, Bach and Mozart. He enjoyed a recent concert at the Esplanade which featured pianist-conductor Vladimir Ashkenazy and local violinist Lee Huei Min.

He catches up with reading books when on vacation, as keeping up with newspapers and periodicals takes up most of his reading time during work weeks.

Unlike his father, who is impatient with what-ifs, the younger DPM

Lee has a philosophical bent. Some days, he wonders how his life would have turned out if he had chosen to be a mathematician, as his tutors in Cambridge University had suggested.

"Once in a while, I go and browse all these maths websites on the Internet. You can't keep abreast of the subject, but you can be sort of a voyeur, reading about what's happening."

He adds: "I think I'll have had quite an enjoyable time and an interesting career... But where does that lead? What difference would I have made?"

His idea of a life well-lived is this: "You have done what you wanted to do and you have made a difference to other people's lives. You can do a lot of things on your own and be satisfied but if you just do it for yourself, well, then it's not quite complete."

THIS IS NOT A FAMILY SHOW

Transcript of interview with Lee Hsien Loong

12 October 2003

Q   What role do you see Prime Minister Goh Chok Tong playing in your Cabinet?

A   I think he will be a very valuable member, for his experience and advice, his feel of the ground and his rapport with the people. I will want to make the most of all that, and also of course his international experience dealing with many leaders in the region and around the world.

Q   So you are likely to want him to remain in Cabinet...

A   Of course, yes.

Q   ...as a senior minister?

A   Well, titles we will think about later on.

Q   And how about the Senior Minister?

A   Well, I hope he will stay on and play the same role he's playing now. He describes it as being a mascot. I think it's a little bit more than a mascot.

He's somebody who's keeping an eye on things from the corner. It's like that picture in the birthday book of quotes where the PM, DPMs and ministers of state were lined up taking photographs and there the SM was, sitting in the corner watching us.

That's the position. We are running the ship, but he keeps an eye on it and if he feels strongly about something, he'll surely let us know and we will consider very carefully his views and then decide what we need to do.

We have to set the direction, steer the ship and manage it. We have to set the agenda because the SM can't do it: He's advising us.

If he were to set the agenda, he would have to go round and make the speeches and do the grassroots dialogues and campaign in the constituencies, at National Day dinners, and so on. It can't be done.

Q But there's a perception that even though Senior Minister is not in the forefront of explaining policies, that he's actually still the main person deciding on the policies and that his influence in the Cabinet may be unduly large.

A I don't think it could work like that. If that were the situation, the present PM would find it very uncomfortable, and the ministers too, because you have to work with the boss, and the boss has to be the PM. How can the centre forward not be taking the lead? You are in the middle of a play and all of a sudden, you're looking to someone else for instructions. You're going to fumble. It doesn't work like that.

On most matters, we just decide. Sometimes, the SM expresses his views, but often we just settle the matter because we've got to carry it.

On very major issues, he will take more interest and sometimes he will have strong views.

Far from holding us back, often he's pushing us to go even further than we are ready to do, because we have to do the selling. He says, 'Let's do the right thing.' We have to say, 'Just a moment, we are not quite ready yet. You're right but let's take it one step at a time and we will get through it in our way.'

Q Do you think it will be awkward to have two former prime ministers sort of looking over your shoulders in Cabinet?

A I think it's quite reassuring in some ways because you have somebody watching you and if they feel strongly, you listen to them. If they say it's okay, that gives you confidence that different minds have been brought to bear and have confirmed your conclusion and judgment.

Q But will you be able to be the boss in your Cabinet with Senior Minister there?

A   Well, as I've said, the Senior Minister's role in the last 10 years has increasingly been to be an adviser and a consultant. I think that is a good relationship. If he is really chief executive without title, like Deng Xiaoping was at one time, then that becomes much more difficult.

Q   What will you do to ensure that the expectations of the Confucian idea of a father-son relationship will not impede your decision-making process and your Cabinet decisions?

A   Decisions are made in Cabinet, not individually. It's a collective responsibility and all the ministers state their views. Some views of course carry more weight than others. And the Cabinet has to discuss these things and decide.

It is not something you can discuss and settle at home and then just inform the other ministers! If that were the way things worked, we would have a totally different Cabinet and a totally different Singapore – and I wouldn't be here answering your questions, I'd have to go and consult on what answers to give you!

Q   But there is a perception nevertheless that some decisions may be made at Lee family councils.

A   No, it cannot be done. Just look at the quality of the people in our team. If you operate in this hole-in-a-corner way, you are not going to get good people to work for you. Are they people of substance? Or are they just your lackeys and stooges who will say three bags full, aye aye sir, and do whatever you instruct them?

We have gone out of our way to find people who have ability, who have standing of their own, who command support and respect, in order to form a strong team whose members have different views from one another, so that we will have diversity and can take a rounded approach to problems. I think we have achieved that.

If this were a family show, you are not going to get people like PM Goh or Tony Tan or S. Jayakumar or Wong Kan Seng or Teo Chee Hean in the team, and you're not going to get new people like Tharman Shanmugaratnam or Khaw Boon Wan or the others joining us. Why should they?

Ministers consulted too

Q   At the same time, it will be quite natural if you were making an important decision and it was weighing very much on your mind, to want to discuss it with those close to you. In a sense, how do you compartmentalise, how do you draw a distinction between matters that are public and matters that are private?

A   Yes, the ministers discuss. We meet formally in Cabinet but we also talk informally to each other and sometimes we talk in smaller groups.

The Prime Minister has what he calls the Political Group or PG, which is the inner group of ministers whom he consults more frequently on sensitive matters. And we have informal contacts.

But it is quite clear that we are discussing matters as ministers responsible for Singapore and not doing family business.

Don't believe all polls

Q   There was a recent Yahoo! poll asking people whether they thought SM should retire from politics, and the majority thought it would be better for Singapore if he did. Do you have a response to that and would you be able to ask the Senior Minister to retire?

A   First of all, I don't believe the Yahoo! poll. If you ask Singaporeans whether they would like SM to retire, I'm quite sure you will have an overwhelming majority saying no. The people who answered Yahoo! polls do not represent Singaporeans.

Secondly, I don't think being able to ask the SM to retire is a problem. As long as he has that edge, few can make the kind of contribution to Cabinet deliberations that he can because of his depth of experience. When he loses that sharp edge, many besides ministers will notice it. I do not see him remaining as a passenger Senior Minister.

The core issue is to be able to get the full benefit of his advice, and for the PM and the Cabinet to take the decision with inputs from the whole Cabinet. And that's been the practice the SM had established when he was PM.

On thorny issues, the whole Cabinet, including SM, thrashes out differing views until finally the PM decides what is the majority view and takes his decision. Thereafter, all ministers must support that decision.

Q   But if there comes a day when you assess that the Senior Minister may be more of a liability than an asset, would you be able to ask him to retire?

A   I would have to do that. That would be my job.

I think that's a very hypothetical question. It's not the real problem. The main issue is, how to manage and tap the Senior Minister's experience and get the maximum contribution from him as long as we can.

Q   May we move on to Madam Ho Ching and whether she will continue as executive director of Temasek?

A   Well, that's up to her boss and the board of Temasek Holdings. Mr S. Dhanabalan is the chairman. Dhanabalan asked her, and had her appointed as the executive director. If he's happy with her, then it continues. If he's not happy or uncomfortable, then it has to stop. But I don't see any reason why my changing jobs should cause her to change jobs.

Q   On the other hand, when she was appointed, Mr Dhanabalan and the Prime Minister both said you had felt uncomfortable about it.

A   Dhanabalan's proposal was to make her the CEO. I wasn't keen to have her directly reporting to me as the Minister for Finance, or reporting to what we call the GLCs [government-linked company] and Competition Policy Committee, which I chaired even before I went to the Finance Ministry.

It's not a conflict of interest problem but it's a problem of one spouse reporting directly to the other. Many organisations try to avoid that because other staff do not feel comfortable and it upsets their working relationships.

But Dhanabalan said he would take responsibility. He's overseeing Temasek and spending a lot of time in Temasek now. He's supposedly in retirement but we dragged him back. Ho Ching works for him, and as long as he's happy, I think the arrangement can stand. If he's not happy, then we have to change it.

Overrule wife? Sure

Q   Do you foresee a day when as Prime Minister with oversight of
sensitive Temasek decisions like investments or appointments
that you may have to overrule or evaluate decisions made by
Madam Ho?

A   Yes, of course. Even now, every time Temasek puts up a proposal,
the Ministry of Finance has to study it and decide or make its
recommendation to me as minister. And often, the ministry
doesn't agree or has a different perspective.

Q   There's no problem, there's no position where there's any
awkwardness?

A   The Ministry of Finance staff have to be quite comfortable,
otherwise we have a big problem. They know that I take their
inputs seriously. Temasek puts up submissions, the ministry staff
have to give their views and if there is a disagreement, the matter
has to be argued out.
    It doesn't mean I always side with the ministry staff against
Temasek, but all positions have to be canvassed. If I always
automatically side with the ministry, that's not right either.

Q   And it's your assessment that they are quite comfortable?

A   I think they have become comfortable. In the beginning, I could
sense that they acted a bit gingerly. But they now know that when
they put up a recommendation, I take them seriously and decide
it on the merits of the issue.
    In fact, sometimes the ministry staff put up proposals arguing
for a certain course of action, and I say, no, I disagree with this.
And they want to rewrite the paper to argue for my conclusion
instead. I say, no, you keep the paper and put on my decision
paragraph on top of that, then we all know where each of us
stands. Otherwise, all the papers reflect my views, and all the
papers get approved, and it's very odd.

Q But is there a potential image problem caused by Madam Ho Ching in Temasek, and could that image problem override the benefits of having her in that job?

A Image problem with whom?

Q Maybe some Singaporeans, increasingly external analysts and commentators.

A It cannot be more awkward than when SM was Prime Minister and I was the minister in the Ministry of Trade and Industry. A Temasek director isn't even in the Cabinet. Temasek is supervising the GLCs and reporting to the Ministry of Finance.

Q What does it say though about Singapore's talent pool if the person most suitable to head Temasek Holdings is the wife of the Prime Minister? Would you have been more comfortable if someone else had been found suitable?

A It would be much easier for her and for me if she had a happy career somewhere else and somebody else is running Temasek and all is working fine. But this is Singapore.

  You asked what it says for talent. Well, we are a society where the jobs have grown in scope and complexity, and the talent pool hasn't expanded as quickly as the jobs.

  It's not unique to us. If you look at Switzerland, which is twice our size – gross domestic product as well as population – or Australia, which is four times our size, they have the same problem.

  If you look at their boards and their key people, the elite is always a small group and you always find the same persons wearing multiple hats sitting on different boards, doing different public service duties. We feel this more acutely than them but it's basically the same problem.

Q There is a view that there could be an over-concentration of power if you're Prime Minister and Senior Minister remains in Cabinet and Madam Ho is at Temasek Holdings. What's your response to that?

A   I would say if the Senior Minister were not in the Cabinet, it wouldn't make the slightest difference to that perception.

Q   It's a perception that will continue regardless.

A   Yes, because SM will be influential whether he's in or out of the Cabinet. In the Cabinet, we explicitly acknowledge that he has a role, it's well defined, it's transparent. He's advising as a minister.

If he were out of the Cabinet, then people will ask why are you talking to him? Or if you are not talking to him, they say why stop talking to him? So, I think it's better to have an explicit arrangement.

'IT'S OKAY TO ARGUE WITH THIS PA'

19 October 2003

Deputy Prime Minister Lee Hsien Loong does not believe in being the heavy-handed Chinese father.

"If we want to go out for a family dinner, we have to make appointments with everybody," he says with a laugh.

Indeed, arranging the family walk on Sunday was a challenge: The Sunday Times was told that DPM Lee and his wife would be at Changi – with "whichever children are available". In the end, only the two younger boys – Hongyi, 16, and Haoyi, 14, could make it. They are both at the Anglo-Chinese School (Independent).

Eldest daughter Xiuqi is now 22 and studying architecture at the National University of Singapore, while son Yipeng, 21, has finished his A levels and is taking a year out before deciding what to do next.

Mr Lee believes in giving them lots of room to grow: "These are minds in the process of growing up, so you have to treat them as people growing up rather than as little children to be nannied."

In fact, they give him grief over education policies. Pet peeves: the way subjects are taught, the volume of stuff which they have to memorise. "They say why don't you change it? What's the point of being a minister if you are not going to change things?"

He argues with them and explains that the system is improving. "But if that doesn't work, my final answer is that when they grow up, they can help to change it," he says with a laugh.

They also talk about current affairs and economics, and science and physics.

Family time at home is often spent around the computer centre, which Mr Lee manages and which is the heart of the LAN network in their home in the Tanglin area. The night before the interview, he spent an hour setting up Xiuqi's new Apple notebook.

Once or twice a year, the family takes a break and heads to Changi, unwinding at a seaside bungalow for a week or so and exploring Changi Village.

Mr Lee and wife Ho Ching are a very private couple and declined to answer questions about their relationship, although Madam Ho said in an interview last year that she liked him for being "humorous" and "kind".

Their courtship had been a whirlwind affair. At their wedding in December 1985, Mr Lee told this story: A friend, told of the impending marriage, had said "good", then "congratulations" and finally, after a pause, added: "So fast!"

At that reception at the Istana, Mr Lee had said: "We have each of us found a companion, a partner in life, someone with whom to make a fresh beginning along a new path together."

Last Sunday at Changi, they walked companionably together, sometimes with arm round each other, as the two boys clattered ahead deep in teenage conversation.

ONE LAST GOODBYE: LOVING WIFE, MOTHER, GRANDMA

Amid the grief and sadness, a celebration of an extraordinary life

7 October 2010

———

In the end, there was just a man who loved his wife till the end.

He walked to her casket and placed a single stalk of red rose, green leaves still on its stem, on her body.

He raised his 87-year-old body and walked half a step towards the head of the casket, supporting himself on the frame.

Then, he bent towards her and reached for her face with his right hand. He brought his hand back to his lips and planted a kiss on her forehead.

As though he could not bear to part, he did that again. And then he walked away, composed and unaided.

Minister Mentor Lee Kuan Yew gave his wife two final kisses as she lay peaceful in her casket at Mandai Crematorium. Madam Kwa Geok Choo – his beloved Choo – had died on Saturday, aged 89, after being bedridden for over two years as a result of a series of strokes.

His kiss was a private gesture of love, but will linger in the memories of those who witnessed it, as a public affirmation of the abiding love they shared.

Earlier, in his eulogy, he spoke of their years together, as starry-eyed lovers at Raffles College and Cambridge University. He spoke too of her support as he fought for independence, and through his many years as Prime Minister as he and his colleagues built a new nation.

He spoke of their public life together, reminding his audience of her role in helping to draft legal documents at pivotal moments in Singapore's history, and of her role as his confidante and adviser.

Of his private feelings at losing his wife, he would only say he would have been a different man without her, with a completely different life, adding at the end, with his head bowed: "I should find solace in her 89 years of her life well lived. But at this moment of the final parting, my heart is heavy with sorrow and grief."

After lying at Sri Temasek for two days, Mrs Lee's casket was borne on a gun carriage to Mandai Crematorium. Hundreds gathered outside the Istana gates to send her off.

Her casket travelled down roads bordering the Central Catchment and nature reserve areas, down Thomson Road past MacRitchie Reservoir where she went courting with her then-fiance more than 60 years ago, past the Lower Peirce Reservoir, down leafy Upper Thomson Road lined with the beautiful albizia, to her final stop at Mandai, a route apt for one who loved botany and enjoyed watching birds in the Istana grounds.

Thousands of Singaporeans and foreign dignitaries had gone to Sri Temasek, the official residence of the prime minister, to pay their respects over the last two days. The crowd included a stenographer she had encouraged to become a lawyer, and a butler's son she had encouraged to become a policeman. Others came to pay their respects to a woman they had never met, but whom they admired for her faithful support of her husband and for her quiet grace in public.

But yesterday's funeral service at Mandai Crematorium Hall 1 was private, a family affair with about 300 guests – colleagues, friends and relatives, as well as representatives from the People's Action Party and grassroots organisations, and the doctors, nurses and others who cared for Mrs Lee over the years.

Mr Lee Hsien Loong spoke not as Prime Minister but as the grieving elder son, clad in mourning garb of plain white T-shirt and black trousers, addressing the Minister Mentor as Papa for the first time in public.

After two days of standing for hours by his mother's casket to receive well-wishers, there were shadows under his eyes. However, his face lit up when he spoke of her hand-knitted sweaters, and his voice swelled with grief when he recalled how she had taken care of his two older children when their mother died.

On behalf of the family, he said: "Over these last few days, I, and my family, have been deeply touched by the outpouring of condolences and fond recollections of people from all walks of life. We stood receiving the visitors, all moved that so many had come."

She was a doting Mama, so attuned to her children's needs, she seemed to know just when daughter Wei Ling needed a toothbrush, or when youngest child Hsien Yang needed medical attention. The family's eulogies gave glimpses into life in the fiercely private Lee family. One highlight was Sunday lunches at Oxley Road with three, or even four, generations – with the grandchildren tending "to eat far too fast and play far too loudly", as grandson Shengwu put it.

Granddaughter Xiuqi, in a fond tribute, celebrated the zest for life her beloved Nai Nai (Chinese for granny) had, relating how she, in her last years, developed a fondness for dessert and ribbons. As Mrs Lee grew frail and her husband became more attentive to her every need, she "acquired the glow of a girl who knew she was adored".

What Mr Lee, a traditional Chinese gentleman in his restraint and composure had declined to reveal, his children and grandchildren chose to say for him, describing how he learnt to care for his wife after she became frail.

As Hsien Yang said, looking teary-eyed: "He adjusted his routine to accommodate her changing circumstances and physical condition. His abiding love, devotion and care must have been a great comfort to her, and an inspiration to Fern and me on how to manage a lifelong partnership, through good health and illness."

His wife Suet Fern, and PM Lee's wife Ho Ching, were present by their husbands' sides throughout the wake and funeral.

Historians will accord Mrs Lee Kuan Yew an illustrious place in Singapore history, for her pioneering legal career, her quiet contributions to constitutional draftsmanship and as the wife of Singapore's founding prime minister.

But in her final journey yesterday, she returned to the roles she most valued – that of wife, mother and grandmother. And listening to her family members' moving tributes, there is no doubt that she loved them all, and was much loved in return.

In the end, there was just a woman who stood by her husband over a lifetime and cared for her children and grandchildren. That woman was Madam Kwa Geok Choo.

MR LEE KUAN YEW'S FUNERAL: FROM PUBLIC MOURNING TO PRIVATE FAMILY FAREWELL AT MANDAI

29 March 2015

Mr Lee Kuan Yew's family said farewell to him on Sunday, March 29, evening, in an emotional ceremony at Mandai Crematorium.

The casket arrived at 6.10pm and was borne aloft to Hall 1. Daughter Lee Wei Ling placed the memorial portrait in front of the casket.

The national flag draping the coffin was then lifted and folded by uniformed officers, in a drill common in state funerals. The flag was then handed to his eldest son Lee Hsien Loong, who is the Prime Minister.

The coffin cover was lifted, in a symbolic move marking the mourning of Mr Lee the public figure, to Mr Lee, the family man.

As his body lay in the open casket, family members took turns to share memories of their father and grandfather.

Prime Minister Lee Hsien Loong, the elder son, said: "We are gathered here to say our final farewells to Papa – Mr Lee Kuan Yew. After the formalities of the Lying in State and the State Funeral Service, in this final hour Papa is with his family, his friends of a lifetime, his immediate staff who served him loyally and well, his security team who kept him safe and sound, and his medical team who took such good care of him.

"So much has been said about Pa's public life in the past few days. His public life is something we share with all of Singapore, with the world. But we were privileged to know him as a father, a grandfather, an elder brother, a friend, a strict but compassionate boss, the head of the family."

PM Lee recalled how Mr Lee taught him to ride a bike. "Once when

I was just getting the hang of balancing on two wheels, he pushed me off. I pedalled off across the field, thinking that he was still supporting and pushing me. Then I looked back and found that actually he had let go, and I was cycling on my own, launched, and he had let go! He was so pleased, and so was I."

Daughter Dr Lee, who wore a black dress, spoke lovingly of the father she is said to resemble most, among her siblings, recalling his stubborn insistence on not using a lift installed for him so he would not need to climb up and down the steps from the verandah at home to the car porch. She had inherited his "pugnacious" trait, she added good-humouredly.

She thanked his staff, especially the security officers who spent so much time with him. She recalled the time three of them had to interlock arms to perform the Heimlich manoeuvre when he nearly choked on a piece of meat. That bought him a few more months of quality life, she said.

Dr Lee, who has shunned the public spotlight in her private grief, said the last week had not been easy. Mr Lee died on Monday, aged 91.

When she saw this morning that the maid had moved Mr Lee's chair away from the dining table and placed it against the wall, she nearly broke down, she said. "But I can't break down, I am a Hakka woman."

Instead, she sat composed, and sometimes bowed her head to hide her emotions as other family members spoke.

Younger son Hsien Yang said: "Papa, thank you for being my own special father. Always there to guide, counsel and advise, every step of the way, but also prepared to step back and let me find my own wings and make my own way."

Li Hongyi, the elder son of PM Lee and wife Ho Ching, told of the one and only present his grandfather – whom he called Ye Ye – had given him: a camera. Hongyi said he went on to take many photographs and had a book printed.

"When Ye Ye gave me that camera years ago, he wrote me a note. It was a simple note without any flowery language or cheap sentiment. He simply told me that he hoped I made good use of it. I hope I have."

All his life, he said, he wanted to emulate his grandfather, to be the kind of man his grandfather was.

He was emotional, tearing up as he said: "Ye Ye showed me that you could make a difference in this world. Not just that you could make a difference, but that you could do it with your head held high. You didn't have to lie, cheat, or steal. You didn't have to charm, flatter, or cajole. You didn't have to care about frivolous things or play silly games. You could do something good with your life, and the best way to do so was to have good principles and conduct yourself honourably."

Li Shengwu, the eldest son of Hsien Yang and wife Suet Fern, spoke of his Ye Ye's influence over the development of his own beliefs. "Ye Ye, you chose to forsake personal gain and the comforts of an ordinary life, so that the people of Singapore could have a better life for themselves, and for their children and for their grandchildren. That Singapore is safe, that Singapore is prosperous, that Singapore is — for this we owe a debt that we cannot repay.

"Ye Ye, we will try to make you proud. Majulah Singapura."

The ceremony was attended by family members, friends and long-time staff of Mr Lee.

After the eulogies, family members filed past the open casket to lay a single red rose each in the coffin. Then the coffin was closed and his security officers who had guarded him in life, bore the coffin aloft and left the hall, accompanying him as long as they could, as he went on his final journey.

Mr Lee's body will be cremated. While alive, he had given instructions for his ashes to be mixed with his wife's. Mrs Lee died in October 2010. "For reasons of sentiment, I would like part of my ashes to be mixed up with Mama's, and both her ashes and mine put side by side in the columbarium. We were joined in life and I would like our ashes to be joined after this life."

OXLEY ROAD DISPUTE: TIME TO REFLECT, AND SEEK THE COMMON GOOD

Those in family dispute should set aside
hurt feelings and self-interest

17 June 2017

On my Facebook, some people are saying that the ongoing feud within the Lee family is like a multi-episode TV drama, with plot twists and characters that could have come straight from a scriptwriter's most overwrought imagination.

There is intrigue; a will – in fact, several wills; accusations and counter claims among siblings; money – always, there is money; feuding women; and a whiff of dynastic ambitions, swiftly denied. Politics, power, money, family drama.

They add to a potent mix. And as accusations levelled at Prime Minister Lee Hsien Loong, the eldest son of founding prime minister Lee Kuan Yew who died in March 2015, swirl, many Singaporeans are following the statements and Facebook posts put out by his sister, Dr Lee Wei Ling, brother Lee Hsien Yang and third-generation Lees, with a mix of prurient interest and concern.

On Facebook, people talk of this being a popcorn moment, like when you settle down for a movie.

It would all make for great entertainment.

Except, of course, it is not.

Because this is clearly not just a "family matter" being played out in public. Matters of public interest have arisen.

First is whether to preserve the Lee family home where the patriarch Mr Lee and his wife Kwa Geok Choo raised three children. This house was also the site of meetings that led to the founding of the People's Action Party, and a frequent meeting place for the first generation of leaders. It has historic value.

Disagreement over whether to demolish the house or have it conserved for history is central to the ongoing spat. It turns out, too, that inheritance shares and value are also involved.

My former colleague Cherian George summed up the issue well in a post on Thursday, when he said of the senior Mr Lee's wish to demolish his house: "This was in line with his well-known abhorrence of emotional pulls in politics, whether in the form of race, religion, language or charismatic personality. He wanted to build legitimacy around performance, not identity, and to train Singaporeans to exercise a more clinical, legal-bureaucratic rationality.

"You don't need to be a disciple of Lee Kuan Yew to recognise this as a worthy principle for Singapore governance. Nor do you have to be a traitor to Lee Hsien Loong to acknowledge the risk, red-flagged by his siblings, that this principle will be compromised by preserving their house as a monument, against their father's wishes."

I was part of a team that interviewed Mr Lee for the book *Hard Truths*. His frugal habits and simple house came up in an interview in August 2009. He immediately said he had told the Cabinet: "When I am dead, demolish it." We probed him for a few minutes on this. But he was quite insistent, citing the cost of preserving it, and the fact that many historic abodes turn into "shambles" after a while.

According to PM Lee, Mr Lee had first stated he wanted the house demolished in earlier wills, but took out that requirement in later wills. In his final will read out after his death, there was a clause which specifically stated that he wished for the house to be demolished.

PM Lee has raised questions about the circumstances in which that last will was made and if Mr Lee was fully aware of the content when he signed it, including the reinstatement of the so-called "demolition clause".

While much is now made of trying to determine what Mr Lee's final, authentic wishes were for the house, ironically it might not matter very much. At least, it should not be the final word on the matter.

Mr Lee believed community and society's needs took precedence over the individual's claims. Just as his Land Acquisition Act rode roughshod over other families' wishes, it is perfectly consistent with the ethos of Mr Lee's regime that the state has power to override Mr Lee's own wishes and those of his family.

This is not to say it should or must.

Whether one comes down on one side or the other of the save-it-or-demolish-it divide, most would agree that the process of deciding this is as important as the outcome.

Mr Lee himself, after all, as a leader and a lawyer, believed in the rule of law and proper government process for all manner of things, including gazetting of national monuments. As for who gains and by how much, should the house be demolished and redeveloped for sale, that is no one's business but the Lees'.

Issues of public interest, such as whether to conserve the house of the founding prime minister, can be resolved calmly, over the long term, by rational discussion and public consultation. There is little value in Facebook wars.

The other issue of public interest that has arisen is the charge made by Mr Lee Hsien Yang and Dr Lee that PM Lee "misused his position".

In words carefully crafted to raise questions without making specific accusations, the post said: "Since the passing of Lee Kuan Yew on March 23, 2015, we have felt threatened by Hsien Loong's misuse of his position and influence over the Singapore Government and its agencies to drive his personal agenda. We are concerned that the system has few checks and balances to prevent the abuse of government.

"We feel big brother omnipresent. We fear the use of the organs of state against us and Hsien Yang's wife, Suet Fern. The situation is such that Hsien Yang feels compelled to leave Singapore."

The post mentions the writers' fear of the use of organs of state, and their concerns over the lack of checks and balances. The one specific accusation made is that PM Lee "misused" his position and influence over the Singapore Government.

These are serious allegations to make, albeit sweeping and vague. Whatever the differences among the Lee siblings, casting doubts and aspersions on the system that Mr Lee had worked his whole life to build with Singaporeans must surely be an unfortunate, even if unintended, blow to his legacy.

Yet, no doubt many will say that the fact that members of the Prime Minister's own family fear that the organs of state might be improperly used against them is not insignificant, especially in view of the Singapore state's past reputation as a police state.

In 2017, that reputation is receding, as citizens have more rights and feel more empowered, and as the Government also becomes more responsive and accountable. But that might be due to voluntary restraint by the executive.

To be sustainable and iron-clad, checks on executive power must reside in institutional mechanisms, such as laws, regulations and scrutiny by other arms of government, not in voluntary self-restraint by those in power.

Many other issues are being thrown into the mix — some of major public interest, many of nothing more than prurient interest.

Maybe it is because I have met Mr Lee many times as a journalist, sat across from him, watched his face, seen his eyes and heard the intonation of his words, as he spoke about the country he so loved and the family so close to his heart.

I can't view this as a popcorn moment; I can't watch this family drama unfold as pure entertainment. As a political journalist, I had the rare, unusual duty of being present at the Mandai crematorium for both Mr Lee's last journey, and that of his wife.

Mr Lee was not only the Lee siblings' father, but also the founding father of Singapore, and many of us as ordinary citizens claim a small – no matter how small – part of him and want to honour his memory.

The public fighting would have grieved him so.

There is a time for everything, and the time for family feuding is not now, when the country faces multiple challenges on the terrorism front and in foreign policy; when we all fear our jobs and livelihoods disappearing as technologies disrupt the workplace.

There is a place for everything, and the place for fighting over a family will and inheritance is not via Facebook and social media.

Singapore is a mature country with a mature polity. There are probate courts. There are family courts. There has been much effort to promote mediation as a means for dispute resolution in tricky cases. There are men and women of integrity and influence who can be appealed to, to mediate.

What is required is that those involved set aside hurt feelings, pride, fears and self-interest and seek to find a common good.

Mr Lee used to talk about "knocking heads" whenever people proved intractable or unyielding to reason. I think he would say that his children need a dose of that right now.

HE CHANGED MY LIFE: MY FATHER AND OUR FOUNDING FATHER

Over time, both distant, disapproving figures
turned into real beings I could relate to

29 March 2015

When I was growing up, God, my father and Lee Kuan Yew all merged into one. I was the youngest child in a Teochew-speaking, working-class Chinese household. My parents were immigrants from China, who ran a hawker stall for much of my formative years.

My father was a stern patriarch who was not averse to using the cane. My mother was a traditional Chinese wife and self-sacrificing mother, with a twinkling sense of humour with those close to her. She tended to our household altar, placing platters of food there on religious or festive days. She prayed to the deity who I found out years later is supposed to be the Kitchen God, assigned by the Emperor of Heaven to report on a family's doings. The offerings were meant to placate the deity and sweeten his tongue when he delivered reports.

As for Lee Kuan Yew, he was just the man who founded the nation that I heard and read about. Like God, he was everywhere in the ether. Like God, he was all-powerful and all-knowing. Lee Kuan Yew didn't affect my family's life much in a direct way, although his policies formed the arc within which ordinary lives like ours were lived.

My parents were street hawkers who were fined repeatedly for peddling their wares. Unlike many hawkers grateful to be relocated, they resisted being put into a centre for years. When the frequency of fines grew too overwhelming, they gave up. By then, choice sites like Newton were taken up; they were sent to Timbuktu — a small hawker centre off Alexandra Road, where they struggled to make enough to raise three children.

Apart from the way big policies of the day intersected with our lives, mine was not a political family. The closest I came to Lee Kuan Yew was hearing my father tell the story of how he was standing close by and witnessed the (to him) historic moment when Mr Lee was pushed into a big monsoon drain at Towner Road, while touring Kallang constituency in 1963.

Lee Kuan Yew close up

I first watched Lee Kuan Yew close up in 1983, when I was 15. By then, my parents could afford a second-hand black-and-white TV set. Sitting in the living room, I watched his National Day Rally speech live.

I didn't know it then, but this was his famous speech on graduate mothers. It went on into the night, and I remember I was riveted, moving from the sofa to toilet reluctantly for pee breaks.

In junior college, we would discuss Lee Kuan Yew and Singapore politics incessantly. At 18, I won a Public Service Commission Overseas Merit Scholarship to study English literature at Cambridge University in England. Like hundreds of exam-smart Singaporeans from poor families, who got government scholarships that opened doors to good careers, I am a beneficiary of the meritocratic scholarship system Mr Lee created.

In my case, though I was contracted to work in the civil service for eight years after my studies, I broke my bond. I approached Singapore Press Holdings (SPH), which agreed to hire me and buy out my bond. I remember walking to the Public Service Commission with the SPH cheque for $140,000 that bought my freedom from the civil service. I have remained grateful to SPH ever since. After 24 years, I still love my job as a journalist.

When I joined The Straits Times Political Desk in 1991, Lee Kuan Yew became less of a myth, and much more real.

Over the years, I would cover Mr Lee on many more occasions, including in Singapore, at Tanjong Pagar and in Parliament, and overseas, in China and Malaysia.

Videos of him in the 1970s show a gruff, thuggish figure with an aggressive chin thrust, given to raised arms, finger-pointing and trouser-hiking. By the time I met him, from the mid-1990s, he was already in his 70s and 80s, and had mellowed considerably.

Fiery rhetoric

But when required, his oratory was just as fiery as ever.

Two parliamentary speeches in the last 20 years stood out for me. One was in November 1994. After hours of debate on the proposal to peg ministers' pay to top private-sector professionals', including a suggestion to put the proposal to a referendum, Mr Lee rose and put an end to it, saying: "I am pitting my judgment after 40 years in politics, and I've been in this chamber since 1955, against all the arguments on the other side... against all the arguments the doubters can muster."

Enough said. Done deal.

In 1996, there were complaints about property purchases by Mr Lee and his son Hsien Loong, then the Deputy Prime Minister. Amid the unhappiness about ministers having an "inside track" to VIP priority bookings for condominiums, it took Mr Lee to call a spade a spade.

Businesses want to get the best customers to help sell and add value to their products, he said, adding: "Let us be realistic... I ask all of you to be honest, including Mr Chiam (See Tong). All ministers who carry weight, all MPs who are popular, you go to a hawker centre. If they gave the other customer one egg, they'll give you two. Count on it."

In words that entered the lexicon of Mr Lee's hard truths, he thundered in the House, telling MPs to be realistic that some people would be given better treatment by businesses than others: "Let's grow up!"

Over the years, I came to know of his reputation for imprisoning political opponents. I read critical biographies of him. I had even covered and written news articles on some of the defamation suits he brought against his critics.

But when I covered him at a press conference, or sat across a table from him in an interview, I would put aside those thoughts and focus on the issue at hand. In any case, I usually had my colleagues around me. I wasn't a political opponent. I was a journalist, and I knew Mr Lee respected the role of journalists. Much as he might berate us or our editors when he disagreed with something we wrote, he knew our job was to ask honest, if difficult, and to him annoying, questions. And while the Singapore Government can be authoritarian, it respects the rule of law.

I once asked if he was satisfied with the level of political contest, or if he should have done more to create the conditions for an alternative in Singapore.

His answer: "We'll be quite happy if we get a small group of equal calibre contesting against us. I mean you look at the NMPs, they talk more sense, right? Would they fight an election? No. So? But they've got the brain power, they've got the knowledge, but they're not prepared to jump into the sea."

My counter: "That's because many people are intimidated by the PAP, the climate of fear, crackdown on dissent and so on."

Mr Lee: "No, no. Are you intimidated?"

Me: "Well, asking you this question, obviously I'm not. I just feel that there's a perception."

Mr Lee went on to add that if a person joined an opposition party, "he takes us on, we'll take him on. But you can't join the Workers' Party and we just let him lambast us away. We'll demolish him as hard as he tries to demolish us. That's part of the game, right? I mean you say that's intimidation?"

Growing fond

I don't remember when exactly I started to get fond of him. It was certainly after my conversion to Christianity, when my concept of God changed from a punitive deity chalking up wrongdoings, to one who loved and sacrificed for humanity.

It was also after my own stern father became an unlikely doting grandfather who chased after his crawling grandson, trying to feed him durian. God and my father were no longer distant, disapproving figures. They had become real beings I could relate to.

And so had Lee Kuan Yew.

A few incidents come to mind. In March 2003, I wrote a long, personal account of my battle with breast cancer. I wanted to destigmatise it, and to encourage people going through terminal illness, and their caregivers, to talk about it, and not to impose on those with serious illness the additional burden of secrecy.

Mr Lee wrote to me a few days later, wishing me good luck and good health, and saying he looked forward to reading my articles.

He also shared about the time his son went through chemotherapy, 11 years earlier, and how one lived with the uncertainty, even in remission, of whether the cancer would return. "The searing experience tempered his character and made him more philosophical about his life. I think it has similarly tempered you."

I was touched by his good wishes for my health.

He also sent me a note in June 2010 to say he enjoyed reading my book *Pioneers Once More*, a history of the Singapore public service. He offered some vignettes of senior civil servants that he said I could include in future editions. Again, I was touched by his generous words, and that he bothered.

I began to see a lot more of Mr Lee from December 2008 to October 2009, when my colleagues and I conducted 16 interviews with him for *Hard Truths*. He was vigorous, engaging, sometimes a little testy, but never rude or nasty.

I heard him speak of his wife and his daily ritual of reading to her when she lay bedridden after a stroke. Devoid of her company, he would converse with the nurses during lunch.

I heard the stoic loneliness in his voice after she died. I saw the indulgent grandfather reluctant to forbid his grandchildren to touch his things when they sniffled, but who would discreetly wipe down his computer with disinfecting wipes after they left so as not to catch their bug. Although he was reputed for having no small talk, he sometimes told us about his ailments or his day.

I covered Mrs Lee's funeral in October 2010 at the Mandai crematorium. He walked up to her coffin with a single red rose. His hand touched his lips, then her forehead, planting a kiss there once, and then, as though he could not bear to part, again.

Somewhere along the line amid those incidents, I grew fond of the old man.

In 2012, I was involved in another round of interviews for the book *One Man's View Of The World*. Last year, we interviewed him a few more times to update the book.

He grew visibly more frail over the years. From open-buttoned jackets, he moved on to buttoned-up ones, sometimes with a scarf round the neck. From walking in his trainers, he had to be supported.

We once had to wait 30 minutes for him to rest and he apologised, saying he had not been able to keep his food down. He had an injury once, and conducted the interview with a heat pad around his thigh. He was on meal supplement Ensure and various medications his security officers would give him. His speech got slurred towards the end. From over two hours, the interviews went down to 45 minutes or less.

It pained me to sit across the table over several years and watch Mr Lee weaken. He was the founding father of Singapore. I liked to remember him as the vigorous Prime Minister in television footage, or at least as the still active Minister Mentor in 2009, who told us no question was off limits, and hurried us to complete our book, chiding us not to let the grass grow under our feet.

But somewhere along the line, I came to see him less as Lee Kuan Yew the mythic figure, the great statesman, the fearsome political leader. I came to see him as a man, a flawed but still great mortal, a man who did his best for his country, for his time, the best he knew how.

Luckily for all of us, his best was enough.